G000107866

EDUCATION OF STUDENTS WITH DISABILITIES

FEDERAL ISSUES AND POLICIES

EDUCATION IN A COMPETITIVE AND GLOBALIZING WORLD

Additional books in this series can be found on Nova's website under the Series tab.

Additional e-books in this series can be found on Nova's website under the e-books tab.

DISABILITY AND THE DISABLED-ISSUES, LAWS AND PROGRAMS

Additional books in this series can be found on Nova's website under the Series tab.

Additional e-books in this series can be found on Nova's website under the e-books tab.

EDUCATION OF STUDENTS WITH DISABILITIES

FEDERAL ISSUES AND POLICIES

HARRISON GARLACH

AND

NATHAN DARST

EDITORS

publishers

New York

NOTICE TO THE READER

The Publisher has taken reasonable care in the preparation of this book, but makes no expressed or implied warranty of any kind and assumes no responsibility for any errors or omissions. No liability is assumed for incidental or consequential damages in connection with or arising out of information contained in this book. The Publisher shall not be liable for any special, consequential, or exemplary damages resulting, in whole or in part, from the readers' use of, or reliance upon, this material. Any parts of this book based on government reports are so indicated and copyright is claimed for those parts to the extent applicable to compilations of such works.

Independent verification should be sought for any data, advice or recommendations contained in this book. In addition, no responsibility is assumed by the publisher for any injury and/or damage to persons or property arising from any methods, products, instructions, ideas or otherwise contained in this publication.

This publication is designed to provide accurate and authoritative information with regard to the subject matter covered herein. It is sold with the clear understanding that the Publisher is not engaged in rendering legal or any other professional services. If legal or any other expert assistance is required, the services of a competent person should be sought. FROM A DECLARATION OF PARTICIPANTS JOINTLY ADOPTED BY A COMMITTEE OF THE AMERICAN BAR ASSOCIATION AND A COMMITTEE OF PUBLISHERS.

Additional color graphics may be available in the e-book version of this book.

Library of Congress Cataloging-in-Publication Data

ISBN: 978-1-62257-996-9

Published by Nova Science Publishers, Inc. † New York

CONTENTS

Preface   **vii**

Chapter 1   The Education of Students with Disabilities:
                Alignment Between the Elementary and Secondary
                Education Act and the Individuals with Disabilities
                Education Act   **1**
                Erin D. Lomax and Ann Lordeman

Chapter 2   The Individuals with Disabilities Education Act
                (IDEA), Part B: Key Statutory and Regulatory
                Provisions   **49**
                Ann Lordeman

Chapter 3   The Individuals with Disabilities Education Act
                (IDEA): Selected Judicial Developments Following
                the 2004 Reauthorization   **91**
                Nancy Lee Jones

Chapter 4   Alternate Assessments for Students with Disabilities   **135**
                Erin D. Lomax

Index   **173**

PREFACE

The largest sources of federal funding for elementary and secondary education are the Elementary and Secondary Act (ESEA), and the Individuals with Disabilities Education Act (IDEA). The ESEA provides funding and services for a broad population of students, including disadvantaged students, migrant students, neglected and delinquent students, and students with limited English proficiency. Approximately 6 million students with disabilities aged 6 through 21 attend elementary and secondary schools; however they are not afforded special services under the ESEA due to their disability status. Both the ESEA and IDEA aim to improve the educational outcomes for students with disabilities. The ways in which they do this sometimes differ, and when the laws are not fully or clearly aligned it can be difficult for educators to plan and execute an appropriate education for these students. This book highlights the federal issues and policies pertaining to the education of students with disabilities.

Chapter 1 – The largest sources of federal funding for elementary and secondary education are the Elementary and Secondary Education Act (ESEA), as amended by the No Child Left Behind Act (NCLB; P.L. 107-110), and the Individuals with Disabilities Education Act (IDEA; P.L. 108-446). The ESEA provides funding and services for a broad population of students, including disadvantaged students, migrant students, neglected and delinquent students, and students with limited English proficiency. Approximately 6 million students with disabilities ages 6 through 21 attend elementary and secondary schools; however, they are not afforded special services under the ESEA due to their disability status. The IDEA provides funding and services specifically for those students with disabilities. Both the ESEA and IDEA aim to improve the educational outcomes for students with disabilities. The ways in which they do this sometimes differ, and when the laws are not fully or clearly aligned it can be difficult for educators to plan and execute an appropriate education for students with disabilities. In the 112th Congress, legislators may consider the reauthorization of the ESEA. This report focuses on four broad policy issues within both the ESEA and IDEA, which potentially create differing expectations or requirements for schools and teachers educating students with disabilities:

- Standards. Under the ESEA, students with disabilities are taught to state academic content standards that apply to all children in the state. Under the IDEA, academic goals are established for each child in an individualized education program (IEP).

- Assessments. Under the ESEA, students with disabilities participate in annual assessments that determine adequate yearly progress toward meeting expectations associated with state academic content and achievement standards. Under the IDEA, students with disabilities are assessed for identification purposes and for monitoring progress toward meeting goals articulated in their IEPs.

- Accountability. The ESEA accountability system primarily measures whether schools and local education agencies are making adequate yearly progress in reading and mathematics achievement. The "students with disabilities" subgroup is expected to make adequate yearly progress. The IDEA monitoring system measures whether states are meeting certain compliance and performance indicators to determine whether the law is being implemented as intended.

- Teachers. Both the ESEA and IDEA have requirements regarding "highly qualified" teachers. The ESEA includes a definition of "highly qualified" teacher as the term relates to teachers of elementary and secondary education. The IDEA also includes a definition of "highly qualified" teacher as the term relates to special education teachers of elementary and secondary education. Because students with disabilities spend the majority of time in the general education classroom, they are affected by both definitions.

This report highlights issues pertaining to alignment and misalignment among ESEA and IDEA provisions within these areas, describes how statutory and regulatory language has sought to clarify these issues, and addresses specific issues that Congress may want to clarify as it considers the reauthorization of ESEA.

Chapter 2 – The Individuals with Disabilities Education Act (IDEA) is both a grants statute and a civil rights statute. As a grants statute, IDEA provides federal funding for the education of children with disabilities and requires, as a condition for the receipt of such funds, the provision of a free appropriate public education (FAPE) (i.e., specially designed instruction provided at no cost to parents that meets the needs of a child with a disability). In FY2011, $12.5 billion was appropriated for IDEA. In the fall of 2009, 5.9 million children ages six through 21 received educational services under IDEA. As a civil rights statute, IDEA contains procedural safeguards, which are provisions intended to protect the rights of parents and children with disabilities regarding the provision of FAPE. These procedures include parental rights to resolve disputes through a mediation process, and present and resolve complaints through a due process complaint procedure, and through state complaint procedures. IDEA's procedural safeguards also address disciplinary issues. In general, a child with a disability is not immune from discipline, but the procedures are not the same as for non-disabled children. To be covered under IDEA, a child with a disability must meet the categorical definition of disability in the act, and the child must require special education and related services as a result of the disability in order to benefit from public education. Once a child meets IDEA's eligibility criteria, FAPE is implemented through the Individualized Education Program (IEP), which is the plan for providing special education and related services by the local educational agency (LEA). The IEP is developed by an IEP team composed of school personnel and parents. IDEA requires that children with disabilities be educated in the least restrictive environment. That is, to the maximum extent appropriate they are to be educated with children who are not disabled. In 2008, over 50% of all children with disabilities served by IDEA spent 80% or more of their time in a regular classroom. To implement IDEA, states and other entities (i.e., the District of Columbia, Puerto Rico, the Bureau of Indian Education, the outlying areas, and the freely associated states) receive grants based on a statutory formula. Most of the federal funds received by states are passed on to LEAs based on a statutory formula. IDEA also contains state and local maintenance of effort (MOE) requirements and supplement, not supplant (SNS) requirements aimed at increasing overall educational spending, rather than substituting federal funds for education spending at the state and local levels. Originally enacted in 1975, IDEA has been the subject of numerous reauthorizations to extend services and rights to children with disabilities. The most recent reauthorization of IDEA was P.L. 108-446 enacted in 2004. Funding for Part B, Assistance for Education of all Children with Disabilities, the largest and most often discussed part of the act, is permanently authorized. Funding for Part C, Infants and Toddlers with Disabilities, and Part D, National Activities, is authorized through FY2011.

Chapter 3 – The Individuals with Disabilities Education Act (IDEA) is the major federal statute for the education of children with disabilities. IDEA both authorizes federal funding for special education and related services and, for states that accept these funds, sets out principles under which special education and related services are to be provided. The cornerstone of IDEA is the principle that states and school districts make available a free appropriate public education (FAPE) to all children with disabilities. IDEA has been the subject of numerous reauthorizations; the most recent reauthorization was P.L. 108-446 in 2004. Congress is currently beginning the process of identifying potential issues for the next reauthorization. Some of the issues raised by judicial decisions include the following:

Chapter 4 – The Elementary and Secondary Education Act (ESEA), as amended by the No Child Left Behind Act of 2001 (NCLB, P.L. 107-110), and the Individuals with Disabilities Education Act (IDEA, P.L. 108-446) both require all students with disabilities to participate in district and state assessments. Because student achievement on state assessments is used to determine Adequate Yearly Progress (AYP) in state accountability systems mandated by NCLB, schools are now held accountable for the achievement of all students, including students with disabilities. The authorization for NCLB expired at the end of FY2008, and the 111th Congress is expected to consider whether to amend and extend the ESEA. One focus of reauthorization may be reexamining how students with disabilities are included in accountability systems. The current NCLB focus on accountability for the achievement of students with disabilities has led educators, administrators, and policymakers to reexamine the appropriateness of the general state assessment for measuring the achievement of certain students with disabilities. Although many students with disabilities are able to participate in the general state assessment, either with or without accommodations, other students with disabilities may not be able to participate fully in the general state assessment because of the nature and severity of their disability. These students may need an alternate assessment that is tailored to their needs and allows them to more accurately demonstrate what they know and can do. There are currently five assessment options for measuring the achievement of students with disabilities: (1) general state assessment, (2) general state assessment with accommodations, (3) alternate assessment based on grade-level standards, (4) alternate assessment based on alternate achievement standards (AA-AAS), and (5) alternate assessment based on modified achievement standards (AA-MAS). The first three assessment options (general state assessment, general state assessment with accommodations, and alternate assessment based on grade-level standards) result in scores that may be counted in AYP calculations in the typical manner, as determined by a state's accountability system. Scores from the second two assessment options (AA-AAS and AAMAS) have restrictions on the way they may be counted in AYP calculations. These restrictions are outlined in regulations issued by the U.S. Department of Education (ED) and have numerous implications for state accountability systems. The purpose of this report is to describe the ED regulations that allow states to use scores from alternate assessments for AYP calculations in accountability systems. This report also describes the current status of state implementation of alternate assessments and examines some of the challenges states have encountered in developing and implementing these assessments. The final section of this report discusses other policy proposals for measuring the achievement of students with disabilities and including them in accountability systems.

In: Education of Students with Disabilities   ISBN: 978-1-62257-996-9
Editors: H. Garlach and N. Darst   © 2013 Nova Science Publishers, Inc.

Chapter 1

THE EDUCATION OF STUDENTS WITH DISABILITIES: ALIGNMENT BETWEEN THE ELEMENTARY AND SECONDARY EDUCATION ACT AND THE INDIVIDUALS WITH DISABILITIES EDUCATION ACT[*]

Erin D. Lomax and Ann Lordeman

SUMMARY

The largest sources of federal funding for elementary and secondary education are the Elementary and Secondary Education Act (ESEA), as amended by the No Child Left Behind Act (NCLB; P.L. 107-110), and the Individuals with Disabilities Education Act (IDEA; P.L. 108-446). The ESEA provides funding and services for a broad population of students, including disadvantaged students, migrant students, neglected and delinquent students, and students with limited English proficiency. Approximately 6 million students with disabilities ages 6 through 21 attend elementary and secondary schools; however, they are not afforded special services under the ESEA due to their disability status. The IDEA

---

[*] This is an edited, reformatted and augmented version of a Congressional Research Service publication, CRS Report for Congress R42070, from www.crs.gov, prepared for Members and Committees of Congress, dated October 31, 2011.

provides funding and services specifically for those students with disabilities.

Both the ESEA and IDEA aim to improve the educational outcomes for students with disabilities. The ways in which they do this sometimes differ, and when the laws are not fully or clearly aligned it can be difficult for educators to plan and execute an appropriate education for students with disabilities.

In the 112th Congress, legislators may consider the reauthorization of the ESEA.

This report focuses on four broad policy issues within both the ESEA and IDEA, which potentially create differing expectations or requirements for schools and teachers educating students with disabilities:

- Standards. Under the ESEA, students with disabilities are taught to state academic content standards that apply to all children in the state. Under the IDEA, academic goals are established for each child in an individualized education program (IEP).
- Assessments. Under the ESEA, students with disabilities participate in annual assessments that determine adequate yearly progress toward meeting expectations associated with state academic content and achievement standards. Under the IDEA, students with disabilities are assessed for identification purposes and for monitoring progress toward meeting goals articulated in their IEPs.
- Accountability. The ESEA accountability system primarily measures whether schools and local education agencies are making adequate yearly progress in reading and mathematics achievement. The "students with disabilities" subgroup is expected to make adequate yearly progress. The IDEA monitoring system measures whether states are meeting certain compliance and performance indicators to determine whether the law is being implemented as intended.
- Teachers. Both the ESEA and IDEA have requirements regarding "highly qualified" teachers. The ESEA includes a definition of "highly qualified" teacher as the term relates to teachers of elementary and secondary education. The IDEA also includes a definition of "highly qualified" teacher as the term relates to special education teachers of elementary and secondary education. Because students with disabilities spend the majority of time in the general education classroom, they are affected by both definitions.

This report highlights issues pertaining to alignment and misalignment among ESEA and IDEA provisions within these areas, describes how statutory and regulatory language has sought to clarify these issues, and addresses specific issues that Congress may want to clarify as it considers the reauthorization of ESEA.

INTRODUCTION

The largest sources of federal funding for elementary and secondary education are the Elementary and Secondary Education Act (ESEA), as amended by the No Child Left Behind Act (NCLB; P.L. 107-110), and the Individuals with Disabilities Education Act (IDEA; P.L. 108-446). In FY2011, the ESEA provided approximately $24.4 billion in funding for education, representing roughly 65% of all federal elementary and secondary education funding.[1] Title I of the ESEA is the largest ESEA program, providing support for the education of disadvantaged students. Over the past two decades, the ESEA has become increasingly focused on promoting educational standards and accountability to help ensure that students in schools receiving Title I funds are consistently held to state developed educational standards, and that these same standards are applied to all groups of students. The ESEA contains high stakes accountability provisions featuring varied consequences[2] for schools in which a sufficient percentage of students or subgroups of students fail to make academic progress in relation to the standards.

In FY2011, the IDEA provided approximately $12.5 billion in funding for the education of students with disabilities, representing roughly 33% of all federal elementary and secondary education funding.[3] The IDEA focuses on ensuring that all elementary and secondary students with disabilities receive a free appropriate public education (FAPE). Part B of the IDEA is the largest program, providing special education and related services to students with disabilities from preschool through high school and ensuring that these students receive an individualized education that is tailored to their needs. IDEA has accountability provisions that are largely focused on ensuring that states comply with various provisions of the law. The IDEA accountability system also requires states to report on various performance indicators that pertain to the academic progress of students with disabilities, but, unlike the ESEA, uniform levels of achievement are not expected.

Approximately 6 million students with disabilities attend elementary and secondary schools.[4] While nearly all students with disabilities are educated to some extent in the general education classroom,[5] almost 60% of students with disabilities spend over 80% of their time in the general education classroom.[6] Since many students with disabilities participate in the general education classroom, they often have the same educational experiences as their non-disabled peers. For example, they are taught to the same academic content standards, in the same classrooms, and by the same teachers. They often take the same annual assessments in reading and mathematics. The educational experiences that students with disabilities share with their non-disabled peers are typically guided by policies set forth in the ESEA. Students with disabilities also have educational experiences that are unique to them and are not shared by their non-disabled peers. For example, they are provided individualized education programs (IEPs) that outline the provision of special education and related services. They are taught by special education teachers and related service providers, such as speech pathologists, audiologists, occupational therapists, and others. Sometimes, students with disabilities take alternate assessments in reading and mathematics instead of the general state assessment.[7] The individualized educational experiences of students with disabilities are typically guided by policies set forth in the IDEA.[8]

Both the ESEA and the IDEA affect the education of students with disabilities and aim to improve educational outcomes for these students. While the goals of the two laws may be similar, the ESEA and the IDEA support students with disabilities differently. In particular, some tension exists with regard to expectations for student learning. Under ESEA, the emphasis is placed on holding all students and all subgroups of students (i.e., "students with disabilities") to the same academic standards, closing gaps between subgroups of students, and expecting 100% proficiency on assessments of reading and mathematics. Under IDEA, the emphasis is placed on assessing individual students, establishing individualized learning goals, and monitoring progress toward meeting these goals.

When the underlying concepts or legislative language of the ESEA and IDEA are not clearly aligned, it can be difficult for educators to plan and execute an appropriate education for students with disabilities. One example of possible misalignment concerns *what* to teach students with disabilities. Under ESEA, general education teachers are expected to teach to grade-level standards to students with disabilities. Under IDEA, special education teachers are expected to teach to individualized goals developed for each student with a disability. The individualized goals developed under the IDEA may not be aligned with the grade-level standards under ESEA. Another example of potential misalignment concerns high school graduation rates. While both ESEA and IDEA require states to report graduation rates for students with disabilities, IDEA allows for a longer period of time to complete high school graduation requirements than is generally allowed under the "four-year" graduation rate reported under the ESEA.

The purpose of this report is to highlight issues of alignment and possible misalignment between the two laws, to describe how statutory and regulatory language has sought to clarify these issues, and to draw attention to issues that

Congress may want to clarify. For the purpose of this report, *alignment* refers to the extent to which the ESEA and IDEA have similar conceptual aims and compatible statutory or regulatory language. *Misalignment* refers to the extent to which ESEA and IDEA have conflicting conceptual aims, conflicting statutory or regulatory language, or introduce specific issues that present difficulties in implementing provisions of both laws simultaneously. Where possible misalignment exists, this report explores the potential consequences of dual implementation of the requirements of the ESEA and the IDEA.

While this report provides some relevant background information on the ESEA and the IDEA, it does not serve as a comprehensive resource on the basic provisions of these laws. Background information on the ESEA and the IDEA is available in other reports.[9] In addition, some of the provisions of the ESEA may be affected by waivers issued by the Secretary of Education (hereafter referred to as the Secretary). In September 2011, the Secretary announced that states may request flexibility on specific ESEA requirements in exchange for certain changes in state-developed plans that are designed to improve educational outcomes, close achievement gaps, increase equity, and improve the quality of instruction.[10] It is not known at this time how the waivers would affect interactions between ESEA and IDEA. The focus of this report, therefore, remains on the statutory and regulatory provisions of the ESEA and how they align with the statutory and regulatory provisions of the IDEA. It does not anticipate potential changes due to the issuance of waivers.

This report is organized around four broad education policy issues that are relevant to both the ESEA and IDEA: standards, assessments, accountability, and teachers. The first three education policy issues are interrelated and comprise the ESEA accountability system. That is, states set academic *standards* for students, *assessments* measure whether students are achieving these standards, and the assessment scores inform the ESEA *accountability* system to determine whether certain goals are being met. The fourth policy issue, teachers, is not directly related to the overall accountability system, but it has important implications for the education of students with disabilities. In particular, the "highly qualified" teacher requirements of the two laws are examined to explore whether the requirements further the goal of meeting the needs of students with disabilities. In addition, this section examines the increasing emphasis on teacher effectiveness and how this may affect students with disabilities. For each policy issue, background information on the relevant statutory and regulatory language of ESEA and IDEA is provided. Then, there is a discussion of alignment, possible areas of misalignment, and specific issues that Congress may want to clarify during the reauthorization debate of the ESEA. *Appendix A* presents a glossary of selected acronyms used in this report.

STANDARDS[11]

Standards are a set of expectations of certain skills and knowledge for students at a particular grade level or developmental level. Recent federal policies have supported standards-based education in an effort to promote equity in academic expectations for all students.[12] In elementary and secondary education, "standards" typically refer to grade-level academic content and achievement standards that are required by the ESEA. State academic content and achievement standards are intended to ensure that all students, including students with disabilities, have access to and make progress in the general education curriculum. In addition to the state academic content and achievement standards, students with disabilities are taught the individualized skills and goals outlined by their IEP as required by the IDEA. In a broad sense, IEP goals can be viewed as a set of individualized "standards" for a student with a disability.

The following section provides background information on the relevant statutory and regulatory language that describes the academic content and achievement standards in the ESEA and IEP goals in the IDEA. This discussion is followed by an analysis of how the two sets of standards are used to guide instruction for students with disabilities and a discussion of alignment options that Congress may consider.

Background

Title I-A of the ESEA requires states to develop a set of academic content and achievement standards in mathematics, reading or language arts (hereafter referred to as reading), and science.[13] The academic content and achievement standards are to be used by the state and its local educational agencies (LEAs) and apply to all public schools and children in the state.[14] The academic content standards are required to "(1) specify what children are expected to know and be able to do; (2) contain coherent and rigorous content; and (3) encourage the teaching of advanced skills."[15] The academic achievement standards are required to be aligned[16] with academic content standards and describe at least three levels of achievement (e.g., basic, proficient, and advanced).[17]

The statutory language of the ESEA specifies that the standards "shall include the same knowledge, skills, and levels of achievement expected of all children."[18] This requirement implies that the academic content and achievement standards apply to all students with disabilities regardless of the type or severity of the disability. Subsequent regulations, however, have allowed states to develop different sets of academic achievement standards for some students with disabilities.[19] Although the majority of students with disabilities are taught to grade-level content and achievement standards, regulations permit states to develop *alternate achievement standards* and *modified achievement standards* for some students with disabilities.

Alternate achievement standards may be developed for students with disabilities[20] who have the "most significant cognitive disabilities."[21] If a state chooses to develop alternate achievement standards, the state must use a "documented and validated standards-setting process" to ensure that alternate achievement standards are aligned with the state's academic content standards, promote access to the general curriculum, and reflect professional judgment of the highest achievement standards possible. While any number of students may be taught to alternate achievement standards, there is a limit to the number of state assessments based on alternate achievement standards that can be counted as proficient in a state's accountability system.[22]

Modified achievement standards may be developed for students with disabilities[23] whose disability has "precluded the student from achieving grade-level proficiency" as demonstrated by the state assessment or other assessments that provide valid results on student achievement.[24] If a state chooses to develop alternate achievement standards, the standards must (1) be aligned with the state's academic content standards for the grade level in which the student is enrolled, (2) be challenging for eligible students, but may be less difficult than the grade-level academic achievement standards, (3) include at least three achievement levels, and (4) be developed through a documented and validated standards-setting process that includes broad stakeholder input. While any number of students may be taught to modified achievement standards, there is a limit to the number of state assessments based on modified achievement standards that can be counted as proficient in a state's accountability system.[25]

Under IDEA, a student with a disability is taught according to his or her IEP. The IEP[26] is a written document provided for each student with a disability to ensure that the student is receiving FAPE.[27] The IEP document includes details about the student and information on the specific special education and related services that are provided to the student. One of the features of the IEP is a statement of annual goals, including academic and functional goals, designed to (1) enable the child to be involved in and make progress in the general education curriculum, and (2) meet each of the student's other educational needs that result from the student's disability.

IEP goals are determined by the student's IEP team, which includes general education teachers, special education teachers, parents, and others.[28] IEP goals are individualized for the student and may be academic, address social or behavioral needs, relate to physical needs, or address other educational needs. Academic goals often focus on the content areas of reading and mathematics. Social and behavioral goals may focus on increasing social skills that promote positive peer relationships or decreasing problem behaviors that inhibit learning. Sometimes, students with disabilities have IEP goals that relate to physical needs in the classroom, such as using scissors, gripping a pencil, typing, and other fine-motor skills.

IEP goals are determined annually and represent what the student may reasonably accomplish in one year.[29] They must be measurable and the student's progress toward achieving the goals must be documented. A description of how the student's progress toward meeting the annual goals will be measured must be included in the IEP, including a description of how often progress will be reported (e.g., quarterly, periodically, concurrent with report cards).

Table 1 provides a comparison of select statutory and regulatory provisions of the ESEA and IDEA discussed above.

Alignment Issues

The education of students with disabilities is affected by both the academic content and achievement standards in the ESEA and individualized IEP goals in the IDEA. Standards in the ESEA and IEP goals in the IDEA, however, serve different purposes for tracking the achievement of students with disabilities.

Standards in the ESEA are used for federal accountability purposes; states, LEAs, and schools are held accountable for the subgroup of "students with disabilities" achieving proficiency with respect to the standards, in the aggregate.

IEP goals in the IDEA are not used for accountability purposes.

Table 1. Comparison of Select Statutory and Regulatory Provisions of the ESEA and IDEA: Standards

Standards	ESEA	IDEA
In General	The ESEA requires states to develop a setof academic content and achievement standards in mathematics, reading, and science. The standards apply to all public schools and children in the state.	Under IDEA, a student with a disability is taught according to his or her individualized education program (IEP). IEP goals are determined annually and represent what the student may reasonably accomplish in one year.
Alternate and Modified Achievement Standards for Students with Disabilities	Under ESEA, alternate achievement standards may be developed for students with disabilities who have the "most significant cognitive disabilities." Under ESEA, modified achievement standards may be developed for students with disabilities whose disability has "precluded the student from achieving grade-level proficiency."	N/A

Source: Table prepared by CRS based on provisions in the Elementary and Secondary Education Act (P.L. 107- 110), the Individuals with Disabilities Education Act (P.L. 108-446), and associated regulations.

Note: Under ESEA regulations, only 1% of scores from state assessments based on alternate achievement standards may count as proficient in a state's accountability system. Similarly, under ESEA regulations, only 2% of scores from state assessments based on modified achievement standards may count as proficient in a state's accountability system.

Data regarding whether students are meeting their IEP goals are used by teachers, parents, and schools to refine the special education and related services that are necessary for meeting those goals. If students are not meeting their IEP goals, the IEP team can revise the goals, revise the type or duration of special education and related services, or discuss alternative educational placements.

For some students with disabilities, the state content and achievement standards may be somewhat aligned with reading and mathematics goals in their IEPs. For example, students with disabilities who are relatively high-achieving may have IEP goals in reading and mathematics that are similar to ESEA grade-level content and achievement standards. In this case, the education of a student with a disability in the general education classroom with instruction provided by the general education teacher may be consistent with other special education and related services that are provided. All service providers (i.e., the general education teacher, special education teacher, and related service providers) are working toward a common goal.

For other students with disabilities, the state content and achievement standards may not be aligned with IEP goals. If there is a lack of alignment between state content and achievement standards and IEP goals, there is potential for confusion over what to teach students with disabilities and what level of mastery should be expected. For example, if a student in fifth grade is reading at a second grade level, his or her IEP goal may require a special education teacher to focus on basic literacy skills that are necessary to move the student from the second grade level to the third grade level. Meanwhile, the student's general education teacher would continue to teach the fifth grade content standards developed by the state. In this case, the education of a student with a disability may be somewhat disjointed. While the general education teacher teaches to the grade-level content standards of the state, the special education teacher and related service providers may be focused on skills that are below grade-level.

There is little federal guidance on the level of alignment that is expected between content and achievement standards in the ESEA and IEP goals in the IDEA. The only explicit connection between state standards and IEP goals refers to students who are taught to modified achievement standards. Regulations specify that if a student's IEP includes goals for a subject assessed against modified achievement standards, "those goals must be based on the academic content standards for the grade in which the student is enrolled."[30] There is no analogous requirement for students with disabilities who are taught to alternate achievement standards to have IEP goals aligned with state academic content standards. Moreover, there is no requirement for students with disabilities who are taught to grade-level state content standards to have IEP goals based on those standards.

As Congress considers ESEA provisions regarding state standards, it may also consider how IDEA provisions regarding IEP goals are aligned with the standards:

- Common vs. differentiated expectations. The ESEA statutory language specifies that all children shall be held to the same state achievement standards; however, ESEA regulatory language allows states to develop alternate achievement standards and modified achievement standards for some students with disabilities. All states currently have some form of alternate achievement standards in place.

In order to align ESEA statutory language with current practice, Congress could authorize the use of alternate achievement standards or modified achievement standards for some students with disabilities. The development and use of alternate achievement standards and modified achievement standards are currently implemented consistent with U.S. Department of Education (ED) regulations regarding possible options for including students with disabilities in the ESEA assessment and accountability system. If Congress chooses to include alternate achievement standards or modified achievement standards in the statute during the reauthorization of ESEA, regulatory language developed by ED could be used as a starting point to outline the requirements of these standards.[31] If Congress does not authorize the use of alternate achievement standards or modified achievement standards and requires students with disabilities to be taught to grade-level standards, it could lead to more schools and LEAs facing consequences for failing to meet annual achievement targets.[32]

- Alignment of state content and achievement standards with IEP goals. Statutory language does not require IEP goals under the IDEA to be aligned with state content and achievement standards under the ESEA. Some students with disabilities have IEP goals that address knowledge and skills that are below the state grade-level academic content and achievement standards. Demonstrating alignment between grade-level state standards and IEP goals for some students with disabilities (i.e., students with disabilities that are taught to grade-level standards or modified achievement standards) may be relatively straightforward. Demonstrating alignment between grade-level state standards and IEP goals for students with the most significant cognitive disabilities (i.e., students with disabilities that are taught to alternate achievement standards) may be difficult to achieve, however, because some of these students may have IEP goals that are several grade levels below the state standards or have IEP goals that cover basic, prerequisite academic skills. For students with the most significant cognitive disabilities, Congress could require IEP goals to be aligned with alternate achievement standards (i.e., not aligned with grade-level standards). For other students with disabilities, Congress could require IEP goals to be aligned with grade-level state standards. In either case, if Congress chooses to include alignment language, ESEA regulatory language that requires the alignment of modified achievement standards to IEP goals could be used as a model.[33] If state standards and IEP goals are aligned, the education of some students with disabilities would be more consistent across general and special education settings because there would be a common set of expectations for the student. Furthermore, if state standards and IEP goals are aligned, it is more likely that both the general education teacher and special education teacher would be providing instruction on the academic content that would be assessed on the state assessment. If state standards and IEP goals are not aligned, however, it is more likely that the general education teacher and special education teacher would be providing fragmented instruction that may or may not be assessed on the state assessment, which may inhibit students with disabilities from performing as well as possible on these assessments.

ASSESSMENTS

Educational assessment is a complex endeavor that involves gathering and analyzing data to support decision-making about students and the evaluation of academic programs and policies.[34] In recent years, federal education legislation has placed an increased emphasis on assessment in elementary and secondary schools. The ESEA and IDEA both have assessment requirements that affect students with disabilities. Under the ESEA, students with disabilities are required to participate in state assessments used within the federal accountability system.[35]

The IDEA also requires students with disabilities to participate in state assessments used for federal accountability.[36] Under the IDEA, however, students with disabilities also take assessments for a variety of other purposes, such as determining the type and severity of their disabilities and monitoring their progress toward achieving IEP goals.

The following section provides background information on the relevant statutory and regulatory language that describes student assessment in the ESEA and IDEA.

This discussion is followed by an analysis of how the purpose of assessment differs between the ESEA and IDEA, an examination of the alignment between the two laws, and a discussion of alignment options that Congress may consider.

Background

Title I-A of the ESEA requires states to develop a set of high-quality, annual academic assessments in mathematics and reading to be administered in grades 3 through 8 and once in high school.[37] Results of these assessments are used to determine whether the state and each of its LEAs are assisting all students in meeting the content and achievement standards established by the state. In practice, the results of state assessments are used within the federal accountability system to determine whether schools and LEAs have made adequate yearly progress (AYP).[38]

States are required to develop at least one alternate assessment for students with disabilities.[39] The requirement that states develop at least one alternate assessment was intended to ensure that all students with disabilities could participate in state assessment and accountability systems, which is required by both the ESEA and the IDEA. There are currently five options for assessing students with disabilities for state accountability purposes: (1) general state assessment, (2) general state assessment with accommodations, (3) alternate assessment based on grade-level standards, (4) alternate assessment based on alternate achievement standards (AA-AAS),[40] and (5) alternate assessment based on modified achievement standards (AA-MAS).[41] The first three assessment options result in scores that may be counted in AYP calculations in the typical manner, as determined by a state's accountability system.[42] Scores from the fourth and fifth assessment options (AA-AAS and AA-MAS) have restrictions on the way they may be counted in AYP calculations. These restrictions are outlined in regulations issued by ED and have numerous implications for state accountability systems.[43]

As mentioned above, the IDEA requires students with disabilities to participate in all district and state assessments. The IDEA statutory language also reinforces the ESEA regulatory language regarding the provision of alternate assessments for students with disabilities.[44] The IDEA, however, requires various assessments for students with disabilities that are not included in the ESEA. For example, LEAs are required to assess students to determine eligibility for special education and related services by conducting an evaluation which uses "a variety of assessment tools and strategies to gather relevant functional, developmental, and academic information" to determine whether the child is a "child with a disability" and provide information to be used in the writing of the child's IEP.[45] In addition, the IDEA requires a student's IEP team to use assessments to determine how the student's progress toward meeting the annual IEP goals is measured.[46]

One of the ESEA requirements of state assessment systems relevant to students with disabilities is that such systems provide for "reasonable" accommodations for students who have been identified with a disability under the IDEA.[47] An accommodation is a change in the testing material or administration procedures that enable students with disabilities to participate in the assessment.[48] The intent of an accommodation is to remove the influence of a student's disability to the greatest extent possible so that the student may demonstrate his or her true level of achievement. ESEA regulations specify that a state assessment system must provide "appropriate accommodations that the student's IEP team determines are necessary to measure the academic achievement of the student relative to the state's academic content and achievement standards ..."[49]

Like the ESEA, the IDEA addresses the use of accommodations for assessment. To remain eligible for IDEA funding, a state must provide assurances to the Secretary that the state has developed guidelines for the provision of appropriate accommodations.[50] In addition, IDEA statutory language requires the IEP team to select accommodations and provide a written statement about any individually appropriate accommodations that are necessary to measure the academic achievement and functional performance of students with disabilities on state and district assessments.[51] IDEA regulations further specify that each state must issue guidance that

1. identifies only those accommodations for each assessment that do not invalidate the score, and
2. instructs the IEP team to select only those accommodations that do not invalidate the score.[52]

Table 2 provides a comparison of select statutory and regulatory provisions of the ESEA and IDEA discussed above:

Table 2. Comparison of Select Statutory and Regulatory Provisions of the ESEA and IDEA: Assessments

Assessments	ESEA	IDEA
In General	The ESEA requires states to administer annual academic assessments in mathematics and reading for grades 3 through 8 and once in high school. States are also required to develop assessments of science	The IDEA also requires students with disabilities to participate in the state assessments required under ESEA. Under IDEA, students with disabilities also take assessments for a variety of other purposes, such as determining the type and severity of their disabilities and

Assessments	ESEA	IDEA
	achievement to be administered once in each of three grade bands (i.e., grades 3 through 5, 6 through 8, and 9 through 12). Students with disabilities are required to participate in these assessments. The purpose of assessment under ESEA is to evaluate student achievement.	monitoring their progress toward achieving Individualized Education Program (IEP) goals.
Alternate Assessments	The ESEA requires states to develop or adopt at least one alternate assessment for students with disabilities.	IDEA references alternate assessment as it pertains to assessments administered under the ESEA. Under IDEA, all children with disabilities are required to be included in ESEA assessment systems, with appropriate accommodations and alternate assessments where necessary. The type of assessment administered under ESEA to a student with a disability is indicated in their IEP. IDEA does not have additional requirements for alternate assessments.
Accommodations	Under ESEA, the state assessment must provide for "reasonable" accommodations for students who have been identified with a disability under the IDEA. (An accommodation is a change in the testing material or administration procedures that enable students with disabilities to participate in the assessment.)	Under IDEA, a state provides assurances to the Secretary of Education that the state has developed guidelines for the provision of appropriate accommodations. The IEP team is responsible for selecting appropriate accommodations. IDEA regulations specify that IEP teams must select only accommodations that do not invalidate the scores on state assessments administered under the ESEA.

Source: Table prepared by CRS based on provisions in the Elementary and Secondary Education Act (P.L. 107- 110), the Individuals with Disabilities Education Act (P.L. 108-446), and associated regulations.

Note: Under ESEA regulations, only 1% of scores from state assessments based on alternate achievement standards may count as proficient in a state's accountability system. Similarly, under ESEA regulations, only 2% of scores from state assessments based on modified achievement standards may count as proficient in a state's accountability system.

Alignment Issues

Both the ESEA and the IDEA require all students with disabilities to participate in state assessments for accountability and both require the state to develop at least one alternate assessment. The ESEA regulations provide two options for alternate assessments (i.e., AA-AAS, and AA-MAS); however, the IDEA statutory language references only one type of alternate assessment (AA-AAS). The omission of AA-MAS from IDEA statutory language is likely due to the timing of ESEA regulations. The ESEA regulations outlining the use of AA-AAS were released in 2003, which was before the 2004 reauthorization of the IDEA. The ESEA regulations outlining the use of AA-MAS, however, were released in 2007, which was after the 2004 reauthorization of the IDEA.

Currently, regulations issued by ED outline the requirements of alternate assessments for students with disabilities. It is unclear whether the requirements regarding AA-AAS and AA-MAS would be incorporated into the ESEA statute during the next reauthorization or whether these requirements would remain in regulations. ED has indicated that the current Administration is interested in maintaining the use of AA-AAS for students with the most significant cognitive disabilities; however, it does not support the continuation of AA-MAS for other students with disabilities.[53] ED has expressed that AA-MAS may not be necessary if states are encouraged to develop assessments consistent with the principles of universal design.[54] ED has not made changes to the original regulations outlining the use of alternate assessments; however, this issue may receive attention from Congress during the reauthorization of the ESEA.

As discussed earlier, the IDEA requires certain assessments for students with disabilities that are not required by the ESEA. Although these assessments required by the IDEA are not "aligned" with the ESEA, they do not necessarily conflict with the ESEA. In general, students with disabilities participate in assessments under the ESEA for the purpose of accountability, which is an *evaluative* purpose of assessment. Students with disabilities participate in assessments required by the IDEA for other purposes, such as *identification* (i.e., assessments to determine eligibility for special education and related services) and *instructional* purposes (i.e., assessments that measure progress toward achieving IEP goals). Because the assessments required by the ESEA and IDEA serve different purposes, they are not necessarily duplicative or incompatible.[55]

In terms of accommodations for students with disabilities on state assessments, there are some areas of alignment between the ESEA and IDEA and other areas of potential misalignment that Congress may want to clarify. For example, while both the ESEA and IDEA require the use of "appropriate" accommodations for students with disabilities on state assessments, the IDEA regulations further specify that and IEP team may select only accommodations that do not invalidate the state assessment score. The IDEA regulations, therefore, place additional restrictions on the use of accommodations that are not present in ESEA statute or regulations, which could be interpreted as an area of misalignment.

The use of accommodations on state assessments is an issue of implementation that can generate conflict between the needs of a student with a disability and the need to collect comparable achievement data for accountability. One difficult issue to resolve is defining what an "appropriate" accommodation is. According to ESEA regulations, the requirement that an accommodation be "appropriate" refers to the concept of "appropriate for the state assessment," not "appropriate for the student." Although selected accommodations must be both "appropriate for the assessment" *and* "appropriate for the student," if a particular accommodation is "appropriate for the student" but not "appropriate for the assessment," it is generally not allowed because the resulting score would be considered invalid for the purpose of accountability under the ESEA.

This concept of "appropriate for the assessment" presents a complicating factor in selecting accommodations for students with disabilities. It may be the case that a student with a disability is provided a certain accommodation during classroom instruction and classroom assessment because it is "appropriate for the student." When selecting accommodations for the state assessment, however, that particular accommodation may not be "appropriate for the state assessment." The student, therefore, must participate in the state assessment without an accommodation that is typically used during classroom instruction and classroom assessment. [56] While the score obtained without the accommodation is a more valid representation of student achievement under standardized conditions, some may argue that it is not an accurate measure of achievement for a student with a disability who is typically provided that accommodation in the classroom.

If an accommodation is used that is not "appropriate for the assessment," it is considered a nonstandard accommodation. Scores from students who take the state assessment with a non-standard accommodation are considered invalid, and these students are counted as "nonparticipants" in the federal accountability system under ESEA.[57] States and LEAs have faced difficulties in defining and using only standard accommodations, causing students with disabilities to be counted as nonparticipants.[58] As a result, schools and LEAs have failed to meet participation requirements in the federal accountability system, which has lead to consequences for the school.[59]

As Congress considers ESEA provisions regarding assessments, it may also consider how ESEA regulations regarding alternate assessments and general issues regarding accommodations are aligned with the IDEA:

- *Common vs. differentiated assessments.* Requirements regarding the development and use of alternate assessments for students with disabilities are primarily outlined in the ESEA regulations and IDEA statute. In order to remain aligned with the IDEA, the reauthorization of the ESEA must continue to include language that requires states to maintain at least one alternate assessment (e.g., AA-AAS, AA-MAS, or some other alternate assessment not currently in use). To maintain alternate assessments for some students with disabilities, Congress could include explicit statutory language within the ESEA regarding the development and use of alternate assessments. If Congress codifies the use of alternate assessments, questions regarding what type of alternate assessment to promote may arise. Congress could choose to continue the use of AA-AAS, AAMAS, or both. As discussed, the Secretary has expressed an interest in maintaining the AA-AAS but discontinuing the AA-MAS. If Congress agrees with the Secretary's approach, fewer students with disabilities would be eligible to participate in alternate assessments, which may have implications for how the scores of students with disabilities are included in the accountability system. That is, more students with disabilities would be expected to participate in the general state assessment and be assessed against grade-level state content and achievement standards. Under the current system, if fewer students with disabilities participated in alternate assessments, it could lead to more schools and LEAs facing consequences for failing to meet annual achievement targets.[60] If Congress continues the use of AA-AAS but discontinues AA-MAS, one alternative may be to increase the number of assessment scores from AA-AAS that may be counted as proficient in the accountability system, which would allow a greater number of students with disabilities to participate in AA-AAS.[61]

- *Appropriate accommodations.* Selecting appropriate accommodations for students with disabilities on state assessments has been a difficult task for some schools and LEAs. During the reauthorization of the ESEA, states may need further statutory guidance from Congress to define an "appropriate accommodation" so that they can create appropriate guidelines regarding the use of accommodations for schools and LEAs. Statutory language could include an explanation of when, if ever, a non-standard accommodation could be used even though its use could result in an invalid test score. If Congress would like to continue the current practice of defining "appropriate accommodations" as "appropriate for the state assessment" in order to ensure the validity of assessment scores, the reauthorization of the ESEA could include the IDEA regulatory language that currently specifies this requirement.[62] It is possible, however, that by requiring only those accommodations that do not invalidate the state assessment score, Congress would be continuing to require some students with disabilities to participate in an assessment without accommodations that are typically afforded to them in classroom instruction and assessment. As such, although the score from the state assessment would be an accurate representation of what a student with a disability can do under standardized conditions, it may not be an accurate reflection of his or her ability under typical classroom conditions. Under the current system, the use of only standard accommodations (i.e., those that do not invalidate the test score) has resulted in schools, districts, and states failing to meet annual achievement targets.[63]

- *Common assessments and accommodations across states.* The American Recovery and Reinvestment Act (ARRA; P.L. 111-5) appropriated funds for the Secretary to administer several competitive grant programs. One of the competitive grant programs is the Race to the Top Assessment Program (RTTT Assessment Program).[64] Through this program, ED has provided federal funds to two state consortia for the development of new common assessments in English language arts and mathematics.[65] The assessments must measure the achievement of all students, including students with disabilities.[66] During the reauthorization of the ESEA, Congress may promote the use of common assessments in the ESEA accountability system. Although most states are participating in one of the consortia to develop common assessments,[67] many of the participating states have not yet committed to adopting these assessments. Because the common assessments are being developed by the states with support from ED, it is not clear whether Congress will support or require the adoption of common assessments during the reauthorization of the ESEA. Moving forward, if common assessments are adopted, Congress could require the development of a list of "common accommodations" that are allowable. If a list of "common accommodations" was developed, however, there would be no guarantee that states would implement these accommodations similarly, which would result in a lack of comparable assessment results across states. Unless mandated by Congress, not all states would administer common assessments, and not all states that do administer common assessments may provide accommodations in a consistent way. As such, even with the use of a common assessment, results for students with disabilities would not likely be comparable across states. Given the complexity of determining the development and implementation of common assessments, Congress could require ED to monitor and evaluate the use of accommodations on common assessments.

ACCOUNTABILITY[68]

Over the last two decades, federal education policy has been moving toward a focus on student achievement as a means of measuring accountability for schools, LEAs, and states. The increased focus on student achievement and other educational indicators is evident in both the ESEA and IDEA. Both laws measure student achievement and other educational indicators and use these data within a state accountability system. During the latest reauthorizations of the ESEA and the IDEA, statutory provisions were added that increased the emphasis on student outcomes and accountability.

The ESEA accountability system was designed to assess whether schools and LEAs are making AYP with respect to reading and mathematics achievement, achievement on another academic indicator, and student participation in assessments. The IDEA "monitoring and enforcement" system was designed to assess whether states are meeting a series of academic and compliance indicators to determine whether the law is being implemented as intended. For the purpose of this report, the IDEA "monitoring and enforcement" system is referred to as an "accountability" system.

It is important to note that the federal government enforces accountability requirements at different levels in the ESEA and the IDEA. Under the ESEA, the federal government directly monitors the progress of states, LEAs, and schools. Consequences of not meeting accountability requirements are targeted at the LEA and school level. Under the IDEA, the federal government directly monitors the progress of states only. States, however, are required by the IDEA to monitor their own LEAs using the same system that the federal government uses to monitor the states. Under the IDEA accountability system, consequences of not meeting accountability requirements are targeted at the state level; however, states are required by the IDEA to implement the same consequences at the LEA level. IDEA does not require states or LEAs to implement consequences at the school level.

The following section provides background information on the relevant statutory and regulatory language that describes accountability systems in the ESEA and IDEA. This discussion is followed by an analysis of how the accountability systems differ, an examination of the alignment between the two laws, and a discussion of alignment options that Congress may consider.

Background

Title I-A of ESEA requires states to develop and implement a state accountability system to ensure that schools and LEAs make progress with respect to student achievement.[69] State accountability systems must be based on the academic standards and assessments discussed above. The accountability system must be the same system for all public schools (except that public schools and LEAs that do not receive Title I-A funds are not subject to outcome accountability requirements), and incorporate rewards and sanctions based on student performance.

A key concept embodied in the outcome accountability requirements of the ESEA is AYP. AYP is determined based on three components: (1) student academic achievement on state reading and mathematics assessments, with a focus on the percentage of students scoring at the proficient level or higher; (2) 95% student participation rates in assessments by all students and for any subgroup for which data are disaggregated; and (3) performance on another academic indicator, which for high schools must be graduation rate.[70] Each state plan submitted under Section 1111 of the ESEA defines annual AYP targets, which are set with the goal of all students becoming proficient in reading and mathematics by school year 2013-2014.

Schools or LEAs meet AYP standards only if they meet the required threshold levels of performance on all three indicators for the "all students" group and any subgroup for which data are disaggregated. The subgroups are specified in statute as economically disadvantaged students, students with limited English proficiency (LEP), students with disabilities, and students in major racial and ethnic subgroups.

The primary purpose of AYP requirements is to serve as the basis for identifying schools and LEAs where performance is inadequate, so that these inadequacies may be addressed through a series of consequences. Consequences applied to schools and LEAs range from providing increased support and opportunities for public school choice and supplemental educational services to corrective action and restructuring.[71] If any subgroup of students or the "all students" group does not meet AYP targets for two consecutive years or more (at the school or LEA level), the school or LEA, respectively, is subject to the statutory consequences, regardless of the number or type of subgroups that did not meet the AYP targets. If the "students with disabilities" subgroup does not meet AYP targets, the consequences apply to the entire school or LEA and consequences are not specifically targeted to the "students with disabilities" subgroup.

IDEA requires the Secretary to monitor each state's implementation of the law based on three priorities: (1) provision of FAPE;[72] (2) general supervisory authority (e.g., child find, effective monitoring, mediation, etc.); and (3) disproportionate representation of racial and ethnic groups in special education and related services, to the extent the representation is the result of inappropriate identification. The Secretary requires the states to monitor each of their LEAs using the same three priorities.[73]

Under IDEA, states are required to establish measureable targets for twenty indicators developed by the Secretary.[74] *Appendix B* provides a table of the IDEA, Part B Indicators. The indicators established by the Secretary are a combination of compliance and performance indicators. For example, compliance indicators measure a state's adherence to appropriate processes, such as the timeliness of an initial evaluation for special education and related services (Indicator 11) or timeliness of due process hearings (Indicator 17). Performance indicators measure student outcomes, such as high school graduation rates (Indicator 1), drop-out rates (Indicator 2), and participation and performance of students with disabilities on state assessments (Indicator 3).

Each state must collect data on the indicators and report annually to the Secretary.[75] Based on the state's performance on these indicators, information obtained through monitoring visits, and any other public information made available, the Secretary makes a determination of the state's implementation of IDEA. The Secretary determines if the state meets requirements, needs assistance, needs intervention, or needs substantial intervention in implementing the requirements of Part B of IDEA.[76] If states are not determined to "meet requirements" for two consecutive years, the Secretary enforces consequences ranging from advising the state to seek technical assistance to withholding funds or referring the case to the Department of Justice.[77]

Table 3 provides a comparison of select statutory and regulatory provisions of the ESEA and IDEA discussed above.

Alignment Issues

The ESEA and the IDEA have separate accountability systems with similar, yet distinct, goals. The primary purpose of the ESEA accountability system is to ensure that all students are proficient in reading and mathematics by 2013-2014. The primary purpose of the IDEA accountability system is to ensure that each child with a disability is provided FAPE, which includes appropriate special education and related services, as well as, procedural safeguards for students and parents.[78]

There is some overlap, however, between the ESEA and IDEA accountability systems. Both systems report achievement levels or performance outcomes for students with disabilities. For example, the first three IDEA indicators are also included in the ESEA accountability system. Indicator 1 and Indicator 2 require states to report high school graduation rates for students with disabilities and drop out rates for students with disabilities.[79] For IDEA reporting purposes, ED requires states to use the graduation rate calculation, dropout data, and timeline established in the ESEA. Indicator 3 requires states to report on the participation and performance of students with disabilities on state assessments, including (1) the percent of LEAs with a disability subgroup that meets the state's minimum "n" size that meets the state's AYP targets for the disability subgroup; (2) the participation rate for children with disabilities; and (3) the proficiency rate for children with disabilities against grade-level, modified, and alternate achievement standards. These data are also required for accountability reporting under Title I-A of the ESEA.

Table 3. Comparison of Select Statutory and Regulatory Provisions of the ESEA and IDEA: Accountability

Accountability	ESEA	IDEA
In General	The ESEA accountability system measures whether schools and local educational agencies (LEAs) are making adequate yearly progress (AYP) in reading and mathematics achievement.	The IDEA "monitoring and enforcement" system assesses whether states are meeting a series of academic and compliance indicators to determine whether the law is being implemented as intended.
Components of Accountability System	AYP is determined based on three components: (1) student academic achievement on state reading and mathematics assessments, with a focus on the percentage of students scoring at the proficient level or higher; (2) 95% student participation rates in assessments by all students and for subgroups (i.e., economically disadvantaged students, LEP students, students with disabilities, and students in major racial and ethnic subgroups); and (3) performance on another academic indicator, which for high schools must be graduation rate. Beginning in school year 2011-2012, schools, LEAs, and states must report the "four-year adjusted cohort graduation rate." States may also propose to use an "extended-year adjusted cohort graduation rate"; however, ED does not require states to do so.	Under IDEA, the Secretary is required to monitor each state's implementation of the law based on three priorities: (1) provision of a Free Appropriate Public Education (FAPE); (2) general supervisory authority (e.g., child find, effective monitoring, mediation, etc.); and (3) disproportionate representation of racial and ethnic groups in special education and related services, to the extent the representation is the result of inappropriate identification. The Secretary requires the states to monitor each of their LEAs using the same three priorities. Under IDEA, states must report the high school graduation rate for students with disabilities. States must use the same graduation rate calculation as reported to ED under the ESEA.
Targets	Each state plan submitted under ESEA defines annual AYP targets, which are set with the goal of all students becoming proficient in reading and mathematics by school year 2013-2014.	Under IDEA, states are required to establish measureable targets for twenty indicators developed by the Secretary. The indicators are a combination of compliance indicators (e.g., the timeliness of an initial evaluation for special education and related services), and performance indicators (e.g.,

Accountability	ESEA	IDEA
		high school graduation rates).
Results	The results of annual academic state assessments are used within the ESEA accountability system to determine whether schools and LEAs have made AYP.	Based on the state's performance on the twenty indicators, information obtained through monitoring visits, and other public information, the Secretary makes a determination of the state's implementation of IDEA. The Secretary determines if the state meets requirements, needs assistance, needs intervention, or needs substantial intervention in implementing the requirements of IDEA.
Consequences	If schools and LEAs fail to meet AYP for two consecutive years or more, the Secretary enforces consequences that range from providing increased support and opportunities for public school choice and supplemental educational services to corrective action and restructuring.	If states are not determined to "meet requirements" for two consecutive years, the Secretary enforces consequences ranging from advising the state to seek technical assistance to withholding funds or referring the case to the Department of Justice.

Source: Table prepared by CRS based on provisions in the Elementary and Secondary Education Act (P.L. 107- 110), the Individuals with Disabilities Education Act (P.L. 108-446), and associated regulations.

Other than IDEA Indicators 1 through 3, the ESEA and IDEA accountability systems do not overlap with respect to student achievement data. The remaining indicators measure the implementation of the IDEA and are not relevant to the implementation of the ESEA. That said, the remaining indicators do not appear to be in conflict with the goals and purposes of the ESEA accountability system.

Two possible areas of misalignment in the accountability systems, however, lie outside of the specific AYP targets and indicators. The first possible area of misalignment concerns IEP goals. As discussed in the "Standards" section above, IEP goals required by the IDEA are not always aligned with state academic content and achievement standards required by the ESEA. Since the ESEA accountability system is based on state academic content and achievement standards and state assessments, misaligned IEP goals can set up a dual system of academic expectations for students with disabilities. If students have IEP goals that are below grade level, it can be difficult for teachers to determine the appropriate instruction to provide to the student. Under the ESEA, teachers would be held accountable for teaching the student grade-level academic content and achievement standards; under the IDEA, teachers and related service providers would be expected to teach the student according to his or her IEP goals.

The second possible area of misalignment concerns the high school graduation rate calculation. ESEA regulations require states to report the four-year adjusted cohort graduation rate. The four-year adjusted cohort graduation rate is the number of students who graduate in four years with a regular high school diploma divided by the number of students who form the adjusted cohort for the graduating class.[80] This graduation rate calculation may not fully account for the educational experiences of students with disabilities in several ways. First, under IDEA, students with disabilities are entitled to receive FAPE from ages 3 through 21 (inclusive).[81] IDEA, therefore, affords students with disabilities more than four years to complete their high school education. In some cases, a student with a disability may take five or six years to fulfill the requirements of a regular high school diploma. Second, some students with disabilities do not work toward a regular high school diploma. Students with disabilities who work toward an alternative diploma, certificate of completion, certificate of attendance, or some other acknowledgment may not be fully represented in the ESEA accountability system.

As Congress considers ESEA provisions regarding accountability systems, it may also consider how IDEA and ESEA accountability systems are aligned:

- *Inclusion of IEP goals in ESEA accountability system.* Several organizations have proposed increasing the role of IEPs in ESEA accountability systems. For example, several organizations proposed allowing states to count students with disabilities as meeting AYP if they successfully completed their IEP goals.[82] In this scenario, states and LEAs would be provided with the flexibility necessary to develop truly individualized education plans for students with disabilities and allow the curriculum, standards, and assessments to be adapted to suit the needs of the student. On the other hand, the focus on meeting IEP goals for AYP may inadvertently lead to setting lower goals for students with disabilities, thereby lowering overall expectations of achievement for students with disabilities. Such an outcome would be inconsistent with the original intent of including students with disabilities in state accountability systems—increasing access to the general education curriculum, and, in turn, increasing expectations and achievement of students with disabilities.[83] ED has commented that IEP goals are not currently appropriate to use for AYP because,

IEP goals may address a broad range of individualized instructional needs, as well as behavioral and developmental needs, and might not be based on the state's academic content standards. IEP goals may cover a range of issues beyond reading/language arts and mathematics, such as behavior, social skills, or the use of adaptive equipment, and, as such, an examination of how well a student met his or her IEP goals is not synonymous with achievement measured by an alternate assessment for AYP purposes.[84]

If Congress chooses to increase the role of IEPs in the ESEA accountability system, statutory language outlining the components of the ESEA system would need to be altered to incorporate the use of IEPs and possibly allow for individualized goals for students with disabilities.[85]

- *Graduation rates and accountability.* ESEA regulations specify that schools and LEAs will be held accountable for the four-year adjusted cohort graduation rate beginning with data collected in school year 2011-2012. As discussed above, the "four year" rate may not fully account for the educational experiences of some students with disabilities because IDEA allows them to receive FAPE in high school through age 21. ESEA regulations further specify that states may apply to ED to use an "extended-year adjusted cohort graduation rate" as part of its accountability system.[86] The extended-year adjusted cohort rate allows a state to give schools and LEAs credit for students who graduate in more than four years with a regular high school diploma. The state may not, however, propose to use the extended-year graduation rate for specific student subgroups (e.g., students with disabilities). In addition, the extended-year adjusted cohort rate would not apply to students with disabilities who do not receive a regular diploma.[87] To become conceptually aligned with the timeline of high school completion under IDEA, Congress could consider allowing or requiring the use of the extended-year graduation rate requirement in statutory language. If extended-year adjusted cohort rates are used by states, more students with disabilities may be included in the high school graduation rate calculation. As such, schools may be accountable for ensuring the graduation of a broader pool of students. If extended-year adjusted cohort rates are not used by states, however, there may be less incentive in the ESEA accountability system for states to assist students with disabilities in graduating from high school if they need more than four years to complete the requirements for a regular high school diploma.

- *Alternative measures of high school completion.* Some students with disabilities work toward other forms of high school completion, which is a decision that is typically made by the student's IEP team. This decision has a direct effect on the high school graduation rate that must be reported for both the ESEA and IDEA accountability systems. Decisions made by an IEP team under IDEA, therefore, may influence whether or not schools and LEAs meet the high school graduation rate targets outlined in their ESEA accountability systems. Some may argue that Congress could consider adding statutory language that would allow other forms of high school completion to be reported along with the ESEA high school graduation rate so that IEP teams do not exercise undue influence over the ESEA accountability system. If information on students with disabilities who receive some other form of high school completion is reported along with graduation rates for the purpose of accountability, more students with disabilities would be included in the ESEA accountability system; however, this practice may provide an incentive for states and IEP teams to set lower graduation goals for students with disabilities.[88]

TEACHERS[89]

A major focus of both the ESEA and the IDEA is to improve academic outcomes for all students, including students with disabilities. It is widely recognized that improving academic outcomes for all students is dependent on the quality of instruction they receive from teachers. As discussed earlier, approximately 60% of students with disabilities spend at least 80% of their instructional time in the general education classroom. Because they receive instruction inside and outside the general education classroom, students with disabilities are taught by both general education teachers and special education teachers. The quality of both general education teachers and special education teachers may influence the achievement of students with disabilities.

Furthermore, collaborative efforts between general education teachers and special education teachers may contribute to the achievement of students with disabilities.

The following section provides background information on the relevant statutory and regulatory language that describes teacher requirements in the ESEA and IDEA. This discussion is followed by an examination of the alignment between the ESEA and IDEA and a discussion of alignment options that Congress may consider.

Background

The ESEA includes a definition of "highly qualified" teacher as the term relates to teachers of elementary and secondary education.[90] In general, the ESEA requires that teachers of core academic subjects:[91] (1) must have full state certification, (2) must not have had any certification waived on an emergency, temporary, or provisional basis, and (3) must have at least a baccalaureate degree.[92] In addition, the definition has various requirements depending on the teacher's level of experience (i.e., new versus experienced) and the grade level taught by the teacher (i.e., elementary, middle, or secondary).

With respect to new teachers, a new *elementary* school teacher must demonstrate subject knowledge and teaching skills in reading, writing, mathematics, and other areas of the basic elementary school curriculum by passing a state test. A new *middle or secondary* school teacher must demonstrate a high level of competency in each of the academic subjects taught in one of the following ways: (1) passing a state academic subject test, or (2) completing an academic major, graduate degree, or coursework equivalent to an undergraduate academic major, or advanced certification credentialing in each of the academic subjects taught.[93] Experienced elementary, middle, or secondary school teachers may meet either the definition of "highly qualified" for new teachers or demonstrate competency in all subjects taught using a "high objective uniform state standard of evaluation" (HOUSSE).[94]

The IDEA also includes a definition of "highly qualified" teacher as the term relates to special education teachers of elementary and secondary education.[95] Under IDEA, for any special education teacher, the term "highly qualified" has the meaning given to the term in the ESEA with several exceptions. First, the IDEA definition of "highly qualified" applies to all special education teachers regardless of whether they teach core academic subjects.[96] All special education teachers (1) must have full state certification, (2) must not have had any certification waived on an emergency, temporary, or provisional basis, and (3) must have at least a baccalaureate degree.[97] Second, the IDEA definition broadens the "highly qualified" requirements with respect to two groups of special education teachers: (1) teachers who teach only core academic subjects exclusively to students with the most significant cognitive disabilities and (2) teachers who teach more than one core academic subject exclusively to students with disabilities.[98]

Teachers who teach core academic subjects exclusively to students with the most significant cognitive disabilities, whether new or not new to the profession, have several options for meeting the "highly qualified" definition: (1) teachers may meet the "highly qualified" definition of the ESEA for any elementary, middle, or secondary teacher; (2) *elementary* teachers may meet the requirements by demonstrating competence on HOUSSE; and (3) *middle and secondary* school teachers may meet the requirements by demonstrating "subject matter knowledge appropriate to the level of instruction being provided, as determined by the State, needed to effectively teach to those standards" (i.e., alternate achievement standards).[99]

Teachers who teach more than one core academic subject exclusively to students with disabilities also have several options for meeting the "highly qualified" definition: (1) teachers may meet the ESEA requirements for each core subject taught; (2) experienced special education teachers may meet the requirements based on the ESEA HOUSSE option, which may include a single evaluation covering multiple subjects; and (3) new special education teachers who are already "highly qualified" in mathematics, language arts, or science have two years from the date of employment to meet the "highly qualified" definition with respect to the other core subjects taught.[100]

Table 4 provides a comparison of select statutory and regulatory provisions of the ESEA and IDEA discussed above.

Alignment Issues

The ESEA provides the definition of "highly qualified" teacher for elementary and secondary school teachers. The IDEA definition of "highly qualified" teacher broadens requirements for special education teachers. The legislative language in the ESEA and the IDEA are aligned conceptually, and the IDEA definition references the ESEA definition. Furthermore, the IDEA states that a teacher who is deemed "highly qualified" under IDEA shall be considered "highly qualified" for the purposes of the ESEA.[101]

One potential area of misalignment related to the "highly qualified" teacher definitions concerns the implementation of the requirements at the school level. ESEA outlines the requirements for general education teachers and IDEA outlines the requirements for special education teachers, which sets up two "tracks" to become "highly qualified." The existence of two tracks seems to imply that students without disabilities are taught by general education teachers and students with disabilities are taught by special education teachers.

In reality, general education teachers and special education teachers share the responsibility for educating most students with disabilities. As previously discussed, almost 60% of students with disabilities spend at least 80% of their time in the general education classroom. Many students with disabilities, therefore, spend the *majority* of their time taught by a general education teacher. Even if a general education teacher is "highly qualified," the teacher may not have any preparation or training in special education.

There is no federal requirement for general education teachers to have specialized preparation or training in special education. The likelihood that a general education teacher has received such preparation or training depends on certification requirements in the state. According to data from the National Association of State Directors of Teacher Education and Certification (NASDTEC), in order for a general education teacher to become certified, 28 states require coursework in special education, 11 states do not require coursework in special education, and 12 states did not report this information.[102] In the 28 states that require coursework in special education, information on the amount and type of coursework is not readily available.

A second potential area of misalignment in teacher policy more broadly concerns the current shift toward "teacher effectiveness."[103] During the implementation of the "highly qualified" teacher definition, this requirement came to be seen as setting minimum qualifications for entry into the profession and was criticized by some for establishing standards so low that nearly every teacher met the requirement.[104]

Meanwhile, policymakers have grown increasingly interested in the output of teachers' work; that is, their performance in the classroom and the effectiveness of their instruction.

A number of federal, state, and local programs have been implemented in an effort to improve teacher performance through alternative compensation systems.[105]

Table 4. Comparison of Select Statutory and Regulatory Provisions of the ESEA and IDEA: Teachers

Teachers	ESEA	IDEA
In General	The ESEA includes a definition of "highly qualified" teacher as the term relates to teachers of elementary and secondary education.	The IDEA also includes a definition of "highly qualified" teacher as the term relates to special education teachers of elementary and secondary education.
Highly Qualified Teacher Requirements	The ESEA "highly qualified" teacher definition requires that teachers of core academic subjects (i.e., English, reading, or language arts, mathematics, science, foreign languages, civics and government, economics, arts, history, and geography): (1) must have full state certification, (2) must not have had any certification waived on an emergency, temporary, or provisional basis, and (3) must have at least a baccalaureate degree. In addition, the definition has various requirements depending on the teacher's level of experience (i.e., new versus experienced) and the grade level taught by the teacher (i.e., elementary, middle, and secondary).	Under IDEA, for any special education teacher, the term "highly qualified" teacher has the meaning given to the term in the ESEA with some exceptions. First, the IDEA definition of "highly qualified" teacher applies to all special education teachers regardless of whether they teach core academic subjects. Second, the IDEA definition broadens the "highly qualified" teacher requirements with respect to special education teachers who teach only core academic subjects exclusively to students with the most significant cognitive disabilities and to teachers who teach more than one core academic subject exclusively to students with disabilities.

Source: Table prepared by CRS based on provisions in the Elementary and Secondary Education Act (P.L. 107-110), the Individuals with Disabilities Education Act (P.L. 108-446), and associated regulations.

The most recent federal effort to promote teacher evaluation systems based on teacher effectiveness is the Race to the Top (RTTT) grant program.106 A significant feature of teacher evaluation systems that measure the output of teachers' work is the concept of "teacher effectiveness." Under the RTTT program, the measurement of teacher effectiveness was required to be based, in part, on student achievement on state assessments.[107]

One concern with the potential policy shift toward teacher evaluation systems based on teacher effectiveness is that it is unclear how special education teachers would be included in these systems.[108] Teacher evaluation systems based on teacher effectiveness must be able to link student achievement data to the teacher who is responsible for instruction. Students with disabilities are educated in multiple settings by multiple teachers. As such, general education teachers and special education teachers share the responsibility of educating students with disabilities. It is unclear whether the general education teacher or the special education teacher would ultimately be held accountable for the student's achievement.[109] It is possible that both general and special education teachers could be held accountable for the student's achievement, but the logistics of "splitting" responsibility for student achievement may complicate teacher evaluation systems. There also may be some complicating factors in terms of measurement. That is, students with disabilities participate in a variety of state assessments (i.e., general state assessments and alternate assessments), and it is unclear whether all types of assessment are appropriate to use in a teacher evaluation system that is based, in part, on student achievement on state assessments.

As Congress considers the ESEA provisions regarding teacher preparation, recruitment, and evaluations, it may also consider how these provisions are aligned with IDEA:

- *Highly qualified teachers providing instruction to students with disabilities.* Several education disability advocacy groups that have promoted maintaining the "highly qualified" teacher definition have called for the reauthorization of the ESEA to include more specific requirements for general educators who teach students with disabilities.[110] Specifically, the Learning Disabilities Association of America (LDA) recommends that "highly qualified" general education teachers should be prepared to deliver scientific, research-based instruction for students with disabilities and be able to modify the curriculum, as necessary.[111] The National Association of State Directors of Special Education (NASDSE) recommends that language be added to the ESEA that requires teachers to "have knowledge and proficiency to work with all types of diverse students, including students with disabilities, in order to be highly qualified."[112] Because many students with disabilities spend the majority of their time in the regular education classroom, the ability of a regular education teacher to address the needs of students with disabilities may directly impact the learning of students with disabilities and their performance on state assessments. Under the current ESEA accountability system, the quality of instruction provided to students with disabilities by general education teachers, therefore, likely contributes to a school's, LEA's, or state's ability to meet AYP targets for students with disabilities.

- *Collaboration between general and special education teachers.* Because many students with disabilities spend the majority of their time in a general education classroom, a common priority of education disability advocacy groups is to increase collaboration between general education teachers and special education teachers.[113] For example, the Council for Exceptional Children (CEC) recommends that ESEA reauthorization support mentoring and induction programs that support collaboration between general and special education. CEC asserts that such collaboration may lead to more successful teaching or co-teaching for students with disabilities and the provision of more appropriate accommodations and modifications for students with disabilities.[114] Similarly, the Council of Administrators of Special Education recommends that ESEA reauthorization include language promoting collaboration so that students with disabilities can receive appropriate instruction in the least restrictive environment.[115] If general education teachers and special education teachers work more collaboratively, it may be more likely that all teachers take responsibility for the achievement of students with disabilities. In addition, a collaborative model may create a system in which the educational needs of students with disabilities are more likely to be met, which may increase the quality of instruction received by students with disabilities. As discussed above, under the current ESEA accountability system, the quality of instruction provided to students with disabilities likely contributes to a school's, LEA's, or state's ability to meet AYP targets for students with disabilities.

- *Teacher effectiveness.* Some organizations, such as CEC and the National Coalition on Personnel Shortages in Special Education and Related Services, assert that special education teachers should be fully included in any teacher evaluation system that measures the effectiveness of general education teachers.[116] There may be difficulties associated with designing one teacher evaluation for all teachers (i.e., general education teachers and special education teachers). Teacher evaluation systems that include the measurement of "teacher effectiveness" rely on the ability to link student achievement data to the teacher or teachers who are responsible for the student's learning. As discussed previously, students with disabilities are often taught in more than one setting by more than one teacher. It may be difficult to determine which teacher should be held accountable for the achievement of students with disabilities. In addition, it may be difficult to incorporate student achievement on alternate assessments into teacher evaluation systems. Some alternate assessments do not measure student achievement and growth in a standard way;[117] therefore, it would be difficult to determine whether a student made appropriate achievement gains that would indicate whether a teacher is "effective."[118] Due to the complexity of assessing teacher effectiveness, Congress may want to require ED to conduct a pilot study or to provide guidance on how to incorporate special education teachers into teacher evaluation systems. Because of the difficulties associated with evaluating special education teachers based on "teacher effectiveness," another model may be to evaluate special education teachers based on whether or not their students achieve their IEP goals. An evaluation system based on IEP goals may be more relevant for special education teachers; however, such an evaluation system may complicate teacher evaluation because it would set up different systems of evaluating general education teachers and special education teachers. It may also provide an incentive for IEP teams to set lower goals for students with disabilities that seem more attainable and may potentially reduce the likelihood that IEP teams set ambitious goals that could lead to increased achievement for students with disabilities. Furthermore, because special education teachers are required to be part of the IEP team, it may be considered a conflict of interest if special education teachers are permitted to influence the IEP goals against which they would be evaluated.[119]

APPENDIX A. SELECTED ACRONYMS

Table A-1. Glossary

AA-AAS	Alternate Assessment based on Alternate Achievement Standards
AA-MAS	Alternate Assessment based on Modified Achievement Standards

Table A-1. (Continued)

APR	Annual Performance Report
ARRA	American Recovery and Reinvestment Act
AYP	Adequate Yearly Progress
CEIS	Coordinated Early Intervening Services
ED	U.S. Department of Education
ESEA	Elementary and Secondary Education Act
FAPE	Free Appropriate Public Education
HOUSSE	High Objective Uniform State Standard of Evaluation
IDEA	Individuals with Disabilities Education Act
IEP	Individualized Education Program
LEA	Local Educational Agency
LEP	Limited English Proficient
MOE	Maintenance of Effort
NCLB	No Child Left Behind
RTTT	Race to the Top
RTTTAssessment Program	Race to the Top Assessment Program
SPP	State Performance Plan

APPENDIX B. IDEA, PART B INDICATORS

Table B-1. IDEA, Part B State Performance Plan (SPP) and Annual Performance Report (APR)
Part B Indicator Measurement Table

Monitoring Priorities and Indicators
1. Percent of youth with IEPsa graduating from high school with a regular diploma. (20 U.S.C. 1416(a)(3)(A))
2. Percent of youth with IEPs dropping out of high school. (20 U.S.C. 1416(a)(3)(A))
3. Participation and performance of children with IEPs on statewide assessments: a) Percent of the districts with a disability subgroup that meets the state's minimum "n" size that meet the state's AYP[b] targets for the disability subgroup. b) Participation rate for children with IEPs. c) Proficiency rate for children with IEPs against grade level, modified, and alternate academic achievement standards. (20 U.S.C. 1416(a)(3)(A))
4. Rates of suspension and expulsion: a) Percent of districts that have a significant discrepancy in the rate of

Monitoring Priorities and Indicators
suspensions and expulsions of greater than 10 days in a school year for children with IEPs; and b)   Percent of districts that have: (a) a significant discrepancy, by race or ethnicity, in the rate of suspensions and expulsions of greater than 10 days in a school year for children with IEPs; and (b) policies, procedures or practices that contribute to the significant discrepancy and do not comply with requirements relating to the development and implementation of IEPs, the use of positive behavioral interventions and supports, and procedural safeguards. (20 U.S.C. 1416(a)(3)(A); 1412(a)(22))
5. Percent of children with IEPs aged 6 through 21 served: a)   Inside the regular class 80% or more of the day; b)   Inside the regular class less than 40% of the day; and c)   In separate schools, residential facilities, or homebound/hospital placements. (20 U.S.C. 1416(a)(3)(A))
6. Percent of children aged 3 through 5 with IEPs attending a: a)   Regular early childhood program and receiving the majority of special education and related services in the regular early childhood program; and b)   Separate special education class, separate school or residential facility. (20 U.S.C. 1416(a)(3)(A))
7. Percent of preschool children aged 3 through 5 with IEPs who demonstrate improved: a)   Positive social-emotional skills (including social relationships); b)   Acquisition and use of knowledge and skills (including early language/ communication and early literacy); and c)   Use of appropriate behaviors to meet their needs. (20 U.S.C. 1416 (a)(3)(A))
8. Percent of parents with a child receiving special education services who report that schools facilitated parent involvement as a means of improving services and results for children with disabilities. (20 U.S.C. 1416(a)(3)(A))
9. Percent of districts with disproportionate representation of racial and ethnic groups in special education and related services that is the result of inappropriate identification. (20 U.S.C. 1416(a)(3)(C))
10. Percent of districts with disproportionate representation of racial and ethnic groups in specific disability categories that is the result of inappropriate identification. (20 U.S.C. 1416(a)(3)(C))

Table B-1. (Continued)

Monitoring Priorities and Indicators
11. Percent of children who were evaluated within 60 days of receiving parental consent for initial evaluation or, if the State establishes a timeframe within which the evaluation must be conducted, within that timeframe. (20 U.S.C. 1416(a)(3)(B))
12. Percent of children referred by Part C prior to age 3, who are found eligible for Part B, and who have an IEP developed and implemented by their third birthdays. (20 U.S.C. 1416(a)(3)(B))
13. Percent of youth with IEPs aged 16 and above with an IEP that includes appropriate measurable postsecondary goals that are annually updated and based upon an age appropriate transition assessment, transition services, including courses of study, that will reasonably enable the student to meet those postsecondary goals, and annual IEP goals related to the student's transition services needs. There also must be evidence that the student was invited to the IEP Team meeting where transition services are to be discussed and evidence that, if appropriate, a representative of any participating agency was invited to the IEP Team meeting with the prior consent of the parent or student who has reached the age of majority. (20 U.S.C. 1416(a)(3)(B))
14. Percent of youth who are no longer in secondary school, had IEPs in effect at the time they left school, and were: a) Enrolled in higher education within one year of leaving high school. b) Enrolled in higher education or competitively employed within one year of leaving high school. c) Enrolled in higher education or in some other postsecondary education or training program; or competitively employed or in some other employment within one year of leaving high school. (20 U.S.C. 1416(a)(3)(B))
15. General supervision system (including monitoring, complaints, hearings, etc.) identifies and corrects noncompliance as soon as possible but in no case later than one year from identification. (20 U.S.C. 1416 (a)(3)(B))
16. Percent of signed written complaints with reports issued that were resolved within 60-day timeline or a timeline extended for exceptional circumstances with respect to a particular complaint, or because the parent (or individual or organization) and the public agency agree to extend the time to engage in mediation or other alternative means of dispute resolution, if available in the state. (20 U.S.C. 1416(a)(3)(B))
17. Percent of adjudicated due process hearing requests that were adjudicated within the 45-day timeline or a timeline that is properly extended by the hearing officer at the request of either party or in the case of an expedited hearing, within

Monitoring Priorities and Indicators
the required timelines. (20 U.S.C. 1416(a)(3)(B))
18. Percent of hearing requests that went to resolution sessions that were resolved through resolution session settlement agreements. (20 U.S.C. 1416(a)(3)(B))
Monitoring Priorities and Indicators
19 Percent of mediations held that resulted in mediation agreements. (20 U.S.C. 1416(a)(3)(B))
20 State reported data (618 and State Performance Plan and Annual Performance Report) are timely and accurate. (20 U.S.C. 1416(a)(3)(B))

Source: IDEA, Part B Measurement Indicator table from the U.S. Department of Education (http://www2.ed.gov/policy/speced/guid/idea/bapr/2010/b2-1820-0624bmeastable111210.pdf).

a)   Individualized Education Program.
b)   Adequate Yearly Progress.

End Notes

[1] For more information on elementary and secondary education funding, see U.S. Department of Education (ED), Summary of Discretionary Funds, FY2008-FY2012 President's Budget: http://www2.ed.gov/about/overview/budget/   budget12/summary/appendix1.pdf.   Other sources of federal funding for elementary and secondary education in FY2011 include the State Fiscal Stabilization Fund, career and technical state grants, and "other K-12."

[2] For more information on the ESEA accountability system, see CRS Report R41533, Accountability Issues and Reauthorization of the Elementary and Secondary Education Act, by Rebecca R. Skinner and Erin D. Lomax and CRS Report RL32495, Adequate Yearly Progress (AYP): Implementation of the No Child Left Behind Act, by Rebecca R. Skinner.

[3] See footnote 1.

[4] See Data Accountability Center, Part B Child Count (2009), Table 1-3 available at http://www.ideadata.org.

[5] See Data Accountability Center, Part B, Educational Environment (2009), Table 2-2 available at http://www.idea.org.

[6] 58.41% of students with disabilities spend at least 80% of their time in the regular education classroom. See footnote 5.

[7] Alternate assessments are discussed in a later section of this report. For more information, see CRS Report R40701, Alternate Assessments for Students with Disabilities, by Erin D. Lomax.

[8] Students receive special education and related services covered by the IDEA in both the general education classroom and the special education classroom.

[9] For background information on the ESEA, see CRS Report RL33960, The Elementary and Secondary Education Act, as Amended by the No Child Left Behind Act: A Primer, by Rebecca R. Skinner; for background information on the IDEA, see CRS Report R41833,

The Individuals with Disabilities Education Act (IDEA), Part B: Key Statutory and Regulatory Provisions, by Ann Lordeman.

[10] For more information on the Secretary's announcement and to see details of the waiver package, see http://www.ed.gov/esea/flexibility.

[11] This section draws on reports previously written by Rebecca Skinner. For more information on academic standards in the ESEA, see CRS Report RL33960, The Elementary and Secondary Education Act, as Amended by the No Child Left Behind Act: A Primer, by Rebecca R. Skinner and CRS Report R41533, Accountability Issues and Reauthorization of the Elementary and Secondary Education Act, by Rebecca R. Skinner and Erin D. Lomax.

[12] For information on the federal government's role in the standards-based reform movement, see CRS Report R41533, Accountability Issues and Reauthorization of the Elementary and Secondary Education Act, by Rebecca R. Skinner and Erin D. Lomax.

[13] ESEA, §1111(b)(1). A content standard specifies what all students should know and be able to do. An achievement standard is a predetermined level of performance that denotes proficiency within or mastery or a given content area.

[14] This report specifically discusses provisions of the ESEA and IDEA that are relevant to public schools.

[15] ESEA, §1111(b)(1)(D)(i).

[16] The ESEA uses the word "align" with respect to standards and assessments. ESEA's use of the word "align" should not be construed to imply alignment between the ESEA and the IDEA. In this report, alignment between the ESEA and the IDEA is specifically discussed under the headers of "Alignment Issues."

[17] Academic achievement standards may describe more than three levels of achievement as long as they describe two levels of high achievement (proficient and advanced) and one level of lower achievement that describes how students are progressing toward achieving proficiency in the standards.

[18] ESEA, §1111(b)(1)(C).

[19] 34 CFR §200.1(d) and §200.1(e). Note that the regulations do not specify that states may develop different content standards for some students with disabilities; the regulations specify that states may develop different achievement standards. Non-regulatory guidance, however, has further specified that "grade-level content may be reduced in complexity or modified to reflect pre-requisite skills" (see http://www2.ed.gov/policy/elsec/guid/altguidance.pdf). In effect, the content standards may be modified for a small subset of students with disabilities (i.e., students with the most significant cognitive disabilities).

[20] As defined by IDEA, §602(3).

[21] Students with the "most significant cognitive disabilities" are not defined by the ESEA or the IDEA. According to non-regulatory guidance, the term "most significant cognitive disability" was not intended to create a new category of disability. ED intended that "the term 'students with the most significant cognitive disabilities' include that small number of students who are (1) within one or more of the existing categories of disability under the IDEA (e.g., autism, multiple disabilities, traumatic brain injury, etc.); and (2) whose cognitive impairments may prevent them from attaining grade-level achievement standards, even with the very best instruction" (see page 23 of http://www2.ed.gov/policy/elsec/guid/altguidance.pdf). States are responsible for defining "most significant cognitive disability" and establishing criteria for identification.

[22] Only 1% of scores from state assessments based on alternate achievement standards may count as proficient in a state's accountability system. Therefore, it is likely that an estimated 1%

of all students (representing 9% of students with disabilities nationwide) would be taught to alternate achievement standards.

[23] As defined by IDEA, §602(3).

[24] See 34 CFR §200.1(e).

[25] Only 2% of scores from state assessments based on modified achievement standards may count as proficient in a state's accountability system. Therefore, it is likely than an estimated 2% of all students (representing approximately 20% of all students with disabilities) would be taught to modified achievement standards.

[26] Requirements of the IEP are outlined in IDEA, §614.

[27] The term "free appropriate public education," or FAPE, is defined in IDEA, §601(9) as "special education and related services that—(A) have been provided at public expense, under public supervision and direction, and without charge; (B) meet the standards of the state educational agency; (C) include an appropriate preschool, elementary school, or secondary school education in the state involved; and (D) are provided in conformity with the individualized education program required under section 614(d) [Individualized Education Program (IEP)]." For more information on FAPE, see CRS Report R41833, The Individuals with Disabilities Education Act (IDEA), Part B: Key Statutory and Regulatory Provisions, by Ann Lordeman.

[28] IDEA, §614 (d)(1)(B).

[29] Although IEP goals are determined annually, they may be rewritten throughout the year to meet the changing needs of a child with a disability.

[30] 34 CFR §200.1 (e)(2)(iii).

[31] See 34 CFR §200.1(d) and (e) for regulatory language outlining the requirements for alternate achievement standards and modified achievement standards.

[32] Under the current ESEA accountability system, meeting annual achievement targets is part of determining whether a school, LEA, or state meets adequate yearly progress (AYP). AYP is discussed in a later section of this report, "Accountability."

[33] See 34 CFR §200.1 (e)(2)(iii).

[34] For more information on general educational assessment, see CRS Report R40514, Assessment in Elementary and Secondary Education: A Primer, by Erin D. Lomax.

[35] ESEA, §1111(b)(3)(C)(ix)(I).

[36] IDEA, §612(a)(16).

[37] States are also required to develop assessments of science achievement to be administered once in each of three grade bands (i.e., grades 3 through 5, 6 through 8, and 9 through 12). Results of the science assessment, however, are not used in the accountability system. For a comprehensive discussion of assessment requirements under Title I of the ESEA, see CRS Report R41670, State Assessments Required by the No Child Left Behind Act: An Analysis of Requirements, Funding, and Cost, by Erin D. Lomax.

[38] AYP is discussed in a later section of this report, "Accountability."

[39] The requirement that states develop alternate assessments for students with disabilities is not explicitly stated in statutory language; however, regulations on the development of these assessments have made the requirement explicit. For a comprehensive report on alternate assessments, see CRS Report R40701, Alternate Assessments for Students with Disabilities, by Erin D. Lomax.

[40] AA-AAS are provided for students with the "most significant cognitive disabilities."

[41] AA-MAS are provided for students with disabilities whose disability has "precluded the student from achieving grade-level proficiency" as demonstrated by the state assessment or other assessments that provide valid results on student achievement.

[42] For more information on the calculation of AYP, see CRS Report RL32495, Adequate Yearly Progress (AYP): Implementation of the No Child Left Behind Act, by Rebecca R. Skinner.

[43] The restrictions on the use of alternate assessments in accountability systems are discussed in a later section of this report, "Accountability." Restrictions on the use of alternate assessments in accountability systems are also discussed in CRS Report R40701, Alternate Assessments for Students with Disabilities, by Erin D. Lomax.

[44] IDEA, §612(a)(16)(C)(ii). In addition to requirements regarding the alternate assessment itself, IDEA statutory language specifies that, "if the state has adopted alternate academic achievement standards permitted under the regulations promulgated to carry out section 1111(b)(1) of the Elementary and Secondary Education Act of 1965, [the alternate assessment shall] measure the achievement of children with disabilities against those standards."

[45] IDEA, §614(b)(2)(A). While the federal government defines broad disability categories in legislation, the IDEA does not provide operational definitions of each disability. Each state has developed its own operational definition of each disability category, and assessments are used to determine whether a child is a "child with a disability" in that state.

[46] IDEA, §614(d)(1)(A)(i)(III).

[47] ESEA, §1111(b)(3)(C)(ix). Accommodations are also provided for students who are not identified as a "child with a disability" under IDEA but who qualify under Section 504 of the Rehabilitation Act of 1973. Students who qualify for accommodations under Section 504 are beyond the scope of this report. For more information on Section 504 of the Rehabilitation Act, see CRS Report RL34041, Section 504 of the Rehabilitation Act of 1973: Prohibiting Discrimination Against Individuals with Disabilities in Programs or Activities Receiving Federal Assistance, by Emily C. Barbour.

[48] Assessment accommodations are often grouped into five categories: (1) presentation (e.g., repeat directions, read aloud, large print, Braille), (2) equipment and materials (e.g., calculator, amplification equipment, manipulatives), (3) response (e.g., mark answers in book, scribe records response, point), (4) setting (e.g., study carrel, student's home, separate room), and (5) timing/scheduling (e.g., extended time, frequent breaks).

[49] 34 CFR §200.6(a). States are also required to develop, disseminate information on, and promote the use of appropriate accommodations. For more information on states' accommodation policies, see http://www.cehd.umn.edu/ NCEO/TopicAreas/ Accommo dations/StatesAccomm.htm.

[50] IDEA, §612(a)(16)(B).

[51] IDEA, §614(d)(1)(A)(i)(VI)(aa).

[52] 34 C.F.R. §300.160(b).

[53] Secretary Duncan stated that "... we are moving away from the 2% rule" at a gala hosted by the American Association of People with Disabilities on March 15, 2011. The "2% rule" refers to AA-MAS because only 2% of the proficient scores from AA-MAS may be counted as proficient in the NCLB accountability system. To read Secretary Duncan's full remarks, see http://www.ed.gov/news/speeches/all-means-all-secretary-duncans-remarks-american-association-people-disabilities.

[54] Statements made about AA-AAS and AA-MAS are based on information provided by the U.S. Department of Education at a meeting with staff from the House of Representatives on March 25, 2010. Universal design is a concept central to disability policy and is currently a focus of assessment design within IDEA. The universal design of assessments is based on a set of principles that promote fairness and equity in educational assessment. For more

information on universal design, see page 30 of CRS Report R40514, Assessment in Elementary and Secondary Education: A Primer, by Erin D. Lomax.

[55] For a discussion of a general assessment framework, including the purposes of assessment, see pp. 2-3 of CRS Report R40514, Assessment in Elementary and Secondary Education: A Primer, by Erin D. Lomax.

[56] Media reports have found that states and LEAs have faced difficulties with certain accommodations that are typically allowed in the classroom but not on state assessments. Accommodations that seem most likely to be disallowed are the read-aloud accommodation, calculators, and scribes. For examples, see Alexa Aguilar, "Many schools fail only in special ed; Some question how students are tested," Chicago Tribune, November 2, 2007; Jeff Cummings, "State board asked to OK calculators for AIMS test," Arizona Daily Star, December 6, 2006; Bill Turque, "D.C. schools cutting back on 'read-aloud,'" D.C. Wire, March 16, 2009.

[57] The federal accountability system requires at least 95% participation on the state assessment. The 95% participation requirement also applies to subgroups, such as students with disabilities. If a substantial number of students with disabilities use non-standard accommodations and are therefore counted as "nonparticipants," the school or LEA may fail to meet the participation requirement of 95% and not meet AYP goals. See U.S. Department of Education, Modified Academic Achievement Standards Non-regulatory Guidance, April 2007, p. 32.

[58] For examples, see Margaret Reist, "'Adequate yearly progress' not achieved at Culler, Everett," Lincoln Journal Star, November 20, 2007; Bruce Pascoe, "No Child Left Behind rules must be changed," Arizona Daily Star, September 10, 2007; Charles Kelly, "Peoria schools gain on U.S. goals; but some still get dinged because of a conflict between two federal laws, district official says," The Arizona Republic, September 7, 2007; Jeff Cummings, "Specialed AIMS help a dilemma for schools," Arizona Daily Star, September 11, 2006.

[59] Consequences for failing to meet the participation requirement in the federal accountability system are discussed in another section of this report, "Accountability."

[60] Under the current ESEA accountability system, meeting annual achievement targets is part of determining whether a school, LEA, or state meets AYP. AYP is discussed in a later section of this report, "Accountability."

[61] Currently, ED regulations allow up to 1% of scores on AA-AAS to be counted as proficient in the ESEA accountability system. Congress could introduce statutory language to raise, lower, or eliminate the 1% cap.

[62] 34 C.F.R. §300.160(b).

[63] Under the current ESEA accountability system, meeting annual achievement targets is part of determining whether a school, LEA, or state meets AYP. AYP is discussed in a later section of this report, "Accountability."

[64] Although the RTTT and RTTT Assessment Program are not currently included in the ESEA, these competitive grant programs have been seen by some as an outline of ED's priorities for the reauthorization of the ESEA. Since elements of the RTTT program and RTTT Assessment program may be relevant for ESEA reauthorization, these programs are relevant to this report. For information on the RTTT Assessment Program, see http://www2.ed. gov/programs/ racetothetop-assessment/index.html.

[65] The common assessments are intended to measure recently developed common standards in English language arts and mathematics. The common standards were developed by the states through a partnership between the National Governors Association and the Council of

Chief State School Officers. For more information on common standards, see http://www.corestandards.org/.

[66] For the purpose of the RTTT Assessment Program, however, state consortia are not required to design assessments for students with the "most significant cognitive disabilities" (i.e., the students who are currently eligible to participate in AA-AAS). In the RTTT Assessment Program, a student with a disability is defined as "a student with a disability under the Individuals with Disabilities Education Act, as amended (IDEA), except for a student with a disability who is eligible to participate in alternate assessments based on alternate achievement standards consistent with 34 CFR §200.6(a)(2)" (U.S. Department of Education, "Overview Information; Race to the Top Fund Assessment Program; Notice Inviting Applications for New Awards for Fiscal Year (FY) 2010," 75 Federal Register 18171-18185, April 9, 2010.). ED continues to support the development of AA-AAS for students with the most significant cognitive disabilities, however, through a separate competitive grant program (see U.S. Department of Education, "Office of Special Education and Rehabilitative Services; Overview Information; Technical Assistance on Data Collection— General Supervision Enhancement Grants: Alternate Academic Achievement Standards; Notice Inviting Applications for New Awards for Fiscal Year (FY) 2010," 75 Federal Register 32435-32440, June 8, 2010.).

[67] The Partnership for Assessment of Readiness for College and Careers (PARCC) is a consortium of 26 states; the SMARTER Balanced Assessment Consortium is a consortium of 31 states. Some states participate in both consortia.

[68] This section draws on reports previously written by Rebecca Skinner. For more information on accountability in the ESEA, see CRS Report RL33960, The Elementary and Secondary Education Act, as Amended by the No Child Left Behind Act: A Primer, by Rebecca R. Skinner and CRS Report R41533, Accountability Issues and Reauthorization of the Elementary and Secondary Education Act, by Rebecca R. Skinner and Erin D. Lomax.

[69] ESEA, §1111(b)(2).

[70] States select the other academic indicator for elementary and middle schools. Generally, states choose to use attendance rates.

[71] For specific information on consequences and rewards based on AYP, see "Performance-Based Accountability: Consequences and Rewards" in CRS Report R41533, Accountability Issues and Reauthorization of the Elementary and Secondary Education Act, by Rebecca R. Skinner and Erin D. Lomax.

[72] See footnote 27.

[73] IDEA, §616(a)(3).

[74] 34 C.F.R. §300.601(a)(3).

[75] 34 C.F.R. §300.601(b)(1).

[76] States are required to make determinations of their LEAs using the same system as the Secretary uses to make determinations of states (see 34 C.F.R. §300.600).

[77] The Secretary has many statutory enforcement options available depending on the severity of a state's difficulty in implementing the requirements of IDEA. See IDEA, §616(e).

[78] For more information on the procedural safeguards of IDEA, see CRS Report R41833, The Individuals with Disabilities Education Act (IDEA), Part B: Key Statutory and Regulatory Provisions, by Ann Lordeman.

[79] Refer to Table B-1 for the list of indicators.

[80] The cohort is adjusted to include students who transfer into the cohort during the 9th grade and the next three years and exclude students who transfer out, emigrate to another country, or die during the same period.

[81] IDEA, §612(a)(1). FAPE is required for students from age 3 through 21 (inclusive) unless this is inconsistent with state law or practice, or the order of any court; or unless state law does not require the provision of special education and related services to students from age 18 through 21 who, in their educational placement prior to incarceration in an adult correctional facility, were not identified as a "child with a disability" under §602 or did not have an IEP.

[82] National Governors Association, Council of Chief State School Officers, and National Association of State Boards of Education, Joint Statement on the Reauthorization of the No Child Left Behind Act (NCLB), http://www.nga.org/files/live/sites/NGA /files/pdf/ 0704NCLBSTATEMENT.PDF.

[83] For more discussion on the consequences of using IEPs in accountability systems, see "Role of IEPs" in CRS Report R40701, Alternate Assessments for Students with Disabilities, by Erin D. Lomax.

[84] U.S. Department of Education, Alternate Achievement Standards for Students with the Most Significant Cognitive Disabilities, August 2005, p. 17, http://www2.ed.gov/policy/ elsec/guid/altguidance.pdf.

[85] If IEP goals are used in the ESEA accountability system, however, it may be necessary for Congress to include requirements in the IEP process under IDEA that would prevent setting lower goals for students with disabilities. For example, Congress could require an external validation of IEP goals. This external review could be a peer-review process conducted by ED, the state, or the LEA.

[86] 34 C.F.R. §200.19(b)(1)(v).

[87] According to ED, "A student with a disability who does not graduate with a regular high school diploma, but instead receives an alternative diploma, certificate of completion, or any other degree or certificate that is not fully aligned with a state's academic content standards may not be counted as graduating in calculating either the four-year or extended-year graduation rate." See U.S. Department of Education, High School Graduation Rate Non-Regulatory Guidance, Washington, DC, December 22, 2008, p. 7, http://www2. ed.gov/policy/elsec/guid/hsgrguidance.pdf.

[88] If other forms of high school completion are counted, it may be necessary for Congress to include requirements in the IEP process under IDEA that would prevent setting lower high school completion or graduation goals for students with disabilities. Congress could require an external validation of the IEP goals regarding high school completion for students with disabilities. This external review could be a peer-review process conducted by ED, the state, or the LEA.

[89] This section draws on reports previously written by Jeffrey Kuenzi. For more information on teacher policy, see CRS Report RL33333, A Highly Qualified Teacher in Every Classroom: Implementation of the No Child Left Behind Act and Reauthorization Issues for the 112th Congress, by Jeffrey J. Kuenzi and CRS Report R41267, Elementary and Secondary School Teachers: Policy Context, Federal Programs, and ESEA Reauthorization Issues, by Jeffrey J. Kuenzi.

[90] ESEA, §9101(23).

[91] Core academic subjects are defined as "English, reading, or language arts, mathematics, science, foreign languages, civics and government, economics, arts, history, and geography" (see ESEA, §9101(11)).

[92] ESEA, §9101(23)(A). The requirement that all teachers have a baccalaureate degree is not mentioned in subsection (A); however, this requirement is mentioned in several places

within the definition, which results in all teachers being required to have a baccalaureate degree.

[93] ESEA, §9101(23)(B).

[94] ESEA, §9101(23)(C). The HOUSSE standard (1) is set by the state for both grade appropriate academic subject matter knowledge and teaching skills; (2) is aligned with challenging state academic content and achievement standards; (3) provides objective, coherent information about the teacher's attainment of core content knowledge in the subjects taught; (4) is applied uniformly to all teachers in the academic subject taught and the same grade level throughout the state; (5) takes into consideration, but not based primarily on, the time the teacher has been teaching the academic subject; (6) is made available to the public upon request; and (7) may involve multiple, objective measures of teacher competency.

[95] IDEA, §602(10).

[96] Recall that "highly qualified" requirements in the ESEA apply exclusively to teachers of core academic subjects.

[97] IDEA, §602(10)(B).

[98] The IDEA definition of "highly qualified" does not amend the ESEA definition of "highly qualified."

[99] IDEA, §602(10)(C)(ii).

[100] IDEA, §602(10)(D).

[101] IDEA, §602(10)(F). ESEA regulations also specify that a special education teacher shall be deemed "highly qualified" under the ESEA if the teacher meets the requirements of the IDEA (see 34 C.F.R. §200.56(d)).

[102] NASDTEC Knowledge Database, Table B1, retrieved by CRS on July 21, 2011.

[103] For more information on teacher effectiveness, see CRS Report R41051, Value-Added Modeling for Teacher Effectiveness, by Erin D. Lomax and Jeffrey J. Kuenzi.

[104] According to a study conducted for the Education Department by the RAND Corporation, "By 2006–07, the vast majority [over 90 percent] of teachers met their states' requirements to be considered highly qualified under NCLB." http://www.ed.gov/rschstat/eval/ teaching/nclb-final/report.pdf.

[105] For more information on these programs, see CRS Report R40576, Compensation Reform and the Federal Teacher Incentive Fund, by Jeffrey J. Kuenzi.

[106] The recent federal effort to promote the use of teacher evaluation systems based on teacher effectiveness was led by the Administration. For more information on the RTTT grant program and how it relates to teacher effectiveness, see CRS Report R41051, Value-Added Modeling for Teacher Effectiveness, by Erin D. Lomax and Jeffrey J. Kuenzi.

[107] For more information on the measurement of teacher effectiveness, see CRS Report R41051, Value-Added Modeling for Teacher Effectiveness, by Erin D. Lomax and Jeffrey J. Kuenzi.

[108] For a discussion of states' work in the area of performance-based compensation with a focus on special educators, see Paula Burdette, Performance-based Compensation: Focus on Special Education Teachers, inForum, April 2011, http://www.projectforum.org/docs/ Performance-basedCompensation-FocusOnSpecialEducationTeachers-final.pdf.

[109] It is possible to design teacher evaluation systems in which groups of teachers are responsible for the achievement of students. Under the RTTT grant program, however, states were required to use the measurement of teacher effectiveness to make individual-level decisions about teachers (e.g., compensation, promotion, tenure, and dismissal), so it is unclear whether a group model would have been permitted. For more information on the requirements of the RTTT grant program (including teacher evaluation systems), see http://edocket.access.gpo.gov/2009/pdf/E9-27426.pdf.

110 See, for example, comments from the LDA (http://www.ldanatl.org/pdf/LDA% 20%20ESEA%20Comments%2003.22.10.pdf) and NASDSE (http://nasdse.org/Portals/ 0/Documents/ Gov%20Relations/ESEA_ reauthorization_principles_2010.pdf).

111 See LDA comments, available at http://www.ldanatl.org/pdf/LDA%20%20ESEA%20 Comments%2003.22.10.pdf.

112 See NASDSE comments, available at http://nasdse.org/Portals/0/Documents/ Gov%20 Relations/ESEA_reauthorization_principles_2010.pdf). NASDSE maintains, however, that no federal requirement should be enforced. Rather, states should continue to have the authority to establish the specific criteria for teachers to be deemed "highly qualified" in their state.

113 See, for example, LDA and NASDSE comments, available at http://www.ldanatl.org/pdf/ LDA%20%20ESEA%20Comments%2003.22.10.pdf and http://nasdse.org/Portals/0/ Documents/Gov%20Relations/ ESEA_reauthorization_principles_2010.pdf; the Council for Exceptional Children (http://www.cec.sped.org/Content/ NavigationMenu/PolicyAdvocacy/ CECPolicyResources/NoChildLeftBehind/CEC_2010_ESEA_Policy_WEB.pdf); and the Council of Administrators of Special Education (http://www.casecec.org/Documents/ CASE_ESEA_Recommendations.pdf).

114 See CEC comments, available at http://www.cec.sped.org/Content/ NavigationMenu/ PolicyAdvocacy/ CECPolicyResources/NoChildLeftBehind/CEC_2010_ESEA_Policy_WEB.pdf.

115 See CASE comments, available at http://www.casecec.org/Documents/ CASE_ESEA_ Recommendations.pdf. For more information on the "least restrictive environment," see CRS Report R41833, The Individuals with Disabilities Education Act (IDEA), Part B: Key Statutory and Regulatory Provisions, by Ann Lordeman.

116 See CEC comments, available at http://www.cec.sped.org/Content/ NavigationMenu/ PolicyAdvocacy/ CECPolicyResources/NoChildLeftBehind/CEC_ 2010_ESEA_Policy_ WEB.pdf;see National Coalition on Personnel Shortages in Special Education and Related Services comments, available at http://specialedshortages.org/ PersonnelShortagesCoalition ESEA Recommendations5_10_10.pdf.

117 For example, some alternate assessments use checklists, teacher observations, or portfolios to document student achievement.

118 NASDSE recommends that, "if teachers are to be rated on their effectiveness in terms of student achievement, consideration must be given to the diversity of their students and their individual growth (e.g., using a growth model) so that teachers who are making gains with challenging students as well as those students who may not make a year's growth in a year's time are recognized for the accomplishments of their students." See NASDSE comments, available at http://nasdse.org/Portals/0/Documents/Gov%20Relations/ESEA_reauthor ization_principles_2010.pdf.

119 If special education teachers are evaluated based on the achievement of IEP goals, it may be necessary for Congress to include requirements in the IEP process of IDEA that would prevent IEP teams from setting lower goals for students with disabilities.

In: Education of Students with Disabilities   ISBN: 978-1-62257-996-9
Editors: H. Garlach and N. Darst   © 2013 Nova Science Publishers, Inc.

Chapter 2

THE INDIVIDUALS WITH DISABILITIES EDUCATION ACT (IDEA), PART B: KEY STATUTORY AND REGULATORY PROVISIONS[*]

Ann Lordeman

SUMMARY

The Individuals with Disabilities Education Act (IDEA) is both a grants statute and a civil rights statute. As a grants statute, IDEA provides federal funding for the education of children with disabilities and requires, as a condition for the receipt of such funds, the provision of a free appropriate public education (FAPE) (i.e., specially designed instruction provided at no cost to parents that meets the needs of a child with a disability). In FY2011, $12.5 billion was appropriated for IDEA. In the fall of 2009, 5.9 million children ages six through 21 received educational services under IDEA.

As a civil rights statute, IDEA contains procedural safeguards, which are provisions intended to protect the rights of parents and children with disabilities regarding the provision of FAPE. These procedures include parental rights to resolve disputes through a mediation process, and present and resolve complaints through a due process complaint procedure, and through state complaint procedures. IDEA's procedural

[*] This is an edited, reformatted and augmented version of a Congressional Research Service publication, CRS Report for Congress R41833, from www.crs.gov, prepared for Members and Committees of Congress, dated May 24, 2011.

safeguards also address disciplinary issues. In general, a child with a disability is not immune from discipline, but the procedures are not the same as for non-disabled children.

To be covered under IDEA, a child with a disability must meet the categorical definition of disability in the act, and the child must require special education and related services as a result of the disability in order to benefit from public education. Once a child meets IDEA's eligibility criteria, FAPE is implemented through the Individualized Education Program (IEP), which is the plan for providing special education and related services by the local educational agency (LEA). The IEP is developed by an IEP team composed of school personnel and parents. IDEA requires that children with disabilities be educated in the least restrictive environment. That is, to the maximum extent appropriate they are to be educated with children who are not disabled. In 2008, over 50% of all children with disabilities served by IDEA spent 80% or more of their time in a regular classroom.

To implement IDEA, states and other entities (i.e., the District of Columbia, Puerto Rico, the Bureau of Indian Education, the outlying areas, and the freely associated states) receive grants based on a statutory formula. Most of the federal funds received by states are passed on to LEAs based on a statutory formula. IDEA also contains state and local maintenance of effort (MOE) requirements and supplement, not supplant (SNS) requirements aimed at increasing overall educational spending, rather than substituting federal funds for education spending at the state and local levels.

Originally enacted in 1975, IDEA has been the subject of numerous reauthorizations to extend services and rights to children with disabilities. The most recent reauthorization of IDEA was P.L. 108-446 enacted in 2004. Funding for Part B, Assistance for Education of all Children with Disabilities, the largest and most often discussed part of the act, is permanently authorized. Funding for Part C, Infants and Toddlers with Disabilities, and Part D, National Activities, is authorized through FY2011.

INTRODUCTION

Background

The Individuals with Disabilities Education Act (IDEA) is the main federal statute governing special education for children from birth through age 21.[1] IDEA protects the rights of children with disabilities to a free appropriate public education (FAPE).

It also supplements state and local funding to pay for some of the additional or excess costs of educating children with disabilities. IDEA is administered by the Office of Special Education Programs (OSEP) in the Office of Special Education and Rehabilitative Services (OSERS) in the Department of Education (ED).

In the fall of 2008, a total of 6.6 million public school students age six though 21 were served by IDEA Part B, representing approximately 13% of all public school students in this age range.[2]

IDEA was originally enacted in 1975 as the Education for All Handicapped Children Act, P.L. 94- 142.[3] At that time, Congress found that more than half of all children with disabilities were not receiving appropriate educational services and that 1 million children with disabilities were excluded entirely from the public school system. Further, Congress found that many of the children participating in regular school programs were prevented from having a successful educational experience because their disabilities were undiagnosed.[4]

In addition to the awareness of the difficulties faced by children with disabilities, there were three other factors that precipitated the enactment of P.L. 94-142: (1) judicial decisions that found constitutional requirements for the education of children with disabilities, (2) the inability of states and localities to fund education for children with disabilities, and (3) potential long-term benefits of educating children with disabilities.[5]

IDEA consists of four parts. Part A contains the general provisions, including the purposes of the act and definitions.

Part B contains provisions relating to the education of school aged children (the grants-to-states program) and state grants program for preschool children with disabilities (Section 619). Part C authorizes state grants for programs serving infants and toddlers with disabilities, while Part D contains the requirements for various national activities designed to improve the education of children with disabilities. *Table 1* shows the structure and funding of IDEA. *Appendix A* provides a more detailed summary of each of the four parts.

Since 1975, IDEA has been the subject of numerous reauthorizations to extend services and rights to children with disabilities. The most recent reauthorization was P.L. 108-446 in 2004.[6] Funding for Part B, Assistance for Education of all Children with Disabilities, is permanently authorized. Funding for Part C, Infants and Toddlers with Disabilities, and Part D, National Activities, is authorized through FY2011.[7]

Table 1. Structure and Funding of IDEA
(funding in thousands of dollars)

IDEA Part	Description	FY2011 Funding	Percentage of Total IDEA Funding
Part A—General Provisions	Includes findings, purposes, and definitions	—	—
Part B—Assistance for Education of all Children with Disabilities	Contains provisions relating to the education of school aged children (the grants-to-states program) and state grants program for preschool children with disabilities (Section 619)	$11,855,551[a]	95%
Part C—Infants and Toddlers with Disabilities	Authorizes state grants for programs serving infants and toddlers with disabilities	$438,548	3%
Part D—National Activities to Improve Education of Children with Disabilities	Contains the requirements for various national activities	$240,734	2%
IDEA Total		$12,534,833[b]	100%

Source: Table prepared by CRS. Funding amounts are from Department of Education budget tables for FY2011, and reflect the 0.2 percent rescission required by Section 1119 of P.L. 112-10.

a) Of this amount, $373.4 million, or 3% of the total IDEA FY2010 appropriation, was appropriated for the state grants program for preschool children with disabilities (Section 619).

b) This amount does not include $8.1 million for the national activity of the Special Olympics education program authorized under the Special Olympics Sport and Empowerment Act of 2004 (P.L. 108-406). While this is not an IDEA activity, it is sometimes shown in the Department of Education's total for Special Education.

Three of the main purposes of IDEA are

(A) to ensure that all children with disabilities have available to them a free appropriate public education that emphasizes special education and related services designed to meet their unique needs and prepare them for further education, employment, and independent living; (B) to ensure that the rights of children with disabilities and parents of such children are protected; and (C) to assist states, localities, educational service agencies, and Federal agencies to provide for the education of all children with disabilities;[8]

The focus of this report will be on how these purposes are to be achieved under Part B of IDEA, hereafter referred to as IDEA. The first purpose is addressed primarily in the section of this report titled "Services for Children with Disabilities." The second is addressed in the section on "Procedural Safeguards ," and the third is addressed in the section on "Funding, Expenditure Requirements, and Compliance."

SERVICES FOR CHILDREN WITH DISABILITIES

Children with disabilities receive specially designed instruction and other services to meet their unique needs.

This section addresses (1) criteria children must meet to receive services under IDEA, (2) how the children are identified and evaluated, and (3) the procedures for developing an individualized plan to provide special education and related services.

Categories of Disabilities

Autism
Deaf-blindness
Deafness
Emotional disturbance
Hearing impairment
Mental retardation
Multiple disabilities
Orthopedic impairment
Other health impairment
Specific learning disability
Speech or language impairment
Traumatic brain injury
Visual impairment

CHILDREN WITH DISABILITIES

To be covered under IDEA, a child with a disability must meet two criteria. First, the child must be in one of several categories of disabilities, and second, the child must require special education and related services as a result of the disability in order to benefit from public education.[9] If a child meets the two criteria, he or she would be eligible to receive specially designed instruction or special education in which the content or the delivery of the instruction is adapted to the needs of the child. If a child has a disability, but does not require special education to benefit from public education, he or she would not be covered under IDEA. The child might be covered, however, under two other acts that address the rights of individuals with disabilities: Section 504 of the Rehabilitation Act[10] or the Americans with Disabilities Act (ADA).[11] These two acts provide broad nondiscrimination protection not limited to education and have identical functional definitions of disability (i.e., disabilities related to such functions as seeing, hearing, walking, thinking) rather than the categorical definition of IDEA. "Several of the most common disabilities of students included under Section 504 and the ADA, but not always covered under IDEA, are attention deficit hyperactivity disorder (ADHD), diabetes, and asthma."[12]

Figure 1 shows the distribution of students with disabilities age six through 21 receiving special education and related services in the fall of 2009. Forty-two percent of students with disabilities have specific learning disabilities (SLD).[13] Learning disabilities include such conditions as perceptual disabilities, brain injury, minimal brain dysfunction, dyslexia, and developmental aphasia.[14]

Free Appropriate Public Education (FAPE)

All children with disabilities between the ages of three and 21, inclusive, residing in a state are entitled to FAPE.[15] The term "free appropriate public education" means

> special education and related services that—(A) have been provided at public expense, under public supervision and direction, and without charge; (B) meet the standards of the state educational agency; (C) include an appropriate preschool, elementary school, or secondary school education in the state involved; and (D) are provided in conformity with

the individualized education program required under section 614(d) [Individualized Education Programs (IEP)].[16]

In addition, FAPE must be available to a child with a disability who has been suspended or expelled from school.[17] FAPE must also be available to a child with a disability who needs special education and related services even though the child has not failed or been retained in a course or grade and is advancing from grade to grade.[18]

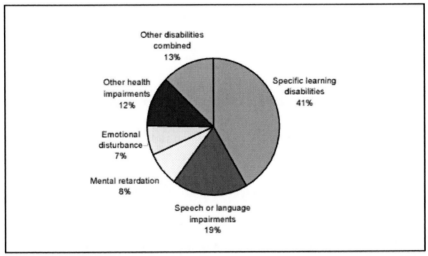

Source: Data Accountability Center, Part B Child Count (2009), MS-EXCEL Table 1-3, https://www.ideadata.org/arc_toc11.asp#partbCC.

Notes: Percentages may not add to 100% because of rounding. Total number of students is 5.9 million. Other disabilities combined include multiple disabilities, hearing impairments, orthopedic impairments, visual impairments, autism, deaf-blindness, traumatic brain injury, and developmental delay.

Figure 1. Disability Distribution for Students ages six through 21 Receiving SpecialEducation and Related Services under IDEA, Part B: Fall 2009.

Identification and Evaluation

Identifying and Evaluating a Child with a Disability
The first step in providing FAPE to children with disabilities is identifying them. Each state must have in effect policies and procedures to ensure that all children with disabilities residing in the state who are in need of special

education and related services are identified, located, and evaluated. These policies and procedures are referred to in statute as "child find."[19] The children include those with disabilities who are

- homeless or wards of the state,
- attending private schools,
- suspected of having a disability, and
- highly mobile children, including migrant children.

A child who has been identified as having (or possibly having) a disability must be evaluated by the LEA before receiving special education and related services to determine whether a child is a child with a disability and to determine the educational needs of the child.[20] Either the parent or the LEA may request an initial evaluation.[21] In general, the LEA must obtain informed consent from the parent before conducting an initial evaluation.[22] Parental consent for an evaluation cannot be construed as consent for special education and related services.[23] The initial evaluation must take place within 60 days of receiving parental consent or within an alternative time frame established by the state.[24]

In conducting the initial evaluation, the LEA must

- use a variety of assessment tools and strategies to gather relevant functional, developmental, and academic information, including information provided by the parent;
- not use any single measure or assessment as the sole criterion for determining whether a child is a child with a disability or determining an appropriate educational program for the child; and
- use technically sound instruments that may assess the relative contribution of cognitive and behavioral factors, in addition to physical or developmental factors.[25]

In addition, assessments and other evaluation materials used to assess a child must be selected and administered so as not to be discriminatory on a racial or cultural basis. They must also be provided and administered in the language and form most likely to yield accurate information on what the child knows and can do academically, developmentally, and functionally.[26]

Upon completion of the evaluation, the determination of whether the child is a child with a disability is made and the educational needs of the child are decided by a team of qualified professionals and by the parent of the child.[27] A copy of the evaluation report and the documentation of determination of eligibility is given to the parent.[28] In making a determination of eligibility, a child shall not be determined to be a child with a disability if the determinant factor is lack of appropriate instruction in reading, lack of instruction in math, or limited English proficiency.[29]

Reevaluations are required if the child's teacher or parent makes a request or if the LEA determines that the child's educational and service needs, academic achievement, or functional performance warrant a reevaluation. For example, a reevaluation might be warranted if the child's performance in school significantly improves, suggesting that he or she no longer requires special education and related services, or if the child is not making progress toward the goals in his or her IEP, indicating that changes are needed in the education or related services the LEA is providing.

A reevaluation may not be done more than once a year unless the parent and LEA agree, and must be done at least once every three years unless the parent and the LEA agree that a reevaluation is not necessary.[30] In general, parental consent is required for reevaluations as well as for the initial evaluation.[31] In addition, the LEA cannot change the eligibility of a child until a reevaluation is done, unless the child graduates from high school with a regular diploma or reaches the age at which state law no longer provides for FAPE.[32]

Identifying and Evaluating a Child with a Specific Learning Disability (SLD)

As noted above, 43% of children with disabilities have SLDs. It is therefore worth noting the procedures required for identifying a child with an SLD. In addition to the procedures addressed above for identifying a child with a disability, the statute and regulations allow additional procedures.[33] In general, a state must adopt criteria for determining whether a child has an SLD, and an LEA must use the state criteria.[34]

The state criteria cannot require the use of a severe discrepancy between intellectual ability and achievement for determining whether a child has a specific learning disability;[35] must permit the use of a process based on the child's response to scientific, research-based intervention;[36] and may permit the use of other alternative research-based procedures for determining whether a child has an SLD.[37]

In general, the group members who determine whether a child has an SLD must include the child's parents, the child's regular education teacher, and at least one person qualified to conduct individual diagnostic examinations of children (e.g., a school psychologist, speech-language pathologist, or remedial reading teacher).[38] The group may determine that a child has an SLD if three criteria are met:[39]

- The child does not achieve adequately for the child's age or meet state-approved grade-level standards in one or more of eight areas[40] when provided with learning experiences and instruction appropriate for the child's age or state-approved grade-level standards.
- The child either does not make sufficient progress to meet age or state-approved grade-level standards in one or more of the eight areas when using a process based on the child's response to scientific, research-based intervention; or the child exhibits a pattern of strengths and weaknesses in performance, achievement, or both, relative to age, state-approved grade-level standards, or intellectual development that is determined by the group to be relevant to the identification of an SLD.
- If the child is found to have an SLD, it is not primarily the result of a visual, hearing, or motor disability; mental retardation; emotional disturbance; cultural factors; environmental or economic disadvantage; or limited English proficiency.

To ensure that underachievement in a child suspected of having an SLD is not due to lack of appropriate instruction in reading or math, the group must consider, as part of the evaluation, (1) data that demonstrate that prior to, or as a part of, the referral process, the child was provided appropriate instruction in regular education settings, delivered by qualified personnel; and (2) data-based documentation of repeated assessments of achievement at reasonable intervals, reflecting formal assessment of student progress during instruction, which was provided to the child's parents.[41]

If prior to a referral for an evaluation, a child has not made adequate progress after an appropriate period of time when provided instruction, an LEA must promptly request parental consent to evaluate the child.[42] The regulations also specify that the child must be observed in the child's learning environment to document the child's academic performance and behavior in the areas of difficulty.[43] Finally, the regulations detail the specific documentation for determining eligibility for a child suspected of having an SLD.[44]

The Individualized Education Program (IEP)

FAPE is implemented through the IEP, which is the plan for providing special education and related services by the LEA to the child with a disability. It is developed by an IEP team composed of school personnel and parents. In general, the IEP team must consider the strengths of the child; the concerns of the parents for enhancing the education of their child; the results of the initial evaluation (or most recent evaluation); and the academic, developmental, and functional needs of the child.[45] The IEP team meets at least once a year to review the IEP to determine if goals are being met and to make necessary changes.[46] The team must meet to develop the initial IEP for a child within 30 days of determining that the child needs special education and related services. In addition, as soon as possible following the development of the IEP, special education and related services must be made available to the child in accordance with the IEP.[47]

Content of IEP[48]

Specifically, IDEA requires that the IEP include the following:

- the child's present levels of academic achievement and functional performance;
- measurable annual goals, including academic and functional goals, designed to
  - meet the child's needs that result from the child's disability to enable the child to be involved in and make progress in the general education curriculum; and
  - meet each of the child's other educational needs that result from the child's disability;
- how the child's progress toward meeting the above annual goals will be measured and when periodic reports on the progress the child is making toward meeting the annual goals will be provided;
- the special education and related services and supplementary aids and services, based on peer-reviewed research to the extent practicable, to be provided to the child, or on behalf of the child, and the program modifications or supports for school personnel that will be provided for the child to
  - advance appropriately toward attaining the annual goals;

- be involved in and make progress in the general education curriculum and participate in extracurricular and other nonacademic activities; and
  - be educated and participate with other children with disabilities and nondisabled children;
- the extent, if any, to which the child will not participate with nondisabled children in the regular class;
- any individual appropriate accommodations49 that are necessary to measure the academic achievement and functional performance of the child on state and district-wide assessments; if the IEP team determines that the child will take an alternate assessment on a particular state or district-wide assessment of student achievement, the IEP should detail why the child cannot participate in the regular assessment and why the particular alternate assessment selected is appropriate for the child;50
- the projected date for the beginning of the assessments and their frequency, location, and duration.

In addition, beginning not later than when the first IEP is in effect when the child is 16, and updated annually thereafter, the IEP must include appropriate measurable postsecondary goals related to training, education, employment, and, where appropriate, independent living skills and the transition services[51] needed to assist the child in reaching those goals.

The IEP Team[52]

Each child identified as a child with a disability must have an IEP developed by an IEP team. In general, the composition of the team includes

- the parents of a child with a disability;
- one or more regular education teachers, if the child is or may be participating in the regular education environment;
- one or more special education teachers;
- a representative of the LEA who is qualified to provide or supervise the provision of special education; is knowledgeable about the general education curriculum; and is knowledgeable about the availability of resources of the LEA;
- an individual who can interpret the instructional implications of evaluation results;

- at the discretion of the parent or the agency, other individuals who have knowledge or special expertise regarding the child, including related services personnel, as appropriate; and
- whenever appropriate, the child with a disability.[53]

Special Education and Related Services

The provision of special education and related services is a key component of FAPE. Special education means "specially designed instruction, at no cost to parents, to meet the unique needs of a child with a disability, including— (A) instruction conducted in the classroom, in the home, in hospitals and institutions, and in other settings; and (B) instruction in physical education."[54] Specially designed instruction, which is delineated in the IEP, means that the content, methodology, or delivery of instruction is adapted to address the unique needs of the child that result from the child's disability. The instruction must ensure the child's access to the general curriculum, so that the child can meet the educational standards that apply to all children. While specially designed instruction is provided at no cost to parents, parents can be required to pay any incidental fees that are normally charged to nondisabled students or their parents as a part of the regular education program.[55]

In general, related services are transportation and those developmental, corrective, and other supportive services required to help a child with a disability to benefit from special education. Both the statute and federal regulations define related services and provide a list of related services.[56] The regulations also further define the services that may be provided to a child with a disability. The list is not exhaustive; other related services could be provided to a child with a disability. Related services include the following:

- speech-language pathology and audiology services;
- interpreting services for children who are deaf, hard of hearing, or deaf-blind;
- psychological services;
- physical therapy and occupation therapy;
- recreation, including therapeutic recreation;
- social work services in schools;
- school health services and school nurse services;
- counseling services, including rehabilitation counseling;

- orientation and mobility services provided to blind or visually impaired children;
- parent counseling and training;
- medical services for diagnostic and evaluation purposes only;[57] and
- early identification and assessment of disabilities through the implementation of a formal plan for identifying a disability.

Coordinated Early Intervening Services (CEIS)

With some restrictions, LEAs may use up to 15% of their allocations[58] "to develop and implement coordinated, early intervening services, which may include interagency financing structures, for students in kindergarten through grade 12 (with a particular emphasis on students in kindergarten through grade 3) who have not been identified as needing special education or related services but who need additional academic and behavioral support to succeed in a general education environment."[59] CEIS may not, however, delay an appropriate evaluation of a child suspected of having a disability.[60]

In its analysis of comments and changes to the final regulations, ED discusses the potential benefits of CEIS as follows:

> The authority to use some Part B funds for early intervening services has the potential to benefit special education, as well as the education of other children, by reducing academic and behavioral problems in the regular educational environment and reducing the number of referrals to special education that could have been avoided by relatively simple regular education interventions.[61]

LEAs may use CEIS funds for both professional development for teachers and other school staff and for educational and behavioral evaluations, services, and supports to students.[62] Funds may also be used to carry out CEIS that are aligned with activities funded by, and carried out under, the Elementary and Secondary Education Act of 1965 (ESEA) if the funds supplement, and do not supplant, ESEA funds.[63]

A state must require an LEA to use up to 15% of its funds for CEIS if the state has determined through statutorily required data collection that "significant disproportionality"[64] based on race and ethnicity is occurring with respect to the identification of children with disabilities; their placement in particular education settings; and the incidence, duration, and type of disciplinary actions, including suspensions and expulsions.[65] The funds are to be used to provide CEIS "to serve children in the LEA, particularly, but not exclusively, children in those groups that were significantly overidentified."[66]

Response to Intervention (RTI)

One way that coordinated early intervening services are provided is through an approach called Response to Intervention (RTI). RTI "is a multi-level framework to maximize student achievement by providing support to students at risk for poor learning outcomes."[67] While there are many models of RTI, ED notes that

> the core characteristics that underpin all RTI models are: (1) students receive high quality research-based instruction in their general education setting; (2) continuous monitoring of student performance; (3) all students are screened for academic and behavioral problems; and (4) multiple levels (tiers) of instruction that are progressively more intense, based on the student's response to instruction.
>
> For example, an RTI model with a three-tier continuum of school-wide support might include the following tiers and levels of support: (1) Tier one (Primary Intervention), for all students using high quality scientific research-based instruction in their general education setting. It would not be appropriate to use EIS funds for these activities since these students do not need additional academic and behavioral support to succeed in a general education environment. (2) Tier two (Secondary Intervention), for specialized small group instruction of students determined to be at risk for academic and behavioral problems. It would be appropriate to use EIS funds to support these activities. (3) Tier three (Tertiary Intervention) for specialized individualized instructional/behavioral support for students with intensive needs. EIS funds could not be used if these students were currently receiving special education or related services.[68]

Highly Qualified Teachers

Each SEA must ensure that each special education teacher who teaches elementary or secondary school is "highly qualified."[69] The term "highly qualified" as defined in IDEA is linked to the definition in ESEA. In brief, ESEA requires that public school teachers of "core academic subjects"[70] obtain full state teaching certification or pass the state teacher licensing examination, or fulfill requirements in a state's charter school law for teachers in charter schools; have not had any certification requirements waived on an emergency, temporary, or provisional basis; and have a bachelor's degree.71 IDEA modifies the ESEA definition as it applies to special education teachers.72 IDEA requires that all special education teachers, whether they teach core academic subjects or not, obtain full state special education teaching certification or pass the state teacher licensing examination, or fulfill requirements in a state's charter school law for teachers in charter schools; have not had any certification requirements waived on an emergency, temporary, or provisional basis; and have a bachelor's degree. In addition, IDEA has specific provisions related to teachers who teach only the most severely disabled children and those who teach more than one core subject.73

The Educational Environment

IDEA requires that children with disabilities be educated in the least restrictive environment possible.[74] In other words, to the maximum extent that is appropriate they are to be educated with children who are not disabled. Further, special classes, separate schooling, or other removal of children with disabilities from the regular educational environment can occur only when the nature or severity of the disability of a child is such that education in regular classes with the use of supplementary aids and services[75] cannot be achieved satisfactorily. Supplementary aids and services could include such things as additional time to take tests or complete assignments, slower-paced instruction, personal aides, peer tutors, and use of a computer.

The LEA must also ensure that there is a continuum of alternate placements that includes instruction in regular classes, special classes, special schools, home instruction, and instruction in hospitals and institutions. This continuum must also make provision for supplementary services to be provided in conjunction with regular class placement.[76]

The specific placement decision for each child with a disability must be made by a group of persons, including the parents, and other persons knowledgeable about the child, the meaning of the evaluation data, and placement options. The child's placement must be (1) determined at least annually, (2) based on the IEP, and (3) as close to home as possible.[77]

As with identification and evaluation, the child's parents must be notified in writing within a reasonable time before the placement.[78] If the parents disagree with the placement decision, they may use the procedural safeguards, such as the mediation and due process complaints discussed in the "Procedural Safeguards " section of this report.

As shown in *Table 2,* 58% of children with disabilities age 6-21 spend 80% or more of their time in the regular classroom; 21% spend between 40% and 79%; 15% spend less than 40%; and 5% are educated in other environments. Other environments are a separate school, a residential facility, a private school placement by the parent, a correctional facility, and a home or hospital. Only 3% of all children with disabilities ages six through 21 receive their education in a separate school and an additional 1% are parentally placed in a private school.

As also shown in *Table 2,* 62% of children with SLDs and 87% with speech and language impairments spend 80% or more their classroom time in the regular classroom, while only 17% of children with mental retardation spend 80% or more of their time in the regular classroom.

Table 2. Percentage of Time Students Ages six through 21 Spend in a Regular Classroom and in Other Environments, under IDEA Part B: Fall 2008

Disability	Percentage Who Spend 80% or More of Time in a Regular Classroom	Percentage Who Spend 40%-79% of Time in a Regular Classroom	Percentage Who Spend Less than 40% of Time in a Regular Classroom	Percentage Who Spend Time in an Environment Other than a Regular Classroom
All disabilities	58%	21%	15%	5%
Specific learning disability	62%	28%	8%	2%
Speech or language impairments	87%	6%	5%	3%
Mental retardation	17%	27%	48%	8%
Emotional disturbance	39%	19%	23%	18%
Other health impairments	60%	24%	11%	4%

Source: Data Accountability Center, Part B Educational Environment (2008), MS-EXCEL Table 2-2, https://www.ideadata.org/arc_toc10.asp#partbLRE.

Notes: Percentages by disability may not add to 100% because of rounding. Total number of students is 5.9 million.

Children with Disabilities in Private Schools[79]

A child with a disability may be placed in a private elementary or secondary school by an LEA as part of an IEP if the IEP team determines that a private school placement is needed to fulfill the FAPE requirements for the child. In this situation, the private school placement is made at no cost to the parents, and the child has all of the rights of a child with a disability who is served in a public school.[80]

A child with a disability may also be unilaterally placed in a private elementary or secondary school by his or her parents.[81] In this situation, the "parentally placed" child is not entitled to FAPE, and the cost of the private school placement is not paid by the LEA unless a court or hearing officer makes certain findings.[82] The LEA must, however, spend a share of its IDEA funds to provide services to children enrolled with disabilities by their parents in private schools located in the LEA based on the proportion of parentally placed children to the total number of children with disabilities in the LEA.[83] Except where there is a court order, the LEA makes the final decision about the services to be provided to parentally placed private school children.[84] In making this decision, the LEA must engage in a consultation process with the private school officials and representatives of parents.[85] The LEA is also responsible for devising a service plan for every parentally placed child with a disability receiving special education or related services from the LEA.[86]

PROCEDURAL SAFEGUARDS

Procedural safeguards[87] are provisions protecting the rights of parents and children with disabilities regarding FAPE. The various types of procedures include parental rights to

- inspect and review educational records;[88]
- participate in meetings related to the identification, evaluation, and educational placement of their child;[89]
- obtain an independent educational evaluation at public expense if the parent disagrees with an evaluation obtained by the LEA;[90]
- receive prior written notice in the native language of the parents when an LEA proposes to initiate or change, or refuses to initiate or change, the identification, evaluation, or educational placement of the child or the provision of FAPE to the child;[91]

- receive a procedural safeguards notice, which is a comprehensive written explanation of IDEA's legal rights and protections for children with disabilities and their parents;[92]
- resolve disputes through a mediation process;[93]
- present and resolve complaints through the due process complaint procedures, which include a right to file suit in federal district court;[94] and
- present and resolve complaints through state complaint procedures.[95]

Three of the procedural safeguards listed above pertain to dispute resolution between parents and the LEA. These are mediation, due process complaint procedures, and state complaint procedures, which are discussed below. IDEA's disciplinary provisions, discussed in this section as well, also include procedural safeguards to protect the rights of children with disabilities to FAPE.

Mediation[96]

Mediation is a process of resolving disputes initiated by either the parent or LEA involving any matter under IDEA. It is a way of resolving complaints without a formal due process hearing, discussed below. Either a parent or an LEA can initiate the mediation process, which must be voluntary for each party. The mediation must be conducted by a qualified and impartial mediator who is trained in effective mediation techniques. The cost of the mediation process is borne by the state.

If the school and parent resolve a dispute through the mediation process, they must execute a legally binding agreement that is signed by the parent and a representative of the LEA. This agreement is enforceable in state or U.S. district court. Discussions that occur during the mediation process must be confidential and may not be used in any subsequent due process hearing or civil proceeding of any federal or state court.

Due Process Complaint Procedures

The due process complaint procedure begins with filing a due process complaint, which is in effect a request for a due process hearing, on matters relating to the identification, evaluation, or educational placement of a child with a disability, or the provision of FAPE to the child.

Generally, unless the SEA or LEA and the parent otherwise agree, the child must remain in his or her current educational placement pending the outcome of the due process complaint procedures or of a court proceeding. This requirement is referred to as "stay put."[97]

Either a parent or an LEA may file a due process complaint.[98] The due process complaint must allege a violation that occurred not more than two years before the date the parent or public agency knew or should have known about the alleged action that forms the basis of the due process complaint, or, if the state has an explicit time limitation for filing a due process complaint, occurred in the time period allowed by state law.[99]

Within 15 days of receiving the due process complaint, the LEA must convene a resolution session to attempt to resolve the issues unless the parents and LEA agree to waive the session. If the issues are not resolved, the due process hearing may occur. If the complaint is not resolved through mediation, a resolution meeting, or a due process hearing, either party to the complaint can file a civil suit.[100]

The due process hearing is conducted by an impartial hearing officer.[101] The decision of the hearing officer is final, except that any party in a state where the hearing is conducted by the LEA may appeal the findings and decision to the SEA, who in turn must conduct an impartial review. If the hearing was held in a state where the SEA conducted the hearing, then either party can file a civil lawsuit. The party filing the lawsuit has 90 days from the date of the decision of the hearing officer or, if applicable, the decision of the state review official, to file the lawsuit; or, if the state has an explicit time limitation for bringing civil action, the lawsuit must be filed in the time period allowed by state law.[102]

State Complaint Procedures[103]

The IDEA regulations require each state to adopt written procedures for resolving complaints that allege LEA violations of the statute or regulations. In its analysis of comments and changes to the final regulations, ED distinguishes between the due process complaint process and the state complaint process as follows:

The due process complaint procedures and the State complaint procedures are separate and distinct. The State complaint procedures remain a viable alternative to the due process procedures for parents to resolve disputes with public agencies in a less formal and more cost effective manner.[104]

Unlike requests for mediation or for complaints filed under due process procedures, where only a parent or an LEA can file a complaint, a state complaint can be filed by any organization or individual, including those from another state.

State complaint procedures must ensure that complaints will be resolved within 60 calendar days from the date the complaint is filed unless an extension is permitted.[105]

Discipline[106]

IDEA's disciplinary provisions are intended to "balance school safety issues with the need to ensure that schools respond appropriately to a child's behavior that was caused by, or directly and substantially related to, the child's disability."[107] IDEA addresses both the school's authority in disciplining students with disabilities and the rights of the students to receive FAPE. In general, a child with a disability is not immune from disciplinary procedures; however, these procedures are not identical to those for children without disabilities.[108]

If a child with a disability commits an action that would be subject to discipline, school personnel have several immediate options. These include

- removing a child from his or her current placement to another setting or suspension for up to 10 school days;[109]
- placing the child in an interim alternative education setting for up to 45 school days for situations involving weapons or drugs, or if the student has inflicted serious bodily injury on another person while at school;[110] and
- asking a hearing officer to order a child to be placed in an interim alternative educational setting for up to 45 school days if the hearing officer determines that maintaining the current placement of the child is substantially likely to result in injury to the child or others.[111]

If an LEA seeks to change the placement of a child with a disability for more than 10 days, the LEA must first determine

> (I) if the conduct in question was caused by, or had a direct and substantial relationship to, the child's disability; or (II) if the conduct in question was the direct result of the local educational agency's failure to implement the IEP.[112]

This determination is referred to as a "manifestation determination." The reason for the determination is IDEA's recognition "that a child with a disability may display disruptive behaviors characteristic of the child's disability and the child should not be punished for behaviors that are a result of the child's disability."[113]

If the child's behavior is not a manifestation of a disability, long-term disciplinary action such as expulsion may occur, except that educational services may not cease.[114]

If the behavior is a manifestation of the disability, the IEP team must conduct a functional behavior assessment and implement a behavior intervention plan for the child, if this has not been done before.[115] If there was a behavioral intervention plan, it must be reviewed and modified as necessary to address the behavior.[116]

Except for certain circumstances involving weapons, illegal drugs, or serious bodily injury, when the conduct is a manifestation of the disability, the child must return to the placement from which he or she was removed unless the parent and the LEA agree to a change of placement as part of the modification of the behavioral intervention plan.[117]

If the parent of a child with a disability disagrees with any decision regarding placement or the manifestation determination, or an LEA believes that maintaining the current placement of the child is substantially likely to result in injury to the child or others, either may request a due process hearing.[118]

Nothing in IDEA is to be construed as prohibiting an LEA from reporting a crime committed by a child with a disability to the appropriate authorities. An LEA reporting a crime committed by a child with a disability will ensure that copies of the special education and disciplinary records of the child are transmitted for consideration by the appropriate authorities to whom the agency reports the crime.[119]

FUNDING, EXPENDITURE REQUIREMENTS, AND COMPLIANCE

IDEA provides federal funding for the education of children with disabilities and imposes certain conditions for the receipt of federal funds. This section addresses state and local (1) funding allocations; (2) expenditure requirements, including maintenance of effort provisions; and (3) compliance with IDEA provisions through federal and state monitoring and enforcement requirements.

Funding

Actual and proposed grants to states are often discussed in terms of the percent of the "excess costs" of educating children with disabilities that the federal government will pay.[120] The metric for determining this excess cost is based on the national average per-pupil expenditure (APPE). In 1975, with the enactment of the Education for All Handicapped Children Act (P.L. 94-142), it was determined that the federal government would pay up to 40% of this excess cost.[121] This 40% of the excess cost is often referred to as "full funding." For FY2011, the Part B grants to states appropriation of $11.5 billion provides an estimated percentage of APPE of 16%.[122]

State Formula Allocations

Of the funds appropriated for IDEA, the Secretary of Education first reserves (1) not more than 1% of the appropriation for the outlying areas and freely associated states,[123] (2) funds for services for Indian children with disabilities,[124] and (3) not more than one-half of 1% of the appropriation up to a maximum of $25 million, adjusted for inflation, to provide technical assistance to improve the capacity of states to meet data collection requirements.[125] The remainder of the funds are allocated by a formula to the 50 states, the District of Columbia, and Puerto Rico. If the amount available for allocations to states for a fiscal year is equal to or greater than the amount allocated to the states for the preceding fiscal year, the formula[126] first requires that each state receive a base grant, which is the amount received by the state for FY1999. The next step is to distribute 85% of the remaining funds among the states based on states' shares of total population ages three to 21[127] and 15% of the remaining funds based on states' shares of poor children in that age range. The third step ensures that states do not receive less than certain minimum amounts or more than certain maximum amounts.[128] If the amount available for allocation to states decreases from the prior year, any amount available for allocation to states above the 1999 level is allocated based on the relative increases in funding that the states received between 1999 and the prior year. If there is a decrease below the amount allocated for 1999, each state's allocation is ratably reduced from the 1999 level.[129]

State-Level Activities

A state may reserve funds from their grants for administration[130] and for a variety of other statewide activities. These include two mandatory activities: (1) monitoring, enforcement, and complaint investigation, and (2) establishing and maintaining a parental mediation process.[131] Other allowable state-level activities include improving the use of technology in the classroom, developing transition programs, and assisting LEAs in meeting personnel shortages.[132] In addition, for the purpose of assisting LEAs in addressing the needs of high-need children (i.e., children who require expensive services, including certain medical expenses), states may establish a risk pool or "high cost" fund. If a state chooses to establish a risk pool, it must use 10% of the funds it reserved for state-level activities.[133] States using a risk pool must develop and annually review a state plan in which the state determines which children with disabilities are high need, set out the procedures by which LEAs participate in the risk pool, and determine how funds are distributed.[134] Funds distributed from the risk pool must only pay for "direct special education and related services" for high need children with disabilities[135] and may not be used for legal fees or related costs.[136] If some funds reserved for the risk pool are not distributed for services for high-need children, they are to be distributed to LEAs according to the substate formula.[137]

LEA Formula Allocations

Funds remaining after funds for state-level activities are set aside are distributed to LEAs based on a formula similar to the state formula. Like the state formula, LEAs are first allocated base grants. Also similar to the state formula, 85% of the remaining funds is allocated based on LEAs' shares of public and private school enrollment and 15% of the remaining funds is allocated based on shares of children living in poverty, as determined by the SEA. There is no minimum or maximum grant.[138]

State and LEA Expenditure Requirements

IDEA state and LEA expenditure requirements are aimed at increasing overall educational spending, rather than substituting federal funds for education spending at the state and local levels. Maintenance of effort (MOE) provisions basically require that a state or an LEA not reduce its support for special education and related services below the level of support it provided the previous fiscal year. Supplement, not supplant (SNS) requirements generally prohibit a state or LEA from using IDEA grants to provide services, purchase equipment, etc., that state, local, or other federal funds currently provide or purchase or, in the absence of the IDEA funds, that those other funds would have provided or would have purchased.

Maintenance of Effort (MOE)

In general, a state may not reduce the amount of its financial support for special education and related services for children with disabilities below the amount of that support for the preceding fiscal year.[139] In any fiscal year in which a state does not meet this MOE requirement, the Secretary of Education is required to reduce the state's subsequent year grant by the same amount by which the state fails to meet the requirement.[140] The Secretary may grant a waiver for one fiscal year at a time in the case of "exceptional or uncontrollable circumstances" such as a natural disaster or a "precipitous and unforeseen decline in the financial resources of the state."[141] In addition, waivers can be granted if the state can provide "clear and convincing evidence" that FAPE is available for all children with disabilities.[142] If a state does not meet its MOE requirement for any year, including any year for which the state was granted a waiver, the state financial support required in future years is not reduced. That is, the state must provide the amount that would have been required in the absence of failing to meet MOE in the previous year.[143]

LEAs may use IDEA funds only for the excess costs[144] of educating children with disabilities, and may not reduce the level of expenditures for the education of children with disabilities made by the LEA from local funds below the level of those expenditures for the preceding fiscal year.[145] In general, the SEA must determine that an LEA meets this requirement (for purposes of establishing the LEA's eligibility for an award for a fiscal year). If the LEA assures the SEA that it will provide at least the same total or per capita amount from either local funds only or a combination of state and local funds for the most recent prior year for which the data are available, then the

LEA would be eligible for funds.[146] IDEA specifies in statute four circumstances in which an LEA may legally reduce its local expenditures. These are in cases of

> (1) voluntary departure, by retirement or otherwise, or departure for just cause, of special education personnel; (2) a decrease in the enrollment of children with disabilities; (3) the termination of the obligation of the agency ... to provide a program of special education to a particular child with a disability that is an exceptionally costly program ... ; or (4) the termination of costly expenditures for long-term purchases, such as the acquisition of equipment or the construction of school facilities.[147]

The regulations establish a fifth circumstance under which an LEA may reduce its local expenditures. If a state establishes a risk pool (i.e., high cost fund) and the state assumes the costs associated with "high cost" children in the LEA, the LEA may reduce its expenditures.[148]

In addition, with some exceptions, an LEA may reduce its local expenditures in certain fiscal years in which its federal allocation exceeds the amount received in the previous fiscal year by not more than 50% of the excess amount.[149] These funds must be used to carry out activities authorized under ESEA.[150] Exceptions include the following: (1) the state is required to prohibit an LEA from reducing its MOE if the SEA has taken responsibility for providing FAPE in the LEA because the LEA is unable to establish and maintain programs of FAPE, or the state has taken action against the LEA under IDEA's enforcement provisions;[151] (2) if in its annual determination on the performance of LEAs, a state determines that an LEA does not meet requirements (i.e., the LEA needs assistance, intervention, or substantial intervention), the state must prohibit the LEA from reducing its MOE;[152] and (3) the amount of funds expended by an LEA for CEIS[153] must count toward the maximum amount of the reduction in expenditures the LEA may make.[154] Consequently, any LEA that is required to use 15% of its allocation on CEIS because the state has determined that "significant disproportionality"[155] based on race and ethnicity is occurring would be prohibited from reducing its MOE.[156]

Supplement, Not Supplant

Both states and LEAs must use IDEA funds to supplement state, local, and other federal funds and not to supplant them.[157] As with the state MOE requirement, the Secretary of Education has authority to grant a waiver of the state-level SNS requirement if the state provides "clear and convincing evidence" that all children with disabilities in the state have FAPE available.[158] If an LEA (or state) maintains its level of local, or state and local, expenditures for special education and related services from year to year, then the LEA has met its MOE and SNS requirements. There are no SNS or MOE waiver provisions for LEAs.[159]

Compliance

Monitoring

The Secretary monitors the implementation of IDEA through the oversight of states' required general supervision of the implementation of IDEA requirements, and through the states' required state performance plans (SPP).[160] These plans evaluate a state's efforts to implement the requirements and purposes of IDEA and describe how the state will improve implementation.[161] The Secretary must enforce IDEA[162] and must also require states to monitor and enforce the implementation of IDEA by LEAs.[163] The primary focus of federal and state monitoring is on improving educational results and functional outcomes for all children with disabilities and ensuring that states meet IDEA program requirements.[164] IDEA specifies three priority areas that are to be monitored by the Secretary regarding states, and by states regarding LEAs, using quantifiable indicators to measure performance. These three monitoring priorities are:

- provision of a free appropriate public education in the least restrictive environment;
- state exercise of general supervisory authority, including child find, effective monitoring, the use of resolution sessions, mediation, voluntary binding arbitration, and a system of transition services; and
- disproportionate representation of racial and ethnic groups in special education and related services, to the extent the representation is the result of inappropriate identification.[165]

As part of an SPP,[166] each state must establish measurable and rigorous targets for the indicators established by the Secretary in the three priority areas.[167] Each state must use the targets established in its SPP and the three priority areas to analyze the performance of each LEA in the state.[168] In addition, each state must report annually to the Secretary on the state's performance under the SPP.[169] Annual state reporting of performance on the SPP indicators is done through the Annual Performance Report (APR).[170] The state must report annually to the public on the performance of each LEA.[171] This annual report must be made as soon as practicable, but no later than 120 days following the state's submission of its APR to the Secretary.[172] The state must also make available through public means the state's SPP, APR, and the state's annual report on the performance of each LEA in the state. At a minimum, the state must post these items on the SEA's website and distribute them to the media and through public agencies.[173]

Enforcement

Based on the information provided by the state in the SPP, information from monitoring visits, and any other public information made available, the Secretary shall determine annually if the state

- meets the requirements and purposes of IDEA Part B,
- needs assistance in implementing the requirements of IDEA Part B,
- needs intervention in implementing the requirements of IDEA Part B, or
- needs substantial intervention in implementing the requirements of IDEA Part B.

If the Secretary makes a determination that a state needs intervention or substantial intervention, the Secretary must provide notice and an opportunity for a hearing.[174]

If the Secretary determines that a state does not meet requirements, IDEA specifies a number of enforcement actions depending on the Secretary's specific determination. These actions range from advising the state of available sources of technical assistance, to requiring the state to prepare a corrective action plan, to withholding, in whole or in part, further IDEA funds to the state. Prior to withholding any funds, the Secretary must provide notice and an opportunity for a hearing.[175] Whenever a state receives notice that the Secretary is proposing to take an enforcement action, the state must, at a minimum, post a notice of the pendency of an action on the SEA's website and distribute the notice to the media and through public agencies.[176]

In its analysis of comments and changes in the regulations, ED notes that

Neither the Act nor these regulations require SEAs to publicly report on enforcement actions taken against LEAs in the State. The decision to report to the public on enforcement actions imposed on an LEA is best left to each State to decide because individual LEA circumstances vary across each State and no one set of requirements is appropriate in every situation ... However, in the interest of transparency and public accountability, the Department encourages States, where appropriate, to report to the public on any enforcement actions taken against LEAs.[177]

The state must make the same four determinations about LEAs that the Secretary makes about the states.[178] In its analysis of comments and changes in the regulations, ED comments that "States should have some discretion in making annual determination on the performance of their LEAs and, therefore, [ED] decline[s] to establish, in regulation, a uniform process for making annual determinations." ED further notes that it has advised states that in making determinations, they must consider (1) LEA performance on SPP compliance indicators,[179] (2) whether data submitted by an LEA are valid and reliable for each indicator, (3) LEA-specific audit findings, and (4) an uncorrected noncompliance from any source. In addition, ED has advised states to consider performance on results indicators, such as an LEA's graduation and dropout rates or the participation rate of students with disabilities in state assessments.[180] However, the consideration of performance indicators in LEA determinations is not required.

The regulations stipulate the specific enforcement mechanisms that a state must use if the LEA does not meet requirements.[181] These mechanisms include a range of actions and are similar to those that the Secretary must use for state enforcement.[182] The regulations also require that when a state identifies LEA noncompliance with IDEA, it must ensure that the noncompliance is corrected as soon as possible, and no later than one year after the state's identification of the noncompliance.[183]

APPENDIX A. STRUCTURE OF IDEA

Part A—General Provisions

Part A includes congressional findings pertinent to the act, the purposes of the act, and definitions. The definitions included in Part A are of critical importance in interpreting the requirements of the act. These definitions include, among others, definitions of child with a disability, specific learning disability, free appropriate public education, core academic subjects, highly qualified, individualized education program, local educational agency, related services, special education, supplementary aids and services, transition services, and excess costs. These terms have been defined throughout the body of this report.

Part B—Assistance for Education of All Children with Disabilities

Part B provides federal funding for the education of children with disabilities and requires, as a condition for the receipt of such funds, the provision of a free appropriate public education (FAPE) to children with disabilities between the ages of three and 21. School districts must identify, locate, and evaluate all children with disabilities, regardless of the severity of their disability, to determine which children are eligible for special education and related services. Each child receiving services has an Individualized Education Program (IEP), created by an IEP team, delineating the specific special education and related services to be provided to meet his or her needs. The statute also contains procedural safeguards, which are provisions to protect the rights of parents and children with disabilities to ensure the provision of FAPE.

Section 619 of IDEA Part B authorizes grants to states for preschool programs serving children with disabilities ages three to five. Since Part B grants to states are used to serve children with disabilities as young as three years of age (as well as school-age children), Section 619 is not so much a separate program as it is supplementary funding for services to this age group. In general, the provisions, requirements, and guarantees under the grants to states program that apply to school-age children with disabilities also apply to children in this age group. As a result, Section 619 is a relatively brief section of the law and deals mostly with the state and substate funding formulas for the grants and state-level activities.

Part C—Infants and Toddlers with Disabilities
The general purpose of Part C is to aid each state in creating and maintaining "a statewide, comprehensive, coordinated, multidisciplinary, interagency system that provides early intervention services for infants and toddlers with disabilities and their families."[184] Services focus on children from birth through age two who are experiencing or have a high probability of experiencing "developmental delay" (as defined by the state) with respect to

physical, mental, or other capacities, and on their families.[185] Services are detailed for each child and his or her family in an Individualized Family Service Plan (IFSP). Services are to be provided, to the maximum extent feasible, in "natural environments," including the home, with other infants and toddlers who are not disabled. States are required to identify a state lead agency, which might be the state educational agency (SEA) but could be other state agencies, to coordinate the program.

Part D—National Activities to Improve Education of Children with Disabilities[186]

Part D authorizes competitive grants to improve the education of children with disabilities in three areas: (1) state personnel development (Subpart 1); (2) personnel preparation, technical assistance, model demonstration projects, and dissemination of information (Subpart 2); and (3) support to improve results for children (Subpart 3).

- Under Subpart 1, competitive grants are made to SEAs for state personnel development grants to assist SEAs "in reforming and improving their systems for personnel preparation and professional development in early intervention, educational, and transitions services ..."[187]

- Under Subpart 2, competitive grants are made to entities such as SEAs, local education agencies (LEAs),[188] institutions of higher education (IHEs), and nonprofit organizations for personnel development to help ensure that there are adequate numbers of personnel with skills and knowledge needed to help children with disabilities succeed,[189] for technical assistance and dissemination of material based on knowledge gained through research and practice,[190] and for studies and evaluations.[191]

- Under Subpart 3, competitive grants are made to nonprofit organizations for parent training and information centers, which provide parents of children with disabilities with needed training and information to work with professionals in meeting the early intervention and special education needs of their children.[192] Also, under Subpart 3, competitive grants are made to entities such as SEAs, LEAs, IHEs, and nonprofit organizations for research, development, and other activities that promote the use of technology in providing special education and early intervention services.[193]

APPENDIX B. COMMONLY USED ACRONYMS

APPE	Average Per Pupil Expenditure
APR	Annual Performance Report
CEIS	Coordinated Early Intervening Services
ED	U.S. Department of Education
ESEA	Elementary and Secondary Education Act
FAPE	Free Appropriate Public Education
IDEA	The Individuals with Disabilities Education Act
IEP	Individualized Education Program
LEA	Local Educational Agency
MOE	Maintenance of Effort
RTI	Response to Intervention
SEA	State Education Agency
SNS	Supplement, Not Supplant
SPP	State Performance Plan

End Notes

[1] 20 U.S.C. § 1400 et seq.

[2] U.S. Department of Education, National Center for Education Statistics, Institute for Education Sciences, The Condition of Education 2010 , May 2010, p.34, http://nces.ed.gov/pubs2010/2010028.pdf.

[3] The name was changed to the Individuals with Disabilities Education Act by P.L. 101-476. The public law also substituted the phrase "children with disabilities" for the phrase "handicapped children" throughout the act.

[4] 20 U.S.C. § 1401(b), P.L. 94-142 § 601(b).

[5] For more information on each of the factors that contributed to the enactment of P.L. 94-142, see CRS Report 95-669, The Individuals with Disabilities Education Act: Congressional Intent, by Nancy Lee Jones.

[6] For a discussion of the 2004 amendments made by P.L. 108-446, see CRS Report RL32716, Individuals with Disabilities Education Act (IDEA): Analysis of Changes Made by P.L. 108-446, by Ann Lordeman and Nancy Lee Jones. For an overview of the IDEA regulations from the Department of Education, see CRS Report RL33649, The Individuals with Disabilities Education Act (IDEA): Final Regulations for P.L. 108-446, and CRS Report R40055, The Individuals with Disabilities Education Act: Final Part B Regulations.

[7] IDEA authorizes appropriations for Part C and Part D programs and activities through FY2010. These authorities were automatically extended for an additional fiscal year by the General Education Provisions Act (GEPA; 20 U.S.C.§1226a).

[8] 20 U.S.C. § 1400(d)(1), P.L. 108-446 § 601(d)(1).

[9] 20 U.S.C § 14001(3)(A), P.L. 108-446 § 602(3)(A), and 34 C.F.R. § 300.8. The statute at § 602(3)(B) also permits the state and LEA to include as a child with a disability a child age

three through nine, or any subset of that range, who is experiencing developmental delays—as defined by the state and as measured by appropriate diagnostic instruments and procedures—in physical, cognitive, communication, social, emotional, or adaptive development. The child must also require special education and related services because of the developmental delay.

[10] 29 U.S.C. §794. For more information on Section 504, see CRS Report RL34041, Section 504 of the Rehabilitation Act of 1973: Prohibiting Discrimination Against Individuals with Disabilities in Programs or Activities Receiving Federal Assistance, by Nancy Lee Jones.

[11] 42 U.S.C. §12101 et seq. For a more detailed discussion of the ADA, see CRS Report 98-921, The Americans with Disabilities Act (ADA): Statutory Language and Recent Issues, by Nancy Lee Jones.

[12] See citation to Rachel A. Holler and Perry A. Zirkel, "Section 504 and Public Schools: A National Survey Concerning 'Section 504-Only' Students," 92 NASSP Bulletin 19, 28 (March 2008) in CRS Report R40123, Education of Individuals with Disabilities: The Individuals with Disabilities Education Act (IDEA), Section 504 of the Rehabilitation Act, and the Americans with Disabilities Act (ADA), by Nancy Lee Jones. For more information on differences among IDEA, Section 504, and the ADA, see this report.

[13] A specific learning disability is defined as "a disorder in 1 or more of the basic psychological processes involved in understanding or in using language, spoken or written, which may manifest itself in the imperfect ability to listen, think, speak, read, write, spell, or do mathematical calculations." 20 U.S.C. §1401(30)(A), P.L. 108-446 §601(30)(A).

[14] 20 U.S.C. §1401(30)(B), P.L. 108-446 §601(30)(B). Specific learning disabilities do not include learning problems that are primarily the result of visual, hearing, or motor disabilities; of mental retardation; of emotional disturbance; or of environmental, cultural, or economic disadvantage. 20 U.S.C §1401(30)(C), P.L. 108-446 §601(30)(C).

[15] The regulations at 34 C.F.R. §300.102 (2010) specify three exceptions to this requirement: (1) children ages 3, 4, 5, 18, 19, 20, or 21 in a state that does not provide a public education to children of those ages, (2) children ages 18 through 21 incarcerated in an adult correctional facility who were not identified as children with disabilities in their last educational placement; and (3) children with disabilities who have graduated from high school with a regular high school diploma.

[16] 20 U.S.C. §1401(9), P.L. 108-446 §601(9). For information on the legal aspects of FAPE, see CRS Report RL33444, The Individuals with Disabilities Education Act (IDEA): Supreme Court Decisions, by Nancy Lee Jones and Carol J. Toland; CRS Report R40521, The Individuals with Disabilities Education Act (IDEA): Selected Judicial Developments Following the 2004 Reauthorization, by Nancy Lee Jones; and CRS Report R40690, The Individuals with Disabilities Education Act (IDEA): Statutory Provisions and Recent Legal Issues, by Nancy Lee Jones.

[17] 34 C.F.R. §300.101(a) (2010).

[18] 34 C.F.R. §300.101(c) (2010).

[19] 20 U.S.C §1412(a)(3), P.L. 108-446 §612(a)(3).

[20] 20 U.S.C. §1414(a), P.L. 108-446 §414(a). This subsection contains the requirements for evaluations, parental consent, and reevaluations.

[21] The LEA may refuse the parent's request for an initial evaluation if it does not suspect that the child has a disability. However, the public agency must provide written notice to the parents, consistent with 34 C.F.R. §300.503(b)(2010) and §615(c)(1) of the act, which explains, among other things, why the public agency refuses to conduct an initial evaluation and the information that was used as the basis to make that decision. The parent may

challenge such a refusal by requesting a due process hearing. (71 Fed. Reg. 46636 (August 14, 2006)).

[22] The term "consent" is defined at 34 C.F.R. §300.9, and means, in part, that "the parent has been fully informed of all information relevant to the activity for which consent is sought, in his or her native language, or other mode of communication"; For more information on parental consent, see also 34 C.F.R. §300.300 (2010).

[23] In addition, at the time of the referral or parent request for evaluation, the LEA must provide the parent with the "Procedural Safeguards Notice," which is a comprehensive written explanation of IDEA's legal rights and protections for children with disabilities and their parents. See 20 U.S.C. §1415(d), P.L. 108-446 §615(d). For further information on procedural safeguards, see "Procedural Safeguards " in this report.

[24] 20 U.S.C §1414(a)(1), P.L. 108-446 §614 (a)(1). 2520 U.S.C. §1414(b)(2), P.L. 108-446 §614 (b)(2).

[26] For all the provisions related to additional requirements, see 20 U.S.C. §1414(b)(3), P.L. 108-446 §614 (b)(3).

[27] 20 U.S.C. §1414(b)(4)(A), P.L. 108-446 §614 (b)(4)(A).

[28] 20 U.S.C §1414(b)(4)(B), P.L. 108-446 §614 (b)(4)(B).

[29] 20 U.S.C. §1414(b)(5), P.L. 108-446 §614 (b)(5).

[30] 20 U.S.C. §1414(a)(2), P.L. 108-446 §614 (a)(2).

[31] 34 C.F.R. §300.300(c) (2010).

[32] 20 U.S.C. §1414(c)(5), P.L. 108-446 §614 (c)(5).

[33] 20 U.S.C. §1414(b)(6), P.L. 108-446 §614 (b)(6), and 34 C.F.R. §300.307 through §300.311 (2010).

[34] 34 C.F.R. §300.307 (2010).

[35] 20 U.S.C. §1414(b)(6)(A), P.L. 108-446 §614 (b)(6)(A), and 34 C.F.R. §300.307(a)(1) (2010). The Senate report in considering the 2004 amendments to IDEA explains the rationale for this provision: The committee believes that the IQ-achievement discrepancy formula, which considers whether a child has a severe discrepancy between achievement and intellectual ability, should not be a requirement for determining eligibility under the IDEA. There is no evidence that the IQ-achievement discrepancy formula can be applied in a consistent and educationally meaningful (i.e., reliable and valid) manner. In addition, this approach has been found to be particularly problematic for students living in poverty or culturally and linguistically different backgrounds, who may be erroneously viewed as having intrinsic intellectual limitations when their difficulties on such tests really reflect lack of experience or educational opportunity. S.Rept. 108-185, 108th Cong., 2d Sess. 26 (2003).

[36] 20 U.S.C. §1414(b)(6)(B), P.L. 108-446 §614 (b)(6)(B).

[37] 34 C.F.R. §300.307(a)(3)(2010). In ED's analysis of comments and changes to the final regulations at 71 Fed. Reg. 46648 (August 14, 2006), ED elaborates on this criterion by stating: "For example, a state could choose to identify children based on absolute low achievement and consideration of exclusionary factors as one criterion for eligibility. Other alternatives might combine features of different models for identification."

[38] 34 C.F.R. §300.308 (2010).

[39] 34 C.F.R. §300.309(a) (2010).

[40] These eight areas are oral expression, listening comprehension, written expression, basic reading skill, reading fluency skills, reading comprehension, mathematics calculation, and mathematics problem solving.

[41] 34 C.F.R. §300.309(b) (2010).

[42] 34 C.F.R. §300.309 (c). In ED's analysis of comments and changes to the final regulations at 71 Fed. Reg. 46658 (August 14, 2006), ED addresses the issue of "an appropriate period of time" by stating "Instructional models vary in terms of the length of time required for the intervention to have the intended effect on a child's progress. It would not be appropriate for the Department to establish timelines ... because doing so would make it difficult for LEAs to implement models specific to their local school districts. These decisions are best left to state and local professionals who have knowledge of the instructional methods used in their school."

[43] 34 C.F.R. §300.310 (2010).

[44] 34 C.F.R. §300.311 (2010).

[45] 20 U.S.C §1414(d)(3)(A), P.L. 108-446 §614 (d)(3)(A).

[46] 20 U.S.C. §1414(d)(4), P.L. 108-446 §614 (d)(4).

[47] 34 C.F.R. §300.323(c) (2010).

[48] 20 U.S.C. §1414(d)(1)(A), P.L. 108-446 §614 (d)(1)(A).

[49] An accommodation is a change in instructional material or assessment practices that enable students with disabilities to reduce barriers to learning.

[50] Although many students with disabilities are able to participate in the general state assessment, other students may need an alternate assessment that is tailored to their needs and allows them to more accurately demonstrate what they know and can do. For information on alternate assessments for students with disabilities, see CRS Report R40701, Alternate Assessments for Students with Disabilities, by Erin D. Lomax.

[51] As defined at 20 U.S.C. §1401(34), P.L. 108-446 §602(34), transition services mean a coordinated set of activities for a child with a disability that—(A) is designed to be within a results-oriented process, that is focused on improving the academic and functional achievement of the child with a disability to facilitate the child's movement from school to post-school activities, including post-secondary education, vocational education, integrated employment (including supported employment), continuing and adult education, adult services, independent living, or community participation; (B) is based on the individual child's needs, taking into account the child's strengths, preferences, and interests; and (C) includes instruction, related services, community experiences, the development of employment and other post-school adult living objectives, and, when appropriate, acquisition of daily living skills and functional vocational evaluation.

[52] 20 U.S.C. §1414(d)(1)(B), P.L. 108-446 §614 (d)(1)(B).

[53] If the purpose of an IEP meeting is to consider the postsecondary goals for the child and transition services, the LEA must invite the child to attend the meeting; 34 C.F.R. §300.321(b)(1) (2010).

[54] 20 U.S.C. §1401(29), P.L. 108-446 §602(29), and 34 C.F.R. §300.39 (2010).

[55] 34 C.F.R. §300.39(b)(1) (2010).

[56] 20 U.S.C. §1401(26), P.L. 108-446 §602(26), and 34 C.F.R. §300.34 (2010).

[57] For a discussion of the legal issues regarding medical services as a related service, see CRS Report R40690, The Individuals with Disabilities Education Act (IDEA): Statutory Provisions and Recent Legal Issues, by Nancy Lee Jones.

[58] An LEA cannot use the full 15% for CEIS when they are also reducing funds under IDEA maintenance of effort (MOE) provisions. See the discussion in this report on "Maintenance of Effort (MOE)" for further explanation.

[59] 20 U.S.C. §1413(f), P.L. 107-110 §613(f). Coordinated Early Intervening Services (CEIS), also referred to in statute as Early Intervening Serving (EIS), should not be confused with Early Intervention Services (EIS) authorized under Part C of IDEA. Part C, EIS, defined in

Section 632(4), is for infants and toddlers with disabilities, while Part B CEIS is for students who are not currently identified as having disabilities but need additional support to succeed in a general education environment. (A student could receive CEIS if he or she had previously received special education, but is not currently identified as needing it. 71 Fed. Reg. 46626 (August 14, 2006) and 34 C.F.R. §300.226 (2010).)

[60] 34 C.F.R. §300.226 (c) (2010).

[61] 71 Fed. Reg. 46626-46627 (August 14, 2006).

[62] For more information on CEIS, see U.S. Department of Education, "Memorandum: Coordinated Early Intervening Services (CEIS) Under Part B of the Individuals with Disabilities Education Act (IDEA)," July 28, 2008, http://www2.ed.gov/policy/speced/guid/idea/ceis-guidance.pdf.

[63] 20 U.S.C §1413(f)(5), P.L. 107-110 §613(f)(5).

[64] The term "significant disproportionality" is defined by each state; 71.Fed. Reg. 46738 (August 14, 2006).

[65] 20 U.S.C. §1418(d), P.L. 108-446 §618(d).

[66] 34 C.F.R. §300.646 (b)(2) (2010).

[67] U.S. Department of Education, Implementing RTI Using Title I, Title III, and CEIS Funds, Key Issues for Decision-maker, p. 11, http://www2.ed.gov/programs/titleiparta/ rtifiles /rti.pdf.

[68] U.S. Department of Education, Questions and Answers on Response to Intervention (RTI) and Early Intervening Services (EIS), January 2007, Question F-5. RTI is one type of scientific, research-based intervention used to identify students with SLD. See "Identifying and Evaluating a Child with a Specific Learning Disability (SLD)."

[69] 20 U.S.C. §1412(a)(14)(C), P.L. 108-446 §612(a)(14)(C).

[70] The term "core academic subjects" as defined in ESEA at 20 U.S.C. §7801(11), P.L. 107-110 §9101(11) means "English, reading or language arts, mathematics, science, foreign languages, civics and government, economics, arts, history, and geography." The IDEA definition of core academic subjects defined at 20 U.S.C. §1401(4), P.L. 108-446 §602(4) has the same meaning as the ESEA definition.

[71] 20 U.S.C. §7801(23), P.L. 107-110 §9101(23). For more information on ESEA requirements, see CRS Report RL33333, A Highly Qualified Teacher in Every Classroom: Implementation of the No Child Left Behind Act and Reauthorization Issues for the 112th Congress, by Jeffrey J. Kuenzi.

[72] For more information on highly qualified teachers under IDEA, see CRS Report RL33649, The Individuals with Disabilities Education Act (IDEA): Final Regulations for P.L. 108-446, by Nancy Lee Jones and Ann Lordeman.

[73] 20 U.S.C. §1401(10), P.L. 108-446 §602(10), and 34 C.F.R. §300.18.

[74] 20 U.S.C. §1412(a)(5), P.L. 108-446 §612(a)(5). For legal issues pertaining to least restrictive environment, see CRS Report R40690, The Individuals with Disabilities Education Act (IDEA): Statutory Provisions and Recent Legal Issues, by Nancy Lee Jones.

[75] 20 U.S.C. §1401(33), P.L. 108-446 §602(33). Supplementary aids and services are defined as "aids, services, and other supports that are provided in regular education classes or other education-related settings to enable children with disabilities to be educated with nondisabled children to the maximum extent appropriate in accordance with section 612(a)(5) [Least Restrictive Environment]."

[76] 34 C.F.R. §300.115.

[77] 34 C.F.R. §300.116.

[78] 34 C.F.R. §300.503.

[79] For more information on this topic, including legal issues, see CRS Report R41678, The Individuals with Disabilities Education Act (IDEA): Private Schools, by Nancy Lee Jones.

[80] 20 U.S.C. §1412(a)(10)(B), P.L. 108-446 §612(a)(10)(B).

[81] 20 U.S.C. §1412(a)(10)(B), P.L. 108-446 §612(a)(10)(B).

[82] 20 U.S.C. §1412(a)(10)(C), P.L. 108-446 §612(a)(10)(C). Specifically, an LEA could be required by a court or a hearing officer to reimburse the parents of a child with a disability who (1) previously received special education and related services from an LEA, and (2) enrolled the child in a private elementary school or secondary school without the consent of or referral by the LEA for the cost of the private school enrollment if the court or hearing officer found that the LEA had not made FAPE available to the child in a timely manner prior to the private school enrollment.

[83] 20 U.S.C. §1412(a)(10)(iii)(I), P.L. 108-446 §612(a)(10)(iii)(I). For example, if an LEA has 250 children with disabilities, 15 of whom were parentally placed in a private school, 6% of federal IDEA Part B funds (i.e., 15/250 * 100) would be spent on the group of children with disabilities in private schools in the LEA. For a more comprehensive hypothetical example, see Appendix B to 34 C.F.R. Part 300. It should be emphasized that no individual parentally placed private school child with a disability is entitled to services.

[84] 20 U.S.C. §1412(a)(10)(A)(iii), P.L. 108-446 §612(a)(10)(A)(iii).

[85] 34 C.F.R. §300.137(b) (2010).

[86] 34 C.F.R. §300.138)(b) (2010).

[87] For information on the legal issues pertaining to procedural safeguards, including burden of proof, parental rights, attorneys' and expert witness fees, see CRS Report R40690, The Individuals with Disabilities Education Act (IDEA): Statutory Provisions and Recent Legal Issues, by Nancy Lee Jones.

[88] 20 U.S.C. §1415(b)(1), P.L. 108-446 §615(b)(1), and 34 C.F.R. §300.501(a) (2010).

[89] 20 U.S.C. §1414(e), P.L. 108-446 §614(e), and 34 C.F.R. §300.501(b) and (c) (2010).

[90] 20 U.S.C. §1415(b)(1), P.L. 108-446 §614(b)(1), and 34 C.F.R. §300.502 (2010). If the LEA asserts that its evaluation is appropriate, it can file a due process complaint to request a hearing. If the final decision is that the agency's evaluation is appropriate, the parent still has the right to an independent education evaluation, but not at public expense.

[91] 20 U.S.C. §1415 (b)(3) and (4), P.L. 108-446 §615(b)(3) and (4), and 34 C.F.R. §300.503(a) and (c) (2010). For the statutory and regulatory provision regarding the content of the notice, see 20 U.S.C. §1415 (c)(1), P.L. 108-446 §615(c)(1), and 34 C.F.R. §300.503(b) (2010).

[92] 20 U.S.C. §1415(d), P.L. 108-446 §615(d), and 34 C.F.R. §300.504 (2010).

[93] 20 U.S.C. §1415(e), P.L. 108-446 §615(e), and 34 C.F.R. §300.506 (2010).

[94] 20 U.S.C. §1415(f) through (j), P.L. 108-446 §615(f) through (j), and 34 C.F.R. §300.507 through §300.518 (2010).

[95] 34 C.F.R. §300.151 through §300.153 (2010). State complaint procedures are not contained in the statute.

[96] 20 U.S.C. §1415(e), P.L. 108-446 §615(e), and 34 C.F.R. §300.506 (2010).

[97] 20 U.S.C. §1415(j), P.L. 108-446 §615(j), and 34 C.F.R. §300.518 (2010).

[98] 20 U.S.C. §1415(b)(7) and (8), and 20 U.S.C. §1415(c)(2), P.L. 108-446 §615(b)(7) and (8), and §615(c)(2), and 34 C.F.R. §300.507 through §300.509 (2010).

[99] There are two exceptions to this timeline. The timeline does not apply if the parent was prevented from requesting a hearing due to specific misrepresentations by the LEA that it had resolved the problem forming the basis of the due process complaint; or the LEA

withheld information from the parent that was required to be provided to the parent. 20 U.S.C. §1415(b)(6), P.L. 108-446 §615(b)(6), and 34 C.F.R. §300.507(a)(2) (2010).

[100] For more detail, see the statutory and regulatory provisions at 20 U.S.C. §1415, P.L. 108-446 §615, and 34 C.F.R. Subpart E (2010).

[101] For information on conducting a due process hearing, see 20 U.S.C. §1415(f), P.L. 108-446 §615(f), and 34 C.F.R. §300.511 through §300.515 (2010). For information on the required qualifications of the hearing officer, see 20 U.S.C. §1415(f)(3), P.L. 108-446 §615(f)(3), and 34 C.F.R. §300.511(c) (2010).

[102] 20 U.S.C. §1415(g) and (i), P.L. 108-446 §615(g) and (i), and 34 C.F.R. §300.514 and §300.516 (2010).

[103] 34 C.F.R. §300.151 through §300.153 (2010).

[104] 71 Fed. Reg. 46700 (August 14, 2006).

[105] An extension of the 60-day time limit may be permitted only if exceptional circumstances exist with respect to a particular complaint or if the complainant and the LEA agree to extend the time to engage in mediation, or to engage in other alternative means of dispute resolution, if available in the state.

[106] For more information on IDEA disciplinary provisions, see CRS Report RL32753, Individuals with Disabilities Education Act (IDEA): Discipline Provisions in P.L. 108-446, by Nancy Lee Jones. For information on legal issues, see discussion of Honig v. Doe in CRS Report RL33444, The Individuals with Disabilities Education Act (IDEA): Supreme Court Decisions, by Nancy Lee Jones and Carol J. Toland.

[107] U.S. Department of Education, Questions and Answers on Discipline Procedures, June 2009, http://idea.ed.gov/ explore/view/p/%2Croot%2Cdynamic%2CQaCorner%2C7%2C.

[108] 20 U.S.C. §1415(k).

[109] 20 U.S.C. §1415(k)(1)(B), P.L. 108-446 §615(k)(1)(B).

[110] 20 U.S.C. §1415(k)(1)(G), P.L. 108-446 §615(k)(1)(G).

[111] 20 U.S.C. §1415(k)(3), P.L. 108-446 §615(k)(3).

[112] To determine if the child's behavior meets either of these criteria, the LEA, the parent, and the relevant members of the IEP team must review all relevant information in the student's file, including the child's IEP, any teacher observations, and any relevant information provided by the parents; 20 U.S.C. §1415(k)(1)(E), P.L. 108-446 §615(k)(1)(E).

[113] 71 Fed. Reg. 46720 (August 14, 2006).

[114] 20 U.S.C. §1415(k)(1)(C), P.L. 108-446 §615(k)(1)(C).

[115] 20 U.S.C. §1415(k)(1)(F)(i), P.L. 108-446 §615(k)(1)(F)(i). In addition, if the conduct of a child with a disability was the direct result of the LEA's failure to implement the IEP, "the LEA must take immediate steps to remedy those deficiencies"; 34 C.F.R. §300.530(e)(3) (2010).

[116] 20 U.S.C. §1415(k)(1)(F)(ii), P.L. 108-446 §615(k)(1)(F)(ii).

[117] 20 U.S.C. §1415(k)(1)(F)(iii), P.L. 108-446 §615(k)(1)(F)(iii).

[118] 20 U.S.C. §1415(k)(3)(A), P.L. 108-446 §615(k)(3)(A).

[119] 20 U.SC. §1415(k)(6), P.L. 108-446 §615(k)(6).

[120] The term "excess costs" is defined at 20 U.S.C. §1401 (8), P.L. 108-446 §602(8).

[121] "In 1975, when the act was originally enacted, Congress established the goal of providing up to 40% of the national average per pupil expenditure to assist states and local educational agencies with the excess costs of educating students with disabilities"; H.Rept. 108-77, p.93.

[122] CRS calculation based on unpublished data from the U.S. Department of Education.

[123] 20 U.S.C. §1411(b)(1), P.L. 108-446 §616(b)(1). The outlying areas are defined in §602(22) as the "United States Virgin Islands, Guam, American Samoa, and the Commonwealth of the Northern Mariana Islands." Freely associated states are defined in §611(b)(3) as "the Republic of the Marshall Islands, the Federated States of Micronesia, and the Republic of Palau."

[124] The statute at §611(b)(2) reserves 1.226% of the Part B appropriation for the Department of the Interior's Bureau of Indian Education (BIE) schools; however, this percentage has been overridden since FY2002 through the appropriations process, which has provided annual increases for BIE schools based on the rate of inflation. For example, see the language in the Special Education account in Title III of Division D of P.L. 111-117 (Consolidated Appropriations Act, 2010).

[125] 20 U.S.C. §1411(c), P.L. 108-446 §616(c).

[126] 20 U.S.C. §1411(d), P.L. 108-446 §616(d).

[127] These age ranges for this population vary from state to state depending on the age range for which each state makes FAPE available.

[128] 20 U.S.C. §1411(d)(3)(B) and 20 U.S.C. §1411(a)(2)(B), P.L. 108-446 §616(d)(3)(B) and P.L. 108-446 §616(a)(2)(B).

[129] 20 U.S.C. §1411(d)(4), P.L. 108-446 §611(d)(4).

[130] 20 U.S.C. §1411(e)(1), P.L. 108-446 §611(e)(1). The amount that a state may reserve for administration is up to the greater of the maximum amount the state could reserve from FY2004 funds, or $800,000, increased by the Secretary for inflation as reflected by the Consumer Price Index for All Urban Consumers.

[131] 20 U.S.C. §1411(e)(2)(B), P.L. 108-446 §611(e)(2)(B).

[132] 20 U.S.C. §1411(e)(2)(C), P.L. 108-446 §611(e)(2)(C).

[133] 20 U.S.C. §1411(e)(3), P.L. 108-446 §611(e)(3). The percentage of a state's allocation that a state may reserve for state-level activities depends on the amount a state uses for state administration and whether or not the state uses a risk pool. A state that uses a risk pool can set aside 10.5% for state level activities if it uses $850,000 or less for state administration, or 10% if it uses $850,000 or more for state administration A state that does not use a risk pool can set aside 9.5% for state level activities if it uses $850,000 or less for state administration, or 9% if it uses $850,000 or more for state administration. For FY2007 and each subsequent fiscal year, each state may reserve the maximum amount the state was eligible to reserve in FY2006, cumulatively adjusted by the rate of inflations as reflected by the Consumer Price Index for All Urban Consumers. See 20 U.S.C. §1411(e)(2)(A), P.L. 108-446 §611(e)(2)(A).

[134] 20 U.S.C. §1411(e)(3)(C), P.L. 108-446 §611(e)(3)(C).

[135] 20 U.S.C. §1411(e)(3)(D)(iii), P.L. 108-446 §611(e)(3)(D)(iii).

[136] 20 U.S.C. §1411(e)(3)(E), P.L. 108-446 §611(e)(3)(E).

[137] 20 U.S.C. §1411(e)(3)(I), P.L. 108-446 §611(e)(3)(I).

[138] 20 U.S.C. §1411(f), P.L. 108-446 §611(f).

[139] 20 U.S.C. §1412(a)(18)(A), P.L. 108-446 §612(a)(18)(A).

[140] 20 U.S.C. §1412(a)(18)(B), P.L. 108-446 §612(a)(18)(B).

[141] 20 U.S.C. §1412(a)(18)(C)(i), P.L. 108-446 §612(a)(18)(C)(i).

[142] 20 U.S.C. §1412(a)(18)(C)(ii), P.L. 108-446 §612(a)(18)(C)(ii).

[143] 20 U.S.C. §1412(a)(18)(D), P.L. 108-446 §612(a)(18)(D).

[144] For information on how an LEA calculates its excess costs, see Appendix A to Part 300, 34 C.F.R.

[145] 20 U.S.C. §1413(a)(2)(A), P.L. 108-446 §613(a)(2)(A).

[146] 34 C.F.R. §300.203(b) (2010). In practice, the MOE requirement is based on a comparison of non-federal expenditures for special education services for pupils with disabilities in the preceding fiscal year to those for the second preceding fiscal year since that would be the most recently available data.

[147] 20 U.S.C. §1413(a)(2)(B), P.L. 108-446 §613(a)(2)(B).

[148] 34 C.F.R. §300.204(e) (2010). See, also, the discussion in the report on "State-Level Activities."

[149] 20 U.S.C. §1413(a)(2)(C)(i), P.L. 108-446 §613(a)(2)(C)(i).

[150] 20 U.S.C. §1413(a)(2)(C)(ii), P.L. 108-446 §613(a)(2)(C)(ii).

[151] 20 U.S.C. §1413(a)(2)(C)(iii), P.L. 108-446 §613(a)(2)(C)(iii).

[152] 20 U.S.C. §1416(f), P.L. 108-446 §616(f). See the section in this report on "Enforcement" for more information on the federal and state performance determinations. Also, see U.S. Department of Education, Modifications to Questions in the April 2009 Guidance on the Individuals with Disabilities Education Act, Part B, April 13, 2009, D-7.

[153] For information on CEIS, see the section of this report on "Coordinated Early Intervening Services (CEIS)".

[154] 20 U.S.C. §1413(a)(2)(C)(iv), P.L. 108-446 §613(a)(2)(C)(iv).

[155] For information on "significant disproportionality," see the section of this report on "Coordinated Early Intervening Services (CEIS)."

[156] U.S. Department of Education, Modifications to Questions in the April 2009 Guidance on the Individuals with Disabilities Education Act, Part B, April 13, 1009, D-7. The amount of funds an LEA uses for CEIS for reducing the MOE in years when there is an increase in the LEA allocation is interrelated. The decision about one use will affect the amount of funds available for the other use. For information on the interaction of CEIS and MOE, see Appendix D to Part 300, 34 C.F.R.

[157] 20 U.S.C. §1412(a)172)(C), P.L. 108-446 §613(a)(17)(C).

[158] Ibid. See 34 C.F.R. §300.164 for standards for applying for this waiver.

[159] U.S. Department of Education, Guidance: Funds for Part B of the Individuals with Disabilities Education Act made Available Under the American Recovery and Reinvestment Act of 2009, April 2009, C-6.

[160] 20 U.S.C. §1416(a)(1)(A), P.L. 108-446 §616(a)(1)(A).

[161] 20 U.S.C. §1416(b)(1)(A), P.L. 108-446 §616(b)(1)(A).

[162] 20 U.S.C. §1416(a)(1)(B), P.L. 108-446 §616(a)(1)(B).

[163] 20 U.S.C. § 1416(a)(1)(C), P.L. 108-446 §616(a)(1)(C).

[164] 20 U.S.C. §1416(a)(2), P.L. 108-446 §616(a)(2).

[165] 20 U.S.C. §1416(a)(3), P.L. 108-446 §616(a)(3). Each state must have in effect policies and procedures designed to prevent the inappropriate over-identification or disproportionate representation by race and ethnicity of children as children with disabilities (20 U.S.C. §1412(a)(24), P.L. 108-446 §612(a)(24)).

[166] Each state must review its SPP at least once every six years and amendments must be submitted to the Secretary; 20 U.S.C. §1416(b(1)(C), P.L. 108-446 §616(b)(1)(C).

[167] 34 C.F.R. §300.601(a)(3) (2010).

[168] 20 U.S.C. §1416(b)(2)(C)(i), P.L. 108-446 §616(b)(2)(C)(i).

[169] 20 U.S.C. §1416(b)(2)(C)(ii)(II), P.L. 108-446 §616(b)(2)(C)(ii)(II).

[170] 20 U.S.C. §1453(d), P.L. 108-446 §653(d).

[171] 20 U.S.C. §1416(b)(2)(C)(ii)(I), P.L. 108-446 §616(b)(2)(C)(ii)(I).

[172] 34 C.F.R. §300.602(b)(i)(A) (2010).

[173] 34 C.F.R. §300.602(b)(i)(B) (2010).

[174] 20 U.S.C. §1416(d), P.L. 108-446 §616(d).

[175] 20 U.S.C. §1416(e), P.L. 108-446 §616(e).

[176] 34 C.F.R. §300.606 (2010). The Secretary also posts the annual determination letters typically issued in June of each year to each state, Puerto Rico, the District of Columbia, and outlying areas on its website at http://www2.ed.gov/fund/ data/report/idea/ partbspap/ allyears.html.

[177] 71 Fed. Reg. 73203 (August 14, 2006).

[178] 20 U.S.C. §1416(a)(1)(C), P.L. 108-446 §616(a)(1)(C)(ii), and 34 C.F.R. §300.600(a)(2) (2010).

[179] Compliance indicators include, among others, the percent of districts with disproportionate representation of racial and ethnic groups in special education and related services that is the result of inappropriate identification, the percent of children with parental consent to evaluate who were evaluated and had eligibility determined within 60 days (or a state established timeframe), and a general supervision system (including monitoring, complaints, hearings, etc.) that identifies and corrects noncompliance as soon as possible but no later than one year from identification.

[180] 73 Fed. Reg. 73021 (August 14, 2006).

[181] 34 C.F.R. §300.600(a)(3), and 34 C.F.R. §300.800 (2010).

[182] Neither the statute nor the regulations require that states permit LEAs to appeal a state decision. According to ED's guidance Questions and Answers on Monitoring, Technical Assistance, and Enforcement, C-11, "Whether a State's determination about an LEA's performance may be appealed is a State decision."

[183] 34 C.F.R. §300.600(e) (2010).

[184] 20 U.S.C. §1431(b)(1), P.L. 108-446 §631(b)(1).

[185] Under certain circumstances, children with disabilities age three and over may continue to receive Part C early intervention services until they are eligible to enter kindergarten; 20 U.S.C. §14345(c), P.L. 108-446 §635(c).

[186] In addition to the statutory provisions in Part D, see the following for more information on these activities: U.S. Department of Education, Fiscal Year 2012, Budget Summary, pp. 34-36; and U.S. Department of Education, Guide to U.S. Department of Education Programs, 2010, pp. 254-262.

[187] 20 U.S.C. §1451(a), P.L. 108-446 §651(a).

[188] The term "local educational agency" means "a public board of education or other public authority legally constituted within a State for either administrative control or direction of, or to perform a service function for, public elementary schools or secondary schools in a city, county, township, school district, or other political subdivision of a State, or for such combination of school districts or counties as are recognized in a State as an administrative agency for its public elementary schools or secondary schools." 20 U.S.C. §14011(19), P.L. 108-446 §601(19). The term "school district" is often used instead of local educational agency.

[189] 20 U.S.C. §1462, P.L. 108-446 §662.

[190] 20 U.S.C. §1463, P.L. 108-446 §663.

[191] 20 U.S.C. §1464, P.L. 108-446 §664

[192] 20 U.S.C. §1471, §1472, and §1473, P.L. 108-446 §671, § 672, and §673.

[193] 20 U.S.C. §1474, P.L. 108-446 §674.

In: Education of Students with Disabilities   ISBN: 978-1-62257-996-9
Editors: H. Garlach and N. Darst   © 2013 Nova Science Publishers, Inc.

Chapter 3

THE INDIVIDUALS WITH DISABILITIES EDUCATION ACT (IDEA): SELECTED JUDICIAL DEVELOPMENTS FOLLOWING THE 2004 REAUTHORIZATION[*]

Nancy Lee Jones

SUMMARY

The Individuals with Disabilities Education Act (IDEA) is the major federal statute for the education of children with disabilities. IDEA both authorizes federal funding for special education and related services and, for states that accept these funds, sets out principles under which special education and related services are to be provided. The cornerstone of IDEA is the principle that states and school districts make available a free appropriate public education (FAPE) to all children with disabilities. IDEA has been the subject of numerous reauthorizations; the most recent reauthorization was P.L. 108-446 in 2004. Congress is currently beginning the process of identifying potential issues for the next reauthorization. Some of the issues raised by judicial decisions include the following:

---

[*] This is an edited, reformatted and augmented version of a Congressional Research Service publication, CRS Report for Congress R40521, from www.crs.gov, prepared for Members and Committees of Congress, dated May 4, 2011.

- What amount of educational progress is required to meet FAPE standards?
- What educational benefits are required to be put in an individualized education program (IEP)?
- What use of seclusion and restraints is allowed (if any) under IDEA?
- Are all settlement agreements enforceable in federal court or only those reached through dispute resolution or mediation?
- Is information disclosed in a resolution session confidential?
- What are the specific rights of a parent of a child with a disability?
- What are the rights of a noncustodial parent of a child with a disability?
- Does the Supreme Court's decision in Schaffer v. Weast correctly allocate the burden of proof in IDEA cases?
- Are compensatory educational services required for the same amount of time that the appropriate services were withheld?
- Does the Supreme Court's decision in Arlington Central School District v. Murphy correctly deny reimbursement for expert witness fees?
- Does there need to be more detailed guidance on systemic compliance complaints?

This report examines the Supreme Court decisions, and selected lower court decisions since July 1, 2005, the effective date of P.L. 108-446.

INTRODUCTION

The Individuals with Disabilities Education Act (IDEA)[1] is the major federal statute for the education of children with disabilities. IDEA both authorizes federal funding[2] for special education and related services[3] and, for states that accept these funds,[4] sets out principles under which special education and related services are to be provided. The requirements are detailed, especially when the regulatory interpretations are considered. The major principles include the following requirements:

- States and school districts make available a free appropriate public education (FAPE)[5] to all children with disabilities, generally between the ages of 3 and 21. States and school districts identify, locate, and evaluate all children with disabilities, regardless of the severity of their disability, to determine which children are eligible for special education and related services.

- Each child receiving services has an individual education program (IEP) spelling out the specific special education and related services to be provided to meet his or her needs. The parent must be a partner in planning and overseeing the child's special education and related services as a member of the IEP team. "To the maximum extent appropriate," children with disabilities must be educated with children who are not disabled; and states and school districts provide procedural safeguards to children with disabilities and their parents, including a right to a due process hearing, the right to appeal to federal district court, and, in some cases, the right to receive attorneys' fees.

IDEA was originally enacted in 1975 in response to judicial decisions holding that when states provide an education for children without disabilities, they must also provide an education for children with disabilities.[6] IDEA has been the subject of numerous reauthorizations; the most recent reauthorization was P.L. 108-446 in 2004. P.L. 108-446 included specific authorizations for appropriations through 2011.[7] Congress is currently beginning the process of identifying potential issues for the next reauthorization.[8] This report examines the Supreme Court decisions, and selected lower court decisions since July 1, 2005, the effective date of P.L. 108-446.[9]

DEFINITION OF DISABILITY

A key component of IDEA is the definition of a child with a disability. Unlike the definitions of disability in the Americans with Disabilities Act (ADA)[10] and Section 504 of the Rehabilitation Act,[11] the IDEA definition is categorical, not functional, and contains a requirement that the child needs special education and related services. The IDEA definition states the following:

CHILD WITH A DISABILITY.—"(A) IN GENERAL.—The term 'child with a disability' means a child—"(i) with mental retardation, hearing impairments (including deafness), speech or language impairments, visual impairments (including blindness), serious emotional disturbance (referred to in this title as 'emotional disturbance'),

orthopedic impairments, autism, traumatic brain injury, other health
impairments, or specific learning disabilities; and "(ii) who, by reason
thereof, needs special education and related services.[12]

In *Hansen v. Republic R-III School District*,[13] the court examined whether
a child who had been diagnosed with conduct disorder, bipolar disorder, and
attention deficit hyperactivity disorder (ADHD) was a child with a disability
under IDEA. Finding that the child met the IDEA definitional categories of
serious emotional disturbance and other health impairments, the court noted
that the child was not "merely socially maladjusted" but struggled to pass his
classes and standardized tests. Similarly, the child was found to have a
diagnosis of ADHD and his educational performance was affected by the
condition.

The need for special education and related services was key in other court
decisions. Several courts of appeal decisions have examined whether a child
who falls within one of the categories of disabilities but whose disability may
have a minimal effect on education is a child with a disability and thus covered
by IDEA. In *L.I. v. Maine School Administrative District No. 55*,[14] the First
Circuit Court of Appeals found that a child with Asperger's Syndrome and an
adjustment disorder with depressed mood was a child with a disability under
IDEA even though she had high grades, generally non-disruptive behavior,
and "undisputed intellectual ability." The court rejected the argument that
IDEA is limited to children whose disabilities "significantly impact
educational performance," noting that neither the statute nor its regulations
contain this limiting language.[15] Similarly, in *Board of Education of
Montgomery County v. S.G.*[16] the school argued that a child with schizophrenia
was not a child with a disability because the disability did not adversely affect
her school performance. The Fourth Circuit Court of Appeals rejected this
argument after finding that the child had missed a substantial amount of school
due to hospitalizations, failed to complete many of her assignments, and, if
returned to the public school environment, would most likely be hearing
voices again.

On the other hand, the Ninth Circuit in *R.B. v. Napa Valley Unified School
District*[17] held that a child with ADHD, depression, reactive attachment
disorder, and post traumatic stress disorder who exhibited violent tendencies
was not eligible for IDEA services since her inappropriate behavior did not
adversely affect her educational performance. The fact that the child received a
Section 504 plan and behavioral supports did not make her eligible under
IDEA. In *Alvin Independent School District v. AD*,[18] the Fifth Circuit also

found no adverse educational effect from the child's ADHD. *Mr. and Mrs. N.C. v. Bedford Central School District*[19] examined whether a child with dysthymic disorder met the requirements of the IDEA regulations for seriously emotionally disturbed and found that the child's behavior fell short of the requirements for seriously emotionally disturbed. The Second Circuit also noted that even if the child qualified as seriously emotionally disturbed, there was insufficient evidence that his educational performance was adversely affected.[20]

CHILD FIND

IDEA requires that in order to receive funds under the statute, a state must submit a plan to the Secretary of Education indicating that a state has certain policies and procedures in effect. Among these is the requirement that all children with disabilities and who are in need of special education, are identified, located, and evaluated.[21] This requirement is referred to as child find. Although this requirement has not been heavily litigated, the ninth circuit held in *Compton Unified School District v. Addison*[22] that a school district who failed to evaluate a ninth grader who failed all her classes, colored with crayons and played with dolls in class failed to meet IDEA's child find requirement and that such a failure could be the subject of a due process complaint. Although the Supreme Court has not yet made a determination regarding whether the case will be heard, the Court did ask the Department of Justice for its views on the issue.[23] The issue as presented to the Court is whether the parent of a child with a disability has a right to a due process hearing alleging negligence because of school officials' failure to arrange an educational program for the child, or if due process suits are only allowed when the school district makes an intentional decision.

FREE APPROPRIATE PUBLIC EDUCATION (FAPE)

Statutory Provision

The core requirement of IDEA is that a state must provide children with disabilities a free appropriate public education in order to receive federal funding under the act.[24] FAPE is defined in the statute as meaning "special education and related services that—(A) have been provided at public expense, under public supervision and direction, and without charge; (B) meet the standards of the State educational agency; (C) include an appropriate preschool, elementary school, or secondary school education in the State involved; and (D) are provided in conformity with the individualized education program required under section 614(d)."[25]

Supreme Court Decision in *Rowley*

A seminal decision on the requirements of FAPE, *Board of Education of the Hendrick Hudson Central School District v. Rowley*,[26] decided in 1982, was the first IDEA case to reach the Supreme Court. The Supreme Court noted that there was no substantive language in IDEA regarding the level of education to be accorded to children with disabilities and observed that "(i)mplicit in the congressional purpose of providing access to a 'free appropriate public education' is the requirement that the education to which access is provided be sufficient to confer some educational benefit upon the handicapped child."[27] The Court concluded that "the 'basic floor of opportunity' provided by the Act consists of access to specialized instruction and related services which are individually designed to provide educational benefit to the handicapped child."[28] The Court held that the requirement of FAPE is met when a child is provided with personalized instruction with sufficient support services to benefit educationally from that instruction. This instruction must be provided at public expense, meet the state's educational standards, must approximate the grade levels used in the state's regular education, and must comport with the child's IEP. The Court found that when a child with a disability is mainstreamed, "the system itself monitors the educational progress of the child.... The grading and advancement system thus constitutes an important factor in determining educational benefit."[29] Therefore, the IEP "should be formulated in accordance with the requirements of the Act and, if the child is being educated in the regular classrooms of the public education system, should be reasonably calculated to enable the child to achieve passing marks and advance from grade to grade."[30] However, the states are not required to "maximize" each child's potential.[31] If the child is progressing from grade to grade and making measurable and adequate gains, the FAPE requirement is met.

The Supreme Court also stated that in ensuring that the requirements of the statute have been met, courts must be careful to avoid imposing their view of preferable educational methods upon the states. The primary responsibility for formulating the education provided was left by IDEA to state and local educational agencies.[32] As the Court noted, determining when children with disabilities are "receiving sufficient educational benefits to satisfy the requirements of the Act presents a more difficult problem"[33] than complying with requirements for access to education. Because of the wide spectrum of disabilities, the Court did not attempt to establish any one test for determining the adequacy of educational benefits and confined its analysis to the facts of the case.

Lower Court Decisions

Rowley remains a key decision under IDEA and is often cited by courts attempting to determine the parameters of a free appropriate public education.[34] However, the lower courts have varied in how expansively they have interpreted Rowley, with some courts interpreting Rowley to support schools' IEPs if the procedural requirements have been met, even if the educational progress is minimal. For example, in Fort Zumwalt School District v. Clynes,[35] the Eighth Circuit emphasized Rowley's "access to education" requirement and held that the IEP was adequate. The court noted that the child was making progress, earning passing marks and advancing to the next grade, despite reading proficiency scores in the second to ninth percentile. However, the dissenting opinion described the child's achievement as "trivial" and argued that "(t)his cannot be the sort of education Congress had in mind when it enacted IDEA."[36] Some courts have emphasized that IDEA requires the provision of educational services and medical services, particularly mental health needs, are not covered.[37]

Other courts have read Rowley more expansively. For example, in Polk v. Cent. Susquehanna Intermediate Unit 16,[38] the Third Circuit examined the "some educational benefit" language in Rowley and held that it required an IEP to provide more than de minimis educational benefit.[39] Similarly, the Fifth Circuit, in Cypress-Fairbanks Indep. School District v. Michael F.,[40] quoted from Rowley and concluded that "the educational benefit that an IEP is designed to achieve must be meaningful."[41] In order to determine whether an IEP meets this standard, the Cypress-Fairbanks court identified four factors: (1) the program is individualized; (2) the program is administered in the least restrictive environment; (3) the services are provided in a coordinated and collaborative manner; and (4) positive academic and nonacademic benefits are demonstrated.[42] Other courts have looked at academic achievement testing, as well as grades, to measure educational benefit. For example, in *Falzett v. Pocono Mountain School District,*[43] the court found that, despite allegations of missed days and limited curriculum, a student whose SAT scores improved and who received excellent grades, qualifying him for the Junior National Honor Society, had received FAPE under IDEA. However, in *Ringwood Board of Education v. K.H.J.,*[44] the Third Circuit found that when a child has above average intellectual ability IDEA requires more than a negligible benefit, and noted that "expecting a child with 'above average' intelligence to perform in the 'average' range hardly qualifies as 'maximizing' that child's potential."[45]

Procedural or other violations do not always give rise to a violation of FAPE.[46] Generally, procedural violations must affect the child's substantive rights.[47] For example, FAPE has been found to require that services mandated by an IEP be implemented as soon as possible after the IEP development, not immediately or within 30 days.[48] Similarly, inaccessible facilities do not necessarily violate FAPE if there is general program accessibility.[49] In addition, FAPE has been found not to be violated when a resolution session is improperly convened if there was not substantial effect on the child's educational opportunities.[50] However, certain procedural violations may be significant enough to be a denial of FAPE. In N.B. and C.B. v. Hellgate Elementary School District,[51] the Ninth Circuit held that the school's failure to evaluate a child in all areas of suspected disability was a procedural error that denied FAPE. A denial of FAPE was also found when the LEA unilaterally scheduled an IEP meeting without attempting to reach a mutually agreed upon time with the parents.[52]

Educational Standards and the No Child Left Behind Act (NCLBA)

The application of the Supreme Court's analysis in *Rowley* to current controversies is somewhat confused by the change in the usage of the term "educational standards." Although the Supreme Court in *Rowley* required that the instruction given to a child with a disability meet the state's educational standards, the term "educational standards" has taken on a different meaning in recent years. Currently, the term "educational standards" is likely to refer to specific content-based standards that delineate what a child should know and be able to perform at various points in his or her educational career.

The 1997 Amendments to IDEA[53] reflected the standards-based education movement. P.L. 105-17 significantly changed the IEP requirements and required that the IEP include, among others, a statement of the child's present levels of educational performance, including the effect of the child's disability on the child's involvement and progress in the general curriculum, and a statement of measurable annual goals designed to enable the child to progress in the general curriculum.[54] In addition, in the statement of findings for the 2004 reauthorization, P.L. 108-446 states that "[a]lmost 30 years of research and experience has demonstrated that the education of children with disabilities can be made more effective by—(A) having high expectations for such children and ensuring their access to the general curriculum in the regular classroom to the maximum extent possible."[55]

Given the fact that the standards-based education movement, as reflected in IDEA and the No Child Left Behind Act (NCLBA),[56] has changed the standards from what was required in the version of the law the Supreme Court interpreted in *Rowley*, questions have been raised concerning the current application of *Rowley*. Parents of students with disabilities have argued that FAPE requirements have been changed by NCLBA in several cases but have not been successful.[57] Similarly, an unsuccessful argument has been made that there is an inherent conflict between IDEA and NCLBA.[58]

Peer-Reviewed Research

The 2004 Amendments to IDEA include a requirement that specially designed instruction and related services be "based on peer-reviewed research to the extent practicable."[59] Commentary to the final regulations indicates that peer-reviewed research "generally refers to research that is reviewed by qualified and independent reviewers to ensure that the quality of the information meets the standards of the field before the research is published."[60] Similar to the educational standards issue discussed above, it could be argued that the peer-reviewed research requirement is difficult to reconcile with *Rowley's* some educational benefit requirement.[61]

At least one court of appeals has addressed this issue. In *Joshua A. v. Rocklin Unified School District,*[62] the student argued that his IEP violated IDEA because it was not based on peer-reviewed research. The court rejected this argument finding that the school's "eclectic approach" was sufficient and noted that "[w]e need not decide whether District made the best decision or a correct decision, only whether its decision satisfied the requirements of the

IDEA."[63] The court also emphasized that courts must be careful to avoid imposing their view of preferable educational methods upon the states.

THE INDIVIDUALIZED EDUCATION PROGRAM (IEP)

Statutory Provisions

After a child has been identified as a child with a disability under IDEA, an Individualized Education Team is formed to write an individualized education program for the child.[64] IDEA contains detailed requirements for the IEP. The IEP must include a statement of the child's present levels of academic achievement and functional performance; a statement of measurable annual goals; a description of how these goals are to be met; a statement of the special education and related services to be provided; and an explanation of the extent to which the child is to be educated with children without disabilities.[65] Since the IEP is the way FAPE is implemented, it is a key component of IDEA and has been the subject of numerous judicial decisions. Generally, these cases have adopted the *Rowley* two-part inquiry: first, the court determines whether IDEA's procedures have been complied with; second, the court determines whether the IEP is reasonably calculated to provide the child with educational benefits.[66]

Lower Court Decisions

The exact parameters of an IEP have been the subject of several decisions. Generally, an IEP does not have to be "perfect" to be in compliance with IDEA, but must be "reasonably calculated to enable the child to receive educational benefits."[67] In *School Board of Independent School District No. 11 v. Joshua Renollett,*[68] the Eighth Circuit court of appeals found that although there were some flaws in the child's IEP, since these flaws did not compromise his right to an appropriate education or deprive him of educational benefits, there was no violation of IDEA.[69]

Similarly, the Second Circuit in *Cabouli v. Chappaqua Central School District*[70] found that the evidence supporting the adequacy of the IEP, including the child's recent social progress, indicated that the child would likely make educational progress under the IEP and, therefore, there was no violation of IDEA. The lack of a functional behavioral assessment in an IEP does not necessarily mean that the IEP is invalid.[71] The Sixth Circuit in *Nack v. Orange City School District*[72] found that procedural violations that did not cause the student any substantive harm were not a violation of IDEA.[73] In addition, the court in *Nack* also held that a lack of progress during one school year does not necessarily indicate an IDEA violation since IDEA does not guarantee success, but requires that a student receive sufficient specialized services to benefit from his or her education.[74]

On the other hand, courts have found that an IEP which does not provide the child with educational benefits violates IDEA. In *A.K. v. Alexandria City School Board,*[75] the Fourth Circuit held that an IEP which stated that the child should be placed at an unidentified private day school was not reasonably calculated to provide educational benefits and, therefore, was a violation of IDEA. And in *M.L. v. Federal Way School District,*[76] the Ninth Circuit found that not including a regular education teacher on the IEP team resulted in a "loss of educational opportunity" that amounted to a denial of FAPE. However, in *R.B. v. Napa Valley Unified School District,*[77] the Ninth Circuit held that IDEA did not require the participation of the child's current special education teacher as long as a special education teacher who has actually taught the child was present.

The input of parents in an IEP has been the subject of several recent decisions. Generally, courts have held that "the right of parents to control the content of the IEP is limited."[78] For example, in *Shelby S. v. Conroe Independent School District,*[79] the Fifth Circuit found that in order to develop an appropriate IEP, the school could perform an independent medical evaluation despite a lack of parental consent. And in *Lessard and Lessard v. Wilton-Lyndeborough Cooperative School District and New Hampshire Department of Education,*[80] the First Circuit held that an IEP was not procedurally deficient due to incompleteness and noted, "[l]ine-drawing is often difficult, and in the IEP context it is impossible to draw a precise line separating healthy requests for parental input from impermissible demands that parents do the school system's work."[81]

Despite the limited control of parents over the IEP, courts have found for the parents in IEP cases. For example, in *County School Board of York County v. A.L.,*[82] the Fourth Circuit found that a lack of prior notice to a proposed IEP change and a failure to inform the parents of their due process rights violated IDEA. Similarly, a finding that the school district determined the child's placement before the IEP meeting was found to violate IDEA's procedural requirements.[83] A school's scheduling of an IEP meeting without first inquiring about the parents' availability and the school's denial of the parents' request to reschedule was found to deny the student FAPE.[84]

RELATED SERVICES

As noted above, IDEA's requirement of a free appropriate public education is the cornerstone of the act. FAPE is defined in part as requiring "special education and related services."[85] Related services are defined as meaning

> transportation, and such developmental, corrective, and other supportive services (including speech-language pathology and audiology services, interpreting services, psychological services, physical and occupational therapy, recreation, including therapeutic recreation, social work services, school nurse services designed to enable a child with a disability to receive a free appropriate public education as described in the individualized education program of the child, counseling services, including rehabilitation counseling, orientation and mobility services, and medical services, except that such medical services shall be for diagnostic and evaluation purposed only) as may be required to assist a child with a disability to benefit from special education, and includes the early identification and assessment of disabling conditions in children.[86]

Two Supreme Court decisions under IDEA have involved the concept of related services, and both have involved the issue of what is a medical service. In *Irving Independent School District v. Tatro*,[87] the Court examined the case of an eight-year-old girl with spina bifida who required clean intermittent catheterization (CIC), and held that the school must provide the service. The Court held that services affecting both the medical and educational needs of a child must be provided under IDEA if (1) the child has a disability so as to require special education; (2) the service is necessary to help a child with a disability benefit from special education; and (3) a nurse or other qualified person who is not a physician can provide the service. Services that could be provided outside the school day would not need to be provided. *Tatro* drew a bright line between services that had to be provided by a doctor and those that could be provided by a person who was not a physician. However, after *Tatro*, some courts of appeal did not apply this bright line but used other factors, such as the nature and extent of services. This set the stage for another Supreme

Court decision in 1999, *Cedar Rapids Community School District v. Garret F.*[88]

Garret F. involved a child who was paralyzed from the neck down as a result of a motorcycle accident when he was four years old. Since the child was ventilator dependent, he required substantial services including providing suction on his tracheotomy tube and manually pumping air through an air bag when suction is being provided. The school denied the parents' request for services, and proposed a test for related services in which the outcome would depend on a series of factors, such as whether the care was continuous and the cost of the services. The Court rejected this proposed test and used the same reasoning it had used in *Tatro*, finding that the medical services exclusion from the definition was limited to the services of physician or a hospital. This holding, the Court stated, was in keeping with the overarching purpose of IDEA "to open the door of public education to all qualified children."[89]

The 2004 reauthorization dealt with this issue by establishing risk pools for high-need children with disabilities.[90] States are permitted to reserve 10% of the funds reserved for other state activities (or 1% to 1.05% of the overall state grant) to establish and maintain a risk pool to assist LEAs serving high-need children with disabilities. Related services have not given rise to a large number of recent IDEA cases. Generally, the cases have emphasized the broad discretion of a federal court to define what services are required to enable a child with a disability to benefit from special education, and have applied the *Tatro* analysis.[91]

LEAST RESTRICTIVE ENVIRONMENT

IDEA requires that children with disabilities, to the maximum extent appropriate, be educated with children who are not disabled and that separate schooling or special classes occur only when the nature or severity of the disability is such that "education in regular classes with the use of supplementary aids and services cannot be achieved satisfactorily."[92]

Several recent courts of appeal decisions have followed a two-pronged approach, first enunciated in *Daniel R.R. v. State Board of Education*,[93] to determine whether an IEP places a student in the least restrictive environment. First, a court must consider whether education in the regular classroom with the use of supplementary services can be achieved satisfactorily. Second, if such placement cannot be achieved satisfactorily, the court must consider whether the school has mainstreamed the child to the maximum extent appropriate. The first prong includes several factors: whether the school district has made reasonable efforts to accommodate the child in the regular classroom; the educational benefits available to the child in the regular classroom as compared to those in a special education classroom; and the possible negative effects of the inclusion of the child on other students in the regular classroom.[94] In A.G. v. Durtan,[95] the Third Circuit examined the effect of the child with a disability on other students, noting the student's frequent, loud vocalizations, combined with removal of shoes and socks, inappropriately clapping and grinding her teeth, having difficulty toileting, and inappropriately touching other students. Although these disruptions were not considered dispositive, the court considered them notable and upheld the district court decision that the student could not be satisfactorily educated full time in a regular classroom.

STAY PUT

In enacting P.L. 94-142, the original version of IDEA, Congress provided grants to the states to help pay for education for children with disabilities, and also delineated specific requirements the states must follow to receive these federal funds. This public law contained a requirement that if there is a dispute between the school and the parents of a child with a disability, the child "stays put" in his or her current educational placement until the dispute is resolved using the due process procedures set forth in the statute. The concept of "stay put" was placed in the statute to help eliminate the then common discriminatory practice of expelling children with disabilities from school. A revised "stay put" provision remains as law in the current version of IDEA.[96]

In 1988, the question of whether there was an implied exception to the "stay put" rule was presented to the Supreme Court in Honig v. Doe.[97] Honig involved emotionally disturbed children, one of whom had choked another student with sufficient force to leave abrasions on the child's neck and who had kicked out a window while he was being escorted to the principal's office. The other child in the Honig case had been involved in stealing, extorting money, and making lewd comments. The school had sought expulsion, but the Supreme Court disagreed finding that "Congress very much meant to strip schools of the unilateral authority they had traditionally employed to exclude disabled students, particularly emotionally disturbed students, from school."[98] However, the Court observed that this holding did "not leave educators hamstrung.... Where a student poses an immediate threat to the safety of others, officials may temporarily suspend him or her for up to 10 school days.... And in those cases in which the parents of a truly dangerous child adamantly refuse to permit any change in placement, the 10- day respite gives school officials an opportunity to invoke the aid of the courts under section 1415(e)(2), which empowers courts to grant any appropriate relief."[99] This statement about the school's right to seek judicial relief has come to be know as a *Honig* injunction.

The Supreme Court's interpretation of IDEA in *Honig* did not quell all concerns about discipline and children with disabilities. In 1994, Congress amended IDEA's "stay put" provision to give schools the unilateral authority to remove a child with a disability to an interim alternative educational setting if the child was determined to have brought a firearm to school. This provision was expanded in the IDEA Amendments of 1997 to include weapons (not just firearms) and drugs, and was further expanded in the 2004 reauthorization to include situations where a student has inflicted serious bodily injury upon another person while at school.

Not all issues regarding the stay put provisions have involved disciplinary actions. Several courts have addressed the issue of whether the stay put requirement applies when a child is transitioning from Part C of IDEA to Part B. Part B of IDEA applies to school-aged children and requires the provision of FAPE as delineated in an IEP; Part C of IDEA applies to infants and toddlers and requires the provision of appropriate early intervention services as set forth in an individualized family service plan (IFSP). Rejecting an opinion by the Office of Special Education Programs (OSEP) of the Department of Education,[100] the Third Circuit in *Pardini v. Allegheny Intermediate Unit*[101] held that the stay put provision requires the child "to continue to receive conductive education until the dispute over its appropriateness for inclusion in her IEP was resolved."[102] However, the Eleventh Circuit in *D.P. v. School Board of Broward County*[103] disagreed, finding that the children in that case were applying for initial admission to a public school program and that they were not entitled to continue to receive services pursuant to their IFSPs.

Other issues regarding the stay put provision have involved mediation, private school placement, a move from a resource room to a classroom, and the appeals process in the courts. *Sammons v. Polk County School Board*[104] raised the issue of whether a request for mediation invokes the stay put provision. The Eleventh Circuit held that the IDEA regulations[105] limited the application of the stay put provision to the pendency of administrative or judicial proceedings and, therefore, it was not applicable to a request for mediation. In *L.M. v. Capistrano Unified School District*,[106] the Ninth Circuit held that a child who had not had an implemented IEP, and had never been placed in a public school, but was unilaterally placed in a private school by his parents, could not use the stay put provision to continue private school placement. Similarly, although the IEP team recommended that a child be placed in a private school in the fall, when the district contested the IEP teams recommendation, the court in *E.Y. v. Elysian Charter School of Hoboken* held that the placement where the child was to "stay put" was the placement for the preceding school year.[107] A child's relocation from a resource room to an inclusion classroom was not found to constitute a change in placement within the meaning of the stay put provision.[108] In *Joshua A. v. Rocklin Unified School District*,[109] the Ninth Circuit held that the stay put provision applied throughout the appeals process in the courts.

An attempt to apply a novel application of the stay put provision failed in *N.D. v. State of Hawaii*.[110] Due to major fiscal concerns, the state of Hawaii decided to furlough teachers and shut down the public schools for 17 Fridays in the 2009-2010 school year. Since this meant an approximate reduction of 10% in instruction days, plaintiffs filed suit, alleging that this reduction violated the stay put provision of IDEA. The Ninth Circuit found no violation, holding that the stay put provision was not intended to cover system-wide changes in public schools that affect children with and without disabilities.[111]

SECLUSION AND RESTRAINTS

The use of seclusion and restraints has been the subject of increased congressional interest, and on March 3, 2010, the House passed H.R. 4247, the "Keeping all Students Safe Act." A similar bill, S. 2860, was introduced in the Senate.[112] IDEA provides that when the behavior of a child with a disability impedes the child's learning or the learning of others, the IEP team must consider "the use of positive behavioral interventions and supports, and other strategies, to address that behavior."[113] Nothing in IDEA specifically addresses the use of seclusion and restraints, and the Department of Education has stated that "[w]hile IDEA emphasizes the use of positive behavioral interventions and supports to address behavior that impedes learning, IDEA does not flatly prohibit the use of mechanical restraints or other aversive behavioral techniques for children with disabilities."[114] The Department also noted that state law may address whether restraints may be used and, if restraints are allowed, the "critical inquiry is whether the use of such restraints or techniques can be implemented consistent with the child's IEP and the requirement that

IEP Teams consider the use of positive behavioral interventions and supports when the child's behavior impedes the child's learning or that of others."[115]

The Supreme Court has not specifically addressed the use of seclusion or restraints under IDEA; however, in *Honig v. Doe,*[116] the Court examined IDEA's requirements for children who exhibited violent or inappropriate behavior, and held that a suspension longer than ten days violated IDEA's "stay-put" provision.[117] In *Honig*, the Court observed that this decision "does not leave educators hamstrung" and that educators may utilize "normal procedures" which "may include the use of study carrels, timeouts, detention, or the restriction of privileges" as well as a ten-day suspension.[118]

Despite the lack of specific language in IDEA regarding the use of restraints and seclusion, cases have been brought alleging that their use violates a child's right to a free appropriate public education.[119] Generally, courts have not found violations of IDEA where the seclusion or restraint was deemed necessary to keep the child from hurting himself or others,[120] or where the child was progressing academically and the school had tailored the child's IEP to address behavioral issues.[121] Courts have examined whether the administrative exhaustion requirements of IDEA apply in situations involving the use of seclusion and restraint. In *C.N. v. Willmar Public Schools,*[122] the child's IEP and behavior intervention plan allowed for the use of seclusion and restraint procedures when the child was a danger to herself or others; however, the parents alleged that these procedures were used improperly and excessively. The parents withdrew their daughter from the school and placed her in another school. After her withdrawal, the parents requested a due process hearing, challenging the adequacy of the educational services. The Eighth Circuit affirmed the district court's dismissal of the case, finding that if the parent was dissatisfied with the child's education, she must follow the IDEA due process procedures and file for a due process hearing while the child was still in the school district against which the complaint was made.[123]

In contrast, IDEA has been used by parents in an attempt to enjoin enforcement of a New York State regulation that banned the use of "aversive interventions."[124] Parents argued in part that "some students' IEP's were being revised without parental consent or simply not revised for the new school year, the effect of which was to deprive those students of aversive therapies."[125] The Second Circuit vacated the district court's injunction against the regulation and remanded for further findings. On remand, the district court upheld the regulations finding that "the regulations represent an informed, rational choice between two opposing schools of thought on the use of aversives.... [T]he regulations are neither arbitrary nor capricious, and are consistent with the purposes of the IDEA."[126]

RETALIATION AND HARASSMENT

Although harassment is not explicitly prohibited in IDEA, the Department of Education has stated that disability harassment may result in a denial of FAPE.[127] Several courts have held that harassment may be so severe that the child with a disability is denied access to educational benefits and that, therefore, IDEA is violated.[128] However, at least one court has found that the claim of harassment must be tied to IDEA and should clearly state that the harassment has denied the child FAPE.[129] In addition, another court held that claims regarding retaliation are subject to IDEA's requirements for exhaustion of administrative remedies.[130]

The Americans with Disabilities Act (ADA) and Section 504 of the Rehabilitation Act[131] may also give rise to actions alleging retaliation for advocacy alleging violations of IDEA. Several circuits have held that "attempting to protect the rights of special education students constitutes protected activity under the Rehabilitation Act."[132]

DUE PROCESS PROCEDURES

Overview

Section 615 of IDEA provides detailed procedural safeguards for children with disabilities and their parents.[133] Procedural safeguards are provisions protecting the rights of parents and children with disabilities regarding a free appropriate public education (FAPE) and include notice of rights, mediation, resolution sessions, and due process procedures. Parents of a child with a disability or a school may file a due process complaint.[134] This complaint may only be presented concerning violations that occurred not more than two years before the date the parent or public agency knew or should have known about the alleged action.[135] The 2004 reauthorization added the provision allowing schools to also file complaints and there have been several instances where a school district has used this authority.[136] After an administrative decision, any party aggrieved by the findings may file suit in district court but must do so within 90 days.[137]

Resolution Sessions and Mediation

In an attempt to resolve issues before the more confrontational due process proceedings, the 2004 reauthorization of IDEA added a requirement for a resolution session prior to a due process hearing. This preliminary meeting involves the parents, the relevant members of the IEP team, and a representative of the local educational agency who has decision making authority. The LEA may not include its attorney unless the parent is accompanied by an attorney.[138] Provisions allowing for mediation of disputes under IDEA were added in the 1997 reauthorization[139] and retained in the current law.[140] In addition, the 2004 IDEA reauthorization provided for judicial enforcement of agreements reached through a resolution session[141] or mediation.[142]

Several judicial decisions have addressed issues regarding the resolution session. One court held that the information disclosed during the resolution session is not confidential since the statute does not specifically confer confidentiality and the resolution session discussions are not settlement discussions.[143] Another decision examined the inclusion of a school board attorney when a parent did not have an attorney present, and found that the limitation on the presence of an attorney is only for the preliminary meeting, not for the writing of a settlement decision.[144] As noted previously, procedural violations in a resolution session do not violate FAPE if there was not a substantial effect on the child's educational opportunities.[145]

Several courts have examined the question of whether all settlement agreements are enforceable in federal court or whether judicial enforcement is limited to agreements reached through dispute resolution or mediation. Generally, the courts have held that the statutory language limits judicial enforcement to those agreements reached through dispute resolution or mediation.[146]

In *Amy S. v. Danbury*,[147] the Sixth Circuit held that mediation agreements signed by the parents, who were represented by counsel, precluded a claim. The parents had alleged that the school had breached the mediation agreement since the agreed upon tutor could no longer transport the child in his car. The court rejected this argument, noting that tutoring services were still available.

Similarly, in *Ballard v. Philadelphia School District*,[148] the court rejected an argument by a parent that a settlement agreement was invalid.

Review of Complaint's Sufficiency

IDEA requires that a due process complaint include, in addition to other information, a description of the nature and the problem, the relevant facts, and a proposed resolution of the problem.[149] In *Knight v. Washington School District*,[150] a district court addressed issues relating to the review of the hearing officer's determination that a due process complaint did not meet IDEA's pleading requirements. The district court quoted from the Senate report language which stated in part that the determination of whether the due process complaint notice met the statutory requirements "shall be made on the face of the complaint" and "[t]here should be no hearing or appeal in regard to the hearing officer's determination."[151] Although finding that it had no jurisdiction to determine the adequacy of the complaint notice, the court noted that this was "an unsatisfying outcome for Plaintiffs" and found it "troubling that a state official's summary dismissal of a complaint founded on federal law, for which federal law provides that applicable standard, appears to be unreviewable in federal court."[152] The Eighth Circuit affirmed the district court's dismissal of the action but modified the dismissal to be without prejudice.[153]

LEA Suits Against the State

Several courts of appeal have addressed the issue of whether an LEA may bring an action against an SEA for its failure to comply with IDEA and found that IDEA does not allow such a private right of action. In *Traverse Bay Area Intermediate School District v. Michigan Department of Education*,[154] the Sixth Circuit held that LEAs did not have statutory authority to challenge a state agency's alleged noncompliance with IDEA's procedural safeguards. Noting that a right to bring suit is created by the text of a statute, the court found that IDEA limited complaints to matters relating to the identifications, evaluation, or educational placement of a child. Similarly, the Ninth Circuit in *Lake Washington School District No. 414 v. Washington State Office of Administrative Hearings*,[155] held that an LEA has no private right of action under IDEA to litigate any issue other than the issues raised by the parents on behalf of their child.

Parental Rights

In *Winkelman v. Parma City School District*,[156] the Supreme Court examined the issue of whether IDEA permits parents who are not attorneys to bring suit in court, either on their own behalf or as representatives of their child. The Court held that such *pro se* suits were permitted for parents suing with regard to their own rights. In an opinion written by Justice Kennedy, the Court concluded that IDEA grants parents independent, enforceable rights that encompass a child's entitlement to a free appropriate public education, and that these rights are not limited to procedural or reimbursement issues.

In arriving at this holding, Justice Kennedy observed that "a proper interpretation of the Act requires a consideration of the entire statutory scheme."

The Court examined IDEA's statutory language, noting that one of the purposes of IDEA is "to ensure that the rights of children with disabilities and parents of such children are protected."[157] This language was found to refer to rights for both parents and children with disabilities. Similarly, the Court found that the establishment of procedural rights was required "to ensure that the rights of children with disabilities and parents of such children are protected."[158]

These provisions were found to support the finding that the parents of a child with a disability have "a particular and personal interest" in the goals of IDEA and that "IDEA includes provisions conveying rights to parents as well as to children."

The rights that IDEA provides for parents were found to encompass not only procedural but also substantive rights. Justice Kennedy observed, "IDEA does not differentiate, through isolated references to various procedures and remedies, between the rights accorded to children and the rights accorded to parents."

It was argued that granting these rights would increase the costs to the states because parents may bring more lawsuits if they do not have the financial constraint of paying for an attorney. However, the Court found that these concerns were not sufficient to support an argument under the Constitution's Spending Clause that IDEA failed to provide clear notice before a new condition or obligation was placed on a recipient of funds. In addition,

Justice Kennedy observed that IDEA specifically allows courts to award attorneys' fees to a prevailing educational agency when a parent has brought an action for an "improper purpose, such as to harass, to cause unnecessary delay, or to needlessly increase the cost of litigation."[159]

The Supreme Court's emphasis on a parent's own rights has led courts to conclude that, although a non-attorney parent cannot pursue claims on behalf of his child, he may amend the complaint to assert his own claims.[160] In addition, a parent was found to have "personal rights to enforce FAPE" and, thus, survived an attempt to dismiss her claim.[161] However, a parent may not use his or her rights in order to circumvent an existing consent decree involving the same issues.[162] In addition, the mere assertion that the rights are those of the parents may not be sufficient. In *Woodruff v. Hamilton Township Public Schools,*[163] the Third Circuit found that although the parents had filed an amended compliant purporting to assert their claims only, the claims asserted were not personal to the parents and, therefore, the parents' complaint was properly dismissed.

Parental rights, as determined by *Winkelman*, have been extended by some courts to cases brought under Section 504 and the ADA as well as IDEA.[164] However, not all courts have agreed with this interpretation. In *D.A. and M.A. v. Pleasantville School District,*[165] the court found that *Winkelman* reflected the specific language and structure of IDEA with its emphasis on parental involvement and was, therefore, not applicable to Section 504 and the ADA.

Other parental rights issues are not as directly tied to the *Winkelman* decision. The issue of whether a parent could recover damages under IDEA for lost earnings and suffering incurred while successfully pursuing her child's IDEA claim was raised in *Blanchard v. Morton School District.*[166] The Ninth Circuit noted that money damages were not available for a child with a disability, and that "IDEA does not contemplate the remedy Blanchard seeks and in that regard creates no right enforceable under §1983."[167] The Second Circuit addressed the issue of the rights of a noncustodial parent in *Fuentes v. Board of Education of New York City.*[168]

IDEA defines the term "parent,"[169] and the IDEA regulations expand upon the statutory language stating that a parent is presumed to be the parent unless he or she does not have legal authority to make educational decisions for the child.[170]

The *Fuentes* court emphasized the regulatory language and found that the noncustodial biological parent did not have the legal authority to make educational decisions.

SECTION 504 AND THE AMERICANS WITH DISABILITIES ACT (ADA)

IDEA is not the only federal statute to address the education of children with disabilities, although it is the most detailed in its provisions. Section 504 of the Rehabilitation Act and the Americans with Disabilities Act (ADA) address the rights of individuals with disabilities to education. Although there is overlap, particularly with Section 504 and the ADA, each statute plays a significant part in the education of individuals with disabilities. IDEA, enacted in 1975, is both a grants statute and civil rights statute and requires programs for children with disabilities that are in addition to those available to children without disabilities. Section 504, enacted in 1973, and the ADA, enacted in 1990, are civil rights statutes that prohibit discrimination against individuals with disabilities. Their coverage is similar, and the ADA was modeled on Section 504 and its regulations; however, Section 504 only applies to entities that receive federal financial assistance, while the ADA has broader coverage, not tied to the receipt of federal funds. As noted in *D.A. v. Houston Independent School District,*[171] "[e]xactly what remedies remain under 504 and the ADA for children whose parents are dissatisfied with the school's determinations under IDEA are unclear."[172] Although a detailed analysis of the educational coverage of these statutes is beyond the scope of this report,[173] it should be noted that several courts have examined issues presented by the interaction of the statutes, noting differences in coverage.[174]

BURDEN OF PROOF

IDEA contains detailed due process requirements to ensure the provision of FAPE. These include the opportunity for an impartial due process hearing.[175] However, the statute contains no specific provision relating to which party has the burden of proof in a due process hearing, and the courts of appeal, prior to the Supreme Court's decision in *Schaffer v. Weast,*[176] were split in their interpretations of who bore the burden of proof.

The Supreme Court in the 2005 case of *Schaffer v. Weast*[177] held that the burden of proof regarding an allegedly inadequate IEP in an IDEA due process hearing rests with the party seeking the relief. The Supreme Court, in an opinion by Justice O'Connor, first observed that "absent some reason to believe that Congress intended otherwise, ... we will conclude that the burden

of persuasion lies where it usually falls, upon the party seeking relief."[178]
Justice O'Connor then examined, and rejected, various reasons advanced to
support the argument that the burden of proof should be on the school system.
The Supreme Court noted that the most plausible argument advanced by the
parents was that, in the interest of fairness, the burden of proof should not be
placed on a party when the facts are "peculiarly within the knowledge of his
adversary."[179] School districts were seen as having a "natural advantage"
regarding the information, but Justice O'Connor did not find this to be
determinative because "Congress addressed this when it obliged schools to
safeguard the procedural rights of parents and to share information with
them."[180] The Court noted that IDEA provides parents with the right to review
records; to have an independent educational evaluation; to have details about
options considered by the school district as well as disclosure of evaluations
and recommendations; and to receive attorneys' fees in the discretion of a
court if they prevail. Justice O'Connor concluded that "[t]hese protections
ensure that the school bears no unique informational advantage."[181]

REMEDIES

Private Schools

Issues concerning what services are required for children with disabilities
placed in private schools, and who is to pay for these services, have been a
continuing source of controversy under IDEA.[182] Under current law, a child
with a disability may be placed in a private school by the local educational
agency (LEA) or state educational agency (SEA) as a means of fulfilling the
FAPE requirement for the child. In this situation, the full cost is paid for by the
LEA or the SEA. A child with a disability may also be unilaterally placed in a
private school by his or her parents. In this situation, the cost of the private
school placement is not paid by the LEA unless a hearing officer or a court
makes certain findings. However, IDEA does require some services for
children in private schools, even if they are unilaterally placed there by their
parents.[183] IDEA, as amended, states in part,

> (ii) REIMBURSEMENT FOR PRIVATE SCHOOL PLACEMENT.—If
> the parents of a child with a disability, who previously received special
> education and related services under the authority of a public agency,
> enroll the child in a private elementary school or secondary school

without the consent of or referral by the public agency, a court or a hearing officer may require the agency to reimburse the parents for the cost of the enrollment if the court or hearing officer finds that the agency had not made a free appropriate public education available to the child in a timely manner prior to that enrollment.[184]

The current statutory provisions regarding private schools are the result of several major amendments, and the majority of the Supreme Court decisions on private schools were decided prior to the statutory changes.[185] However, two recent Supreme Court cases have addressed the question of whether IDEA allows for tuition reimbursement for parents who placed their child in a private school without ever having received special education from the public school. In the 2007 decision *Board of Education of the City School District of the City of New York v. Tom F.*,[186] the Court, dividing 4-4, allowed an appeals court ruling on private school reimbursement to stand. The court of appeals had held that parents of a child with a disability are entitled to private school reimbursement even though the student had never received special education services from the school district. The Court's *per curiam* decision did not set a precedent for lower courts, and therefore the issue about whether reimbursement for private school tuition may be made when the child has not received public special education services remained unsettled. On October 15, 2007, the Supreme Court denied *certiorari* in another case presenting the same issue.[187] However, on June 22, 2009, the Supreme Court held in *Forest Grove School District v. T.A.*[188] that IDEA authorized reimbursement for private special-education services when a public school fails to provide a FAPE and the private-school placement is appropriate, regardless of whether the child previously received special-education services through the public school.

Recent lower court decisions have held that if the child is making some educational progress and the public school has provided an IEP calculated to provide for continued progress, the requirements of FAPE are met and the child is not entitled to a private school placement.[189] For example, in *M.H. and J.H. v. Monroe-Woodbury Central School District*,[190] the court found that the child's IEP was adequate and, therefore, the parents were not entitled to tuition reimbursement for a private school placement. These same standards have been applied when parents seek to place their child in a private school different from the private school where the school district has placed the child.[191] In addition, if a private school does not adequately address the child's educational needs, the court may not require private school tuition reimbursement.[192] However, the mere fact that the private school contains a large percentage of children with disabilities does not make it an inappropriate placement despite IDEA's preference for educating children with disabilities in the least restrictive environment.[193]

Courts have held that reimbursement for private school tuition is barred if parents arrange for private school educational services without notifying the LEA of their problems with their child's IDEA services.[194] Reimbursement is also barred if the parents act unreasonably in their relations with the school[195] or if the allegation concerns procedural violations that do rise to a level of substantive harm.[196] The parents are not barred from private school tuition reimbursement, however, if the child has not previously received special education services.[197]

Compensatory Education

If a school district is found to have deprived a child with a disability of FAPE, the child may be entitled to private school reimbursement, as was discussed previously, or the child may be entitled to receive compensatory education. Essentially, compensatory education is the award of prospective educational services designed to compensate for a previous inadequate program, and is derived from the 1985 Supreme Court's private school ruling in *School Committee of the Town of Burlington v. Department of Education of Massachusetts.*[198]

In *Burlington*, the Court held that parents who place a child in a private school when the public school program violates FAPE may obtain reimbursement for the private school tuition. Lower courts have used this holding to find that if financial reimbursement is allowed, compensatory services must also be allowed.[199]

However, allowing such a remedy is not without some ambiguity. Courts have differed in how the award of compensatory education is to be made. Some courts have found that the child is entitled to compensatory education for the same amount of time that appropriate services were withheld.[200] Other courts have adopted an "equitable focus" which rejects a day for day approach and emphasizes the need of the student to be appropriately educated under IDEA.[201] In addition, the IEP applicable to children receiving compensatory education may also need to provide more services than might be required in a general IEP since the IEP for children receiving a compensatory education must be created to compensate for the denial of appropriate education.[202]

Section 1983 Actions

Section 1983 authorizes suits against state officials and others acting "under color" of state law for deprivation of rights derived from the "Constitution and laws" of the United States.[203] Generally, courts have found that the IDEA procedural remedies must be exhausted prior to the filing of a §1983 action.204 The application of section 1983 with its damages for pain and suffering to IDEA is unclear. Some courts have held that IDEA's statutory scheme does not allow for damages.205 However, other courts have allowed damages.[206]

ATTORNEYS' FEES

Background

Although the original version of IDEA, P.L. 94-142, contained no specific provision for attorneys' fees, prevailing parties used section 505 of the Rehabilitation Act of 1973,[207] or section 1988 of the Civil Rights Attorneys' Fees Award Act,[208] to seek fees. However, the Supreme Court in *Smith v. Robinson*[209] held that the only remedies for prevailing parties under IDEA were those contained in that statute. The statute was described as "a comprehensive scheme set up by Congress to aid the States in complying with their constitutional obligations to provide public education for handicapped children."[210] The Court further noted that allowing the use of other statutes to provide for attorneys' fees would "be inconsistent with Congress' carefully tailored scheme."[211]

The Court's decision in *Smith v. Robinson* was controversial. In response, Congress in 1986 enacted the Handicapped Children's Protection Act, which provided for attorneys' fees under IDEA.[212] These provisions were amended in 1997. The P.L. 105-17 amendments allowed the reduction of attorneys' fees if the attorney representing the parents did not provide the LEA with timely and specific information about the child and the basis of the dispute, and specifically excluded the payment of attorneys' fees for most individualized education plan (IEP) meetings. The 2004 IDEA reauthorization, P.L. 108-446, kept many of the previous provisions on attorneys' fees but also made several additions. These include allowing attorneys' fees for the state educational agency (SEA) or the local educational agency (LEA) against the parent or the parent's attorney in certain situations.[213]

The ADA allows a court, in its discretion, to award attorneys' fees to a prevailing party. In *Buckhannon Board and Care Home, Inc., v. West Virginia Department of Human Resources*,[214] the Supreme Court addressed the "catalyst theory" of attorneys' fees which posits that a plaintiff is a prevailing party if the lawsuit brings about a voluntary change in the defendant's conduct. The Court rejected this theory finding that attorneys' fees are only available where there is a judicially sanctioned change in the legal relationship of the parties.[215]

Lower Court Decisions

Courts have consistently applied *Buckhannon* to the attorneys' fees provision in IDEA. In several cases, attorneys' fees have been given to the party who prevailed in administrative proceedings, provided that result was legally enforceable,[216] although attorneys' fees have not been awarded for resolution sessions.[217] Additionally, attorneys' fees have been given to the prevailing party in judicial proceedings, even if the party prevails because of a dismissal on the merits.[218] Attorney fees have also been awarded without a finding of a denial of FAPE when an LEA has misclassified the child's disability.[219] However, where a child has not yet been determined to be a child with a disability under IDEA, attorneys' fees have not been awarded, even where the fees were sought for a failure to refer for assessments to determine eligibility and failure to identify the child as a child with a disability.[220]

Courts will only award attorneys' fees for relief obtained through a settlement agreement if that agreement received judicial approval.[221] Attorneys' fees will not be awarded for voluntary settlements[222] or purely private settlement agreements[223] that are not judicially sanctioned or do not require judicial approval to take effect. Also, in *Drennan v. Pulaski County Special School District*,[224] a party was not awarded attorneys' fees when it had not performed certain duties that were ordered by the court as a precondition of receiving relief from the school district. Attorneys' fees also will not be awarded to parties for representation by consultants[225] or by parent-attorneys.[226] However, attorneys' fees may be awarded to relatives other than parents, such as a grandparent.[227]

Courts have great discretion when deciding the amount of attorneys' fees to award to a prevailing party.[228] Based on the degree of success that is achieved by a party, a court may decide to award less than the full amount of attorneys' fees requested by the party.[229] Courts have denied or reduced the party's attorneys' fees because the party rejected a settlement offer from the school district but accomplished little more in court than was offered in the proposed settlement.[230] However, the Fifth Circuit has held that refusal to attend a meeting when a proposed settlement has not been offered does not mean that the award should be reduced because the plaintiff unreasonably protracted the proceedings.[231] Additionally, Congress first imposed a fee cap on IDEA cases brought in the District of Columbia in FY1999 through a provision in the annual District of Columbia Appropriations Act, and a cap has been part of every subsequent D.C. appropriations act since that time.[232]

The 2004 IDEA reauthorization added a provision stating that in "any action or proceeding brought under this section, the court, in its discretion, may award reasonable attorneys' fees ... to a prevailing party who is a State educational agency or local educational agency against the attorney of a parent who files a complaint or subsequent cause of action that is frivolous, unreasonable, or without foundation, or against the attorney of a parent who continued to litigate after the litigation clearly became frivolous, unreasonable, or without foundation.... " [233] In *El Paso Independent School District v. Berry,*[234] the Fifth Circuit found that the award of attorneys' fees to the LEA was permissible against a lawyer who refused to accept all offered relief, and used stonewalling tactics to refuse to allow the district to evaluate the student. However, the sixth circuit found that this fee-shifting provision did not apply to private schools.[235] The mere fact that the parents do not prevail in court does not make the parents' action frivolous.[236] The Ninth Circuit noted that "[l]awyers would be improperly discouraged from taking on potentially meritorious IDEA cases if they risked being saddled with a six-figure judgment for bringing a suit where they have a plausible, though ultimately unsuccessful, argument...."[237]

Several of the cases discussing the fee-shifting provision have examined whether the LEA was the prevailing party. In *El Paso Independent School District v. Richard R,*[238] the Fifth Circuit held that although the school district prevailed in successfully arguing for a reduction in the attorneys' fees awarded to the plaintiff, the school district did not prevail on the educational issues and thus was not entitled to attorneys' fees. Similarly, in *District of Columbia v. Straus,*[239] the D.C. Court of Appeals refused to award fees for the school district because the school district was not found to be a prevailing party. The hearing officer had dismissed the case after the school district had agreed to pay for the requested evaluation, and the court noted that "[i]f the District were considered a prevailing party under these circumstances, then DCPS could ignore its legal obligations until parents sue, voluntarily comply quickly, file for and receive a dismissal with prejudice for mootness, and then recover attorney's fees from the parents' lawyers."[240]

EXPERT WITNESS FEES

Although there is no specific provision allowing a court to award to expert witness fees to prevailing parents, the language regarding attorneys' fees has been interpreted by some lower courts to allow such an award. IDEA's statutory language states in relevant part: "in any action or proceeding brought under this section, the court, in its discretion, may award reasonable attorneys' fees as part of the costs—(I) to a prevailing party who is the parent of a child with a disability."[241] The parents in *Arlington Central School District v. Murphy*[242] argued that the language on costs encompassed the payment of expert witness fees. To support this argument, they pointed to the legislative history of the Handicapped Children's Protection Act,[243] which stated that "[t]he conferees intend that the term 'attorneys' fees as part of the costs' include reasonable expenses and fees of expert witnesses."[244] The Supreme Court, in a decision written by Justice Alito, held that IDEA does not authorize prevailing parents to recover fees they have paid to experts. The majority opinion first observed that the holding was "guided by the fact that Congress enacted the IDEA pursuant to the Spending Clause."[245] This was seen as significant because if Congress attaches conditions to a state's acceptance of funds, the conditions must be unambiguous and provide clear notice. The majority concluded that IDEA's statutory language did not provide this clear notice and that the legislative history was unconvincing and "simply not enough" under these circumstances.[246]

H.R. 1208 and S. 613 were introduced in the 112th Congress to amend IDEA to include the fees of expert witnesses. They specifically provided that "the term 'attorneys' fees' shall include the fees of expert witnesses, including the reasonable costs of any test or evaluation necessary for the preparation of the parent or guardian's case in the action or proceeding."

SYSTEMIC COMPLIANCE COMPLAINTS

IDEA has two separate means of resolving disputes: (1) the impartial due process procedures[247] and (2) the state complaint resolution system,[248] and the state complaint regulations specifically allow complaints by "any organization or individual."[249] In addition, the Department of Education is responsible for monitoring implementation of IDEA.[250] At least one court of appeals decision has addressed a systemic complaint under IDEA's due process procedures.[251] In addition, the Ninth Circuit in *Lake Washington School District No. 414 v. Washington State Office of Administrative Hearings,*[252] rejected an LEA's suit against the SEA finding that it had no private right of action to challenge a state's "systematic violation of the IDEA."[253]

In 1975, Congress established a protection and advocacy system (P & A's) to advocate and protect the rights of individuals with developmental disabilities.[254] Many of the court cases filed by P & A's are class action lawsuits aimed at systemic violations of the rights of an individual and a number of these cases have involved special education students.[255] These cases have often involved issues concerning the P & A's access to student records.[256]

End Notes

[1] 20 U.S.C. §1400 et seq. For a more detailed discussion of IDEA, see CRS Report RS22590, The Individuals with Disabilities Education Act (IDEA): Overview and Selected Issues, by Ann Lordeman and Nancy Lee Jones.

[2] Although funding issues are beyond the scope of this report, it should be noted that the Ninth Circuit, in Arizona State Board for Charter Schools v. U.S. Department of Education, 464 F.3d 1003 (9th Cir. 2006), examined whether a for-profit charter school was eligible for federal funds under IDEA and held that a "a natural reading of the [statutory] text conveys clear congressional intent that all schools, including charter schools, must be non profit to receive IDEA and ESEA funds." For a discussion of this case and the use of IDEA funds for charter schools see Mark D. Evans, "An End to Funding of For-Profit Charter Schools?" 70 U. Colorado L. Rev. 617 (2008). For a discussion of IDEA funding generally see CRS Report RL32085, Individuals with Disabilities Education Act (IDEA): Current Funding Trends, by Ann Lordeman.

[3] Related services (for example, physical therapy) assist children with disabilities to help them benefit from special education (20 U.S.C. §1401(26), P.L. 108-446 §602(26)).

[4] Currently, all states receive IDEA funding.

[5] It should be emphasized that what is required under IDEA is the provision of a free appropriate public education. The Supreme Court, in Board of Education of the Hendrick Hudson Central School District v. Rowley, 458 U.S. 176 (1982), held that this requirement is satisfied when the state provides personalized instruction with sufficient support services to permit a child to benefit educationally from that instruction, and that this instruction should be reasonably calculated to enable the child to advance from grade to grade. IDEA does not require that a state maximize the potential of children with disabilities.

[6] PARC v. State of Pennsylvania, 343 F.Supp. 279 (E.D. Pa. 1972); Mills v. Board of Education of the District of Columbia, 348 F.Supp. 866 (D.D.C. 1972). For a discussion of the history

of IDEA see CRS Report 95-669, The Individuals with Disabilities Education Act: Congressional Intent, by Nancy Lee Jones.

[7] 20 U.S.C. §1411(i). For years after 2011, P.L. 108-446 authorized "such sums as may be necessary for fiscal year 2012 and each succeeding fiscal year."

[8] The Department of Education and other groups have begun to look at issues surrounding IDEA reauthorization. See The Brookings Institution, "Building on IDEA: Policy Solutions to Improve U.S. Special Education" (January 18, 2011), http://www.brookings.edu/~/media/Files/events/2011/0118_special_education/20110118_special_education.pdf.

[9] The lower court cases were identified by a LEXIS search using the term "individuals with disabilities education act and date aft 2004" and a LEXIS search for "P.L. 108-446." It should be emphasized that although P.L. 108-446 was enacted in December 2004 and had a July 1, 2005, effective date, many of the cases located by the LEXIS search dealt with events that occurred prior to the effective date of P.L. 108-446, and were therefore subject to the previous statutory language. Generally, these cases are not discussed except where they raise a significant issue that was not resolved by the 2004 reauthorization. It should also be noted that a number of the cases examined concerned whether P.L. 108-446 applied retroactively, and held that the 2004 reauthorization was not retroactive. See e.g., Anna Hood v. Encinitas Union School District, 486 F.3d 1099 (9th Cir. 2007); Anthony v. District of Columbia, 463 F. Supp. 2d 37 (D.D.C. 2006); Tereance D. v. School District of Philadelphia, 570 F. Supp. 2d 739 (2008).

[10] 42 U.S.C. §12102, as amended by P.L. 110-325.

[11] 29 U.S.C. §705(20), as amended by P.L. 110-325.

[12] 20 U.S.C. §1401(3).

[13] 632 F.3d 1024 (8th Cir. 2011).

[14] 480 F.3d 1 (1st Cir. 2007).

[15] Id. at 38.

[16] 230 Fed Appx. 330 (4th Cir. 2007).

[17] 496 F.3d 932 (9th Cir. 2007).

[18] 503 F.3d 378 (5th Cir. 2007).

[19] 300 Fed. Appx. 11 (2d Cir. 2008).

[20] See also, Marshal Joint School District No. 2 v. C.D., 616 F.3d 632(7th Cir. 2010), where the court found that a child with Ehlers-Danlos Syndrome (EDS), a genetic disease characterized by joint hyper-mobility, was a not a child with a disability under IDEA since his educational performance was not adversely affected. Although he needed physical therapy, the court, citing the IDEA regulations at 34 C.F.R. §300.8(a)(2)(i), emphasized that physical therapy is a related service that the school is not required to provide unless the child is a child with a disability under IDEA who need special education.

[21] 20 U.S.C. §1412(a)(3); 34 C.F.R. §300.111 (2010).

[22] 598 F.3d 1181 (9th Cir. 2010), Petition for certiorari filed (Jan. 6, 2011) (No.10-886).

[23] 2011 U.S. LEXIS 2986; 79 U.S.L.W. 3591 (April 18, 2011),

[24] 20 U.S.C. §1412(a)(1).

[25] 20 U.S.C. §1401(9).

[26] 458 U.S. 176 (1982).

[27] Id. at 200.

[28] Id. at 201.

[29] Id at 203.

[30] Id. at 203-204.

[31] Id. at 198.

[32] In Lessard v. Wilton-Lyndeborough Cooperative School District, 592 F.3d 267 (1st Cir. 2010), the First Circuit cited Rowley emphasizing that "an ideal or perfect plan is not required" and that deference to the educational authorities is required.

[33] Id. at 202.

[34] The 2004 reauthorization of IDEA has been found not to affect the Rowley standard. See Mr. and Mrs. C. v. Maine School Administrative District No. 6, 538 F. Supp. 2d 298 (D. Me.2008). An argument that the 1997 IDEA reauthorization, P.L. 105-17, changed the "educational benefit" standard of Rowley was rejected by the Ninth Circuit in J.L., M.L. and K.L. v. Mercer Island School District, 592 F.3d 938 (9th Cir. 2010).

[35] 119 F.3d. 607 (8th Cir. 1997), cert. denied, 523 U.S. 1137 (1998).

[36] Id. at 617 (dissenting opinion by Judge Gibson). For a more detailed discussion of Fort Zumwalt see Charlene K. Quade, "A Crystal Clear Idea: The Court Confounds the Clarity of Rowley and Contorts Congressional Intent," 23 Hamline J. Pub. L. and Policy 37 (2001).

[37] See Shaw v. Weast, 364 Fed. Appx. 47 (4th Cir. 2010), where the Fourth Circuit found that a student whose emotional and mental needs required a level of care beyond her current placement was not entitled to state funding of those needs when the student's educational needs were being addressed. Similarly, the Ninth Circuit in Ashland School District v. Parents of Student E.H., 587 F.3d 1175 (9th Cir. 2009), and Ashland School District v. Parents of Student R.J., 588 F.3d 1004 (9th Cir. 2009), affirmed the district court decisions that the students' residential placements were not for educational needs. But see Alleyne v. New York State Education Department, 691 F.Supp 2d 322(N.D.N.Y. 2010).

[38] 853 F.2d 171 (3d Cir. 1988), cert. denied, 488 U.S. 1030 (1989).

[39] Id. at 180-185. See also R.H. v. Plano Independent School District, 607 F.3d 1003(5th Cir. 2010), Cert. den. 2011 U.S. LEXIS 1330, 79 U.S.L.W. 3475 (U.S. Feb. 22, 2011).

[40] 118 F.3d 245 (5th Cir. 1997), cert. denied, 522 U.S. 1047 (1998).

[41] Id. at 248.

[42] Id. at 253.

[43] 152 Fed. Appx. 117 (3d Cir. 2005). See also A.H. v. Department of Education of the City of New York, 394 Fed. Appx. 718 (2d Cir. 2010), where the court stated that "the relevant inquiry was not whether the proposed IEP provided all possible support to ensure that J.H. did not lose focus, but rather whether objective evidence indicated that the child was likely to progress, not regress, under the proposed plan."; Thompson R2-J School District v. Luke P., 540 F.3d 1143 (10th Cir. 2008), cert. den. 129 S. Ct. 1356 (Feb. 23, 2009), where the progress made by a student with autism was found to be sufficient.

[44] 258 Fed. Appx. 399 (3d Cir. 2007).

[45] Id. at 410. Similarly, in D.S. v. Bayonne Board of Education, 602 F.3d 553 (3d Cir. 2010), the court found that high grades did not necessarily mean that FAPE was provided, especially when the high grades were achieved in special education classes.

[46] A.H. v. Department of Education of the City of New York, 394 Fed. Appx. 718 (2d Cir. 2010); Fitzgerald v. Fairfax County School Board, 556 F.Supp.2d 543 (E.D. Va. 2008); School Board of Independent School District No. 11, Anoka-Hennepin, Minnesota v. Renollett, 440 F.3d 1007 (8th Cir. 2006).

[47] T.T. v. District of Columbia, 2007 U.S. Dist. LEXIS 52547 (July 23, 2007); Hunter v. District of Columbia, 2008 U.S. Dist. LEXIS 70009 (September 17, 2008); Kingsmore v. District of Columbia, 466 F.3d 118 (D.C. Cir. 2006).

[48] DD v. New York City Board of Education, 465 F.3d 503 (2d Cir. 2006), rehearing denied, 480 F.3d 138 (2d Cir. 2007).

[49] Logwood v. Louisiana Department of Education, 197 Fed. Appx. 302 (5th Cir. 2006). The fact that certain parts of the school facilities were inaccessible to a student in a wheelchair did not deny the student a meaningful educational benefit and thus violate FAPE since he had an alternative route to his classrooms and activities on the stage of the auditorium would have been moved to the accessible gymnasium if necessary.

[50] O.O. v. District of Columbia, 573 F.Supp.2d 41 (2008).

[51] 541 F.3d 1202 (9th Cir. 2008).

[52] Drobnicki v. Poway Unified School District, 358 Fed. Appx. 788 (9th Cir. 2009).

[53] P.L. 105-17.

[54] P.L. 105-17 §614(d)(1)(A), 20 U.S.C. §1414(d)(1)(A). The 2004 IDEA reauthorization, P.L. 108-446, continued the standards-based requirements of P.L. 105-17.

[55] 20 U.S.C. §1400(c)(5)(A).

[56] 20 U.S.C. §§6301-6777. For a discussion of the requirements of the NCLBA, see CRS Report RL31284, K-12 Education: Highlights of the No Child Left Behind Act of 2001 (P.L. 107-110), coordinated by Wayne C. Riddle. For a discussion of the relationship between the NCLBA and the IDEA, see CRS Report RL32913, The Individuals with Disabilities Education Act (IDEA): Interactions with Selected Provisions of the No Child Left Behind Act (NCLB), by Ann Lordeman and Nancy Lee Jones.

[57] See e.g., Leighty v. Laurel School District, 457 F.Supp.2d 546 (W.D. Pa. 2006). "Although the IDEA clearly conditions the States' receipt of IDEA funds on the inclusion of disabled children in the assessments mandated by the NCLBA, it does not require that FAPE determinations be based on the results of those assessments, nor does it require that the IEP's prepared for disabled children be designed specifically to enhance their scores on standardized tests. While it is clear that both the IDEA and the NCLBA require recipient States to include disabled children in the assessments, with the modifications necessitated by their disabilities, neither statute indicates that FAPE determinations under the IDEA are controlled by the performance of disabled children on assessments required under the NCLBA." At 40-41. Fisher v. Stafford County Township Board of Education, 2007 U.S. Dist. LEXIS 14003 (February 27, 2007), aff'd 289 Fed. Appx. 520 (3d Cir. 2008). "There is absolutely no support in the statutes or case law for Fisher's attempt to engraft the achievement standards references in the NCLB Act onto the IDEA." At 42. Kirby v. Cabell County Board of Education, 2006 U.S. Dist LEXIS 67254 (S.D. W.Va. September 19, 2006). "While the statutory language of 20 U.S.C. §6311 requires that state plans are coordinated with the IDEA along with other programs under Title 20 ... , there is no language in the Act that places additional obligations on the development or assessment of a child's IEP.... The obligations contained in the section referenced by the plaintiffs are placed on the state in regards to all students. It does not contain specific obligations to children with disabilities nor does it alter the Court's standard of review in regards to the IEP in question." At 20. For a discussion of this issue see Robin Bucaria, "Expanding the Definition of FAPE under NCLB: Why Courts Give FAPE the Slip and Leave it Swimming in a Sea of Alphabet Soup," 10 J. L. Fam. Studies 237 (2007).

[58] Board of Education of Ottawa Township High School District 140 v. Spellings, 517 F.3d 922 (7th Cir. 2008). See also State of Connecticut v. Duncan, 612 F.3d 107 (2d Cir. 2010), Cert. den., 131 S.Ct. 1471, 179 L.Ed.2d 360, 2011 U.S. LEXIS 1115, 79 U.S.L.W. 3418 (U.S. Feb. 22, 2011).

[59] 20 U.S.C. §1414(d)(1)(A)(i)(IV).

[60] 71 FED. REG. 46665 (August 14, 2006).

[61] For a discussion concluding that "[t]he conservative 'some benefit' interpretation of Rowley, as applied to maintain the school district status quo, appears to be antithetical to the outcome based goals which led to the inclusion of PRR in IDEA 2004," see Ilene Young, "Peer-Reviewed Research (PRR)—What Effect on FAPE? From the Parents' Bar," Lehigh University 37th Annual Special Education Law Conference, http://documents.jdsupra.com/7eab09a0-cb63- 4b26-851a-32ae53b6f56d.pdf.

[62] 319 Fed Appx. 692 (9th Cir. 2009).

[63] Id. at 695.

[64] 20 U.S.C. §1414(d).

[65] Id.

[66] See Board of Education of the Hendrick Hudson School District v. Rowley, 458 U.S. 176, 206-207 (1982).

[67] Board of Education of the Hendrick Hudson Central School District v. Rowley, 458 U.S. 176 (1982).

[68] 440 F.3d 1007 (8th Cir. 2006).

[69] Similarly, in Bradley v. Arkansas Department of Education,443 F.3d 965 (8th Cir. 2006), the court found that although the child's IEP and its implementation may not have been perfect, the IEP was reasonably calculated to provide educational benefits and thus did not violate IDEA. See also Mr. and Mrs. B v. East Granby Board of Education, 201 Fed. Appx. 834 (2d Cir. 2006), rejecting the argument that the child's IEPs violated IDEA since they did not include the recommendations of experts retained by the parents. The IEPs were found to be reasonably calculated to provide educational benefit. In G.N. and S.N. v. Board of Education of the Township of Livingston, 309 Fed. Appx. 542 (3d Cir. 2009), the absence of a requested modification to the IEP did not mean that the IEP was not reasonably designed to confer a meaningful educational benefit. There is also no requirement that the IEP name a specific school location. See T.Y. v. New York City Department of Education, 584 F.3d 412 (2d Cir. 2009), cert. den. 130 S. Ct. 3277 (May 17, 2010).

[70] 202 Fed. Appx. 519 (2d Cir. 2006).

[71] A.C. and M.C. v. Board of Education of the Chappaqua Central School District, 553 F.3d. 165 (2d Cir. 2009).

[72] 454 F.3d 604 (6th Cir. 2006).

[73] See also A.H. v. Department of Education of the City of New York, 394 Fed. Appx. 718 (2d Cir. 2010), where the court concluded that the absence of the child's special education teacher from the IEP meeting "did not impede the child's right to a free appropriate education, limit the parents' ability to participate in the decision making process, or result in the denial of educational benefits." At 720.

[74] Id. at 22. See also Lathrop R-II School District v. Gray, 611 F.3d 419 (8th Cir. 2010), cert. den. 131 S.Ct. 1017, 179 L.Ed.2d 843, 2011 U.S. LEXIS 812 (Jan. 18, 2011), where the court held that even if there was a technical violation regarding the scheduling of an IEP meeting, it did not affect the IEP or deprive the child of educational benefit, and thus was not a violation of IDEA.

[75] 484 F.3d 672 (4th Cir. 2007).

[76] 394 F.3d 634 (9th Cir. 2004).

[77] 496 F.3d 932 (9th Cir. 2007). See also, A.G. v. Placentia-Yorba Linda Unified School District, 320 Fed. Appx. 519 (9th Cir. March 20, 2009); Mahoney v. Carlsbad Unified School District, 2011 U.S. App. LEXIS 8728 (9th Cir. April 28, 2011).

[78] J.R. v. Sylvan Union School District, 2008 U.S. Dist. LEXIS 18168 (March 10, 2008). See also, A.E. v. Westport Board of Education,454 F.3d 450 (5th Cir. 2006),where the court

held that an IEP may be valid even if there is not consensus on all its aspects and, since the IEP was reasonably calculated to enable the child to receive educational benefits, there was no violation of IDEA. See also Systema v. Academy School District No. 20, 538 F.3d 1306 (10th Cir. 2008), where the court found that the fact that the parents had not signed a draft IEP did not affect its status. In J.W. v. Fresno Unified School District, 626 F.3d 431 (9th Cir. 2010), the parents' insistence during the IEP meeting that their child be mainstreamed supported the court's determination that the child's mainstream placement did not violate IDEA despite the parents' later arguments for a private school placement.

[79] 454 F.3d 450 (5th Cir. 2006).

[80] 518 F.3d 18 (1st Cir. 2008).

[81] Id. at 20.

[82] 194 Fed. Appx. 173 (4th Cir. 2006).

[83] H. Berry v. Las Virgenes Unified School District, 370 Fed. Appx. 843 (9th Cir. 2010).

[84] Drobnicki v. Poway Unified School District, 358 Fed. Appx. 788 (9th Cir. 2009).

[85] 20 U.S.C. §1401(9).

[86] 20 U.S.C. §1401(26) (emphasis added).

[87] 468 U.S. 883 (1984).

[88] 526 U.S. 66 (1999).

[89] Id. at 78.

[90] 20 U.S.C. §1411(e)(3).

[91] See M.K. v. Sergi, 554 F.Supp.2d 201 (D.Conn. 2008), where the court held that medical services are only covered if they are intended for diagnostic and evaluative purposes, not on-going monitoring of a medication regimen.

[92] 20 U.S.C. §1412(a)(5).

[93] 874 F.2d 1036 (5th Cir. 1989).

[94] P. v. Newington Board of Education, 546 F.3d 111 (2d Cir. 2008); T.W. v. Unified School District No. 259, Wichita, Kansas, 136 Fed. Appx. 122 (10th Cir. 2005); R.H. v. Plano Independent School District, 607 F.3d 1003 (5th Cir. 2010), Cert. denied, 131 S.Ct. 1471, 179 L.Ed.2d 300, 2011 U.S. LEXIS 1330, 79 U.S.L.W. 3475 (U.S. Feb. 22, 2011). Although Daniel R.R. was not cited, a similar standard was used in L.E. v. Ramsey Board of Education, 435 F.3d 384 (3d Cir. 2006), and B.S. v. Placentia-Yorba Linda Unified School District, 306 Fed. Appx. 397 (9th Cir. 2009).

[95] 374 Fed. Appx. 330 (3d Cir. 2010).

[96] 20 U.S.C. §1415(j). For a detailed discussion of "stay put," see CRS Report RL32753, Individuals with Disabilities Education Act (IDEA): Discipline Provisions in P.L. 108-446, by Nancy Lee Jones.

[97] 484 U.S. 305 (1988).

[98] 484 U.S. 305, 323 (1988) (emphasis in the original).

[99] Id. at 325-326.

[100] Letter to Klebanoff, 28 IDELR 478 (July 1, 1997). "Since the dispute in this case involved the child's initial public school placement, the district was not obligated to maintain the child's private nursery school program pending resolution of the dispute about his placement."

[101] 420 F.3d 181 (3d Cir. 2005).

[102] 420 F.3d 181, 192 (3d Cir. 2005).

[103] 483 F.3d 725 (11th Cir. 2007), cert. den. 552 U.S. 1142 (2008).

[104] 165 Fed. Appx. 750 (11th Cir. 2006).

[105] 34 C.F.R. §300.518.

[106] 556 F.3d 900 (9th Cir. 2009), cert. den. 130 S.Ct. 90, 175 L.Ed.2d 28 (U.S. 2009).

[107] 384 Fed. Appx 58 (3d Cir. 2010).

[108] In re: Educational Assignment of Joseph R. v. Mars Area School District, 318 Fed. Appx. 113 (3d Cir. 2009).

[109] 559 F.3d 1036 (9th Cir. 2009).

[110] 600 F.3d 1104 (9th Cir. 2010).

[111] Apparently a plan has been agreed upon to prevent another 17 furlough days for the next school year by using state hurricane relief funds and a $10 million interest-free line of credit from local banks. http://www.nasbe.org/index.php/ hlr-archive/995-headline-review-for-week-ending-52810.

[112] For a more detailed discussion of the use of seclusion and restraints in public schools see CRS Report R40522, The Use of Seclusion and Restraint in Public Schools: The Legal Issues, by Nancy Lee Jones and Jody Feder.

[113] 20 U.S.C. §1414(d)(3)(B).

[114] Letter to Anonymous, 50 IDELR 228 (OSEP March 17, 2008).

[115] Id.

[116] 484 U.S. 305 (1988).

[117] Generally, IDEA requires that if there is a dispute between the school and the parents of a child with a disability, the child "stays put" in his or her current educational placement until the dispute is resolved using the due process procedures set forth in the statute. 20 U.S.C. §1415(j). For a more detailed discussion of Honig and the "stay put" provision see CRS Report RL32753, Individuals with Disabilities Education Act (IDEA): Discipline Provisions in P.L. 108-446, by Nancy Lee Jones.

[118] 484 U.S. 305, 325 (1988).

[119] For a report on restraint and seclusion in schools see National Disability Rights Network, "School is not Supposed to Hurt: Investigative Report on Abusive Restraint and Seclusion in Schools," (January 2009) http://www.napas.org/sr/ SR-Report.pdf. Rep. George Miller has asked the Government Accountability Office to investigate the use of restraint and seclusion in schools. "House Education Committee Chairman asks GAO to Investigate Restraint, Seclusion," 42 Education Daily 3 (January 28, 2009).

[120] Melissa S. v. School District of Pittsburgh, 183 Fed. Appx. 184 (3d Cir. 2006).

[121] CJN v. Minneapolis Public Schools, 323 F.3d 630 (8th Cir. 2003), cert. den. 540 U.S. 984 (2003).

[122] 591 F.3d 624 (8th Cir. 2010).

[123] See also Payne v. Pennisula School District, 598 F.3d 1123 (9th Cir. 2010), where the court dismissed IDEA claims relating to the use of a seclusion room since IDEA's administrative remedies were not exhausted. However, this decision was vacated and a rehearing, en banc, was granted. Payne v. Peninsula Sch. Dist., 621 F.3d 1001 (9th Cir. 2010); Doe v. S&S Consolidated I.S.D., 149 F.Supp.2d 274 (E.D. Texas 2001), aff'd 309 F.3d 307 (5th Cir. 2002), where the court, in a case that also presented constitutional issues, dismissed the IDEA claims relating to restraints since IDEA's administrative procedures had not been exhausted.

[124] Alleyne v. New York State Education Department, 516 F.3d 96 (2d Cir. 2008). Aversive interventions were defined as including "skin shocks, 'contingent' food programs, and physical restraints." Id. at 98.

[125] Id. at 99.

[126] Alleyne v. New York State Education Department, 691 F.Supp2d 322 (N.D. N.Y. 2010).

[127] http://www.ed.gov/about/offices/list/ocr/docs/disabharassltr.html.

[128] M.L. v. Federal Way School District, 394 F.3d 634 (9th Cir. 2005), cert. den. 545 U.S. 1128 (2005); Shore Regional High School Board of Education v. P.S., 381 F.3d 194 (3d Cir. 2004).

[129] Geoffrey Stringer v. St. James R-1 School District, 446 F.3d 799 (8th Cir. 2006).

[130] M.T.V. v. DeLalb County School District, 446 F.3d 1153 (11th Cir. 2006). For a discussion of harassment and IDEA see David Ellis Ferster, "Deliberately Different: Bullying as a Denial of a Free Appropriate Public Education under the Individuals with Disabilities Education Act," 43 Ga. L. Rev. 191 (Fall 2008); Brandy L. Wagstaff, "Disabling Incentives: How A.W. v. Jersey City Public Schools has the Wrong 'Idea' for Deterring Disability Harassment in the Public Schools," 19 Geo. Mason U. Civil Rights L. J. 169 (Fall 2008).

[131] These statutes are discussed in more detail in a subsequent section.

[132] Reinhardt v. Albuquerque Public School Board of Education, 595 F.3d 1126, 1132 (10th Cir. 2010). See also, Barker v. Riverside County Office of Education, 584 F.3d 821, 824-826 (9th Cir. 2009); Montanye v. Wissahickon School District, 218 Fed.Appx. 126, 131 (3d Cir. 2007).

[133] 20 U.S.C. §1415. Generally, exhaustion of IDEA's administrative procedures is required before a civil action is brought. See e.g., Z.F. v. Ripon Unified School District, 365 Fed. Appx. 77 (9th Cir. 2010); Levine v. Greece Central School District, 353 Fed. Appx. 461 (2d Cir. 2009), cert. denied, 130 S. Ct. 3411 (May 17, 2010).

[134] For a discussion of the state due process systems see Perry A. Zirkel and Gina Scala, "Due Process Hearing Systems Under the IDEA: A State-by-State Survey, " 21 J. of Dis. Policy Studies 3 (2010), http://www.directionservice.org/ cadre/pdf/Due%20Process% 20 Hearing%20Systems.pdf.

[135] 20 U.S.C. §1415(b)(6). The third circuit has held that this statute of limitations does not apply retroactively. Steven I. v. Central Bucks School District, 618 F.3d 411 (3d Cir. 2010), Cert. den., 131 S.Ct. 1507, 179 L.Ed.2d 307, 2011 U.S. LEXIS 1405, 79 U.S.L.W. 3476 (U.S. Feb. 22, 2011).

[136] See e.g., Bethlehem Area School District v. Diana Zhou, 2010 U.S. Dist. LEXIS 74404 (E.D. Pa. July 23, 2010), where the district court ruled that the school district could proceed with a suit against a mother who allegedly tried to increase legal fees against the district.

[137] 20 U.S.C. §1415(i). Courts have examined the 90-day statute of limitations, and found that it does not apply to counterclaims. Ruben A. v. El Paso Independent School District, 2011 U.S. App. LEXIS 3906 (5th Cir. March 1, 2011); Jonathan H. v. The Souderton Area School District, 562 F.3d 527 (3d Cir. 2009).

[138] 20 U.S.C. §1415(f)(1)(B).

[139] P.L. 105-17, §615(e).

[140] 20 U.S.C. §1415(e).

[141] 20 U.S.C. §1415(f)(1)(B)(iii).

[142] 20 U.S.C. §1415(e)(2)(F)(iii).

[143] Friendship Edison Public Charter School Chamberlain Campus v. Ebony Smith, 561 F.Supp.2d 74 (D.D.C. 2008).

[144] Mr. and Mrs. S. v. Rochester Community Schools, 2006 U.S. Dist. LEXIS 71432 (W.D. Michigan October 2, 2006).

[145] O.O. v. District of Columbia, 573 F.Supp.2d 41 (2008).

[146] See e.g., 2006 U.S. Dist. LEXIS 53467 (D.D.C. Aug. 2, 2006).

[147] 174 Fed. Appx. 896 (6th Cir. 2006).

[148] 273 Fed. Appx. 184 (3d Cir. 2008), cert. den. 129 S. Ct. 1317 (Feb. 23, 2009).

[149] 20 U.S.C. §1415(b)(7)(A)(ii).

[150] 2010 U.S. Dist. LEXIS 45433 (E.D. Mo. May 10, 2010).

[151] S.Rept. 108-185, at 35, 108th Cong. (2003).

[152] 2010 U.S. Dist. LEXIS 45433 (E.D. Mo. May 10, 2010).

[153] 2011 U.S. App. LEXIS 8640 (April 27, 2011).

[154] 615 F.3d 622 (6th Cir. 2010).

[155] 2011 U.S. App. LEXIS 3464 (9th Cir. February 22, 2011).

[156] 550 U.S. 516 (2007).

[157] 20 U.S.C. §1400(d)(1)(B).

[158] 20 U.S.C. §1415(a).

[159] 20 U.S.C. §1415(i)(3)(B)(i)(III).

[160] KLA v. Windham Southeast Supervisory Union, 348 Fed. Appx. 604 (2d Cir. 2009).

[161] Tereance D. v. School District of Philadelphia, 548 F.Supp.2d 162 (E.D. Pa. 2008).

[162] Muse B. v. Upper Darby School Dist., 282 Fed. Appx. 986 (3d Cir. 2008).

[163] 305 Fed. Appx. 833 (3d Cir.2009).

[164] Blanchard v. Morton School District, 509 F.3d 934 (9th Cir. 2007), cert den. 552 U.S. 1231 (2008); K.F. v. Frances Howell R-III School District, 2008 U.S. Dist. LEXIS 20700 (E.D. Missouri March 17, 2008).

[165] 2009 U.S. Dist. LEXIS 30104 (D.N.J. April 6, 2009).

[166] 509 F.3d 934 (9th Cir. 2007), cert. den., 552 U.S. 1231 (2008).

[167] Id. at 937.

[168] 540 F.3d 145 (2d Cir. 2008), cert den. 129 S. Ct. 1357 (Feb. 23, 2009). See also Cumberland Regional High School District Board of Education v. Freehold Regional High School District Board of Education, 293 Fed. Appx. 900 (3d Cir. 2008), where two school districts were required to share the costs of providing FAPE to a child of divorced parents who shared joint legal and physical custody.

[169] 20 U.S.C. §1401(23).

[170] 34 C.F.R. §300.30(b).

[171] 629 F.3d 450 (5th Cir. 2010).

[172] Id. at 460.

[173] For a more detailed discussion see CRS Report R40123, Education of Individuals with Disabilities: The Individuals with Disabilities Education Act (IDEA), Section 504 of the Rehabilitation Act, and the Americans with Disabilities Act (ADA), by Nancy Lee Jones.

[174] See for example, Andrew M. v. Delaware County Office of Mental Health and Mental Retardation, 490 F.3d 337 (3d Cir. 2007), where the court found that although a violation of IDEA Part B claim is generally also a violation of Section 504, a violation of IDEA Part C, which provides for services for infants and toddlers with disabilities, is not also a violation of Section 504. See also Mark H. ex rel. Michelle H. and Natalie H. v. Lemahieu, 513 F.3d 922 (9th Cir. 2008). But see E.H .and K.H. v. Board of Education of the Shenendehowa Central School District, 361 Fed. Appx. 156 (2d Cir. 2009), where the court stated that a violation of IDEA is insufficient by itself to support a claim of discrimination under the ADA or section 504. Similarly, in Mark H. v. Hamamoto, 620 F.3d 1090 (9th Cir. 2010), the Ninth Circuit held that "simply establishing a violation of the right to a FAPE under IDEA is not sufficient to prevail in a §504 claim for damages."

[175] 20 U.S.C. §1415(f).

[176] 546 U.S. 49 (2005). Chief Justice Roberts took no part in the decision. For a more detailed discussion of Weast, see CRS Report RS22353, The Individuals with Disabilities Education Act (IDEA): Schaffer v. Weast Determines Party Seeking Relief Bears the Burden of Proof, by Nancy Lee Jones.

[177] Id.

[178] Id. at 57-58.

[179] Id. at 60, citing United States v. New York, N.H. & H.R. Co., 355 U.S. 253, 256, n.5 (1957).

[180] Id.

[181] Id. at 61.

[182] For a discussion of these issues under current law, see CRS Report RS22044, Individuals with Disabilities Education Act (IDEA): Services in Private Schools under P.L. 108-446, by Nancy Lee Jones, and CRS Report RL33368, The Individuals with Disabilities Education Act (IDEA): Parentally Placed Children in Private Schools, by Richard N. Apling and Nancy Lee Jones.

[183] 20 U.S.C. §1412(a)(10).

[184] 20 U.S.C. § 1412(a)(10)(C)(ii).

[185] For a discussion of all the Supreme Court decisions on IDEA and private schools see CRS Report RL33444, The Individuals with Disabilities Education Act (IDEA): Supreme Court Decisions, by Nancy Lee Jones and Carol J. Toland.

[186] 552 U.S. 1 (2007).

[187] Board of Education of the Hyde Park Central School District v. Frank G., 459 F.3d 356 (2d Cir. 2006), cert. den. 522 U.S. 985 (2007).

[188] 557 U.S. __ ,129 S.Ct. 2484, 174 L.Ed.2d 168 (2009).

[189] Thompson R2-J School District v. Luke P., 540 F.3d 1143 (10th Cir. 2008), cert. den. 557 U.S. __, 129 S.Ct. 1356, 176 L.Ed. 590 (2009); K.J. v Fairfax County School Board, 39 Fed. Appx. 921 (4th Cir. 2010).

[190] 250 Fed. Appx. 428 (2d Cir. 2007). See also, N.M. v. The School District of Philadelphia, 394 Fed. Appx. 920 (3d Cir.2010).

[191] M.H. and J.H. v. Monroe-Woodbury Central School District, 296 Fed. Appx. 126 (2d Cir. 2008), cert. den. 557 U.S. __, 129 S.Ct. 1584, 173 L.Ed. 2d 676 (2009).

[192] Lauren P. v. Wissahickeon School District, 310 Fed. Appx. 552 (3d Cir. Feb. 12, 2009). Similarly, if the private placement is determined to be for medical, not educational, reasons, reimbursement is not required. Courtney v. School District of Philadelphia, 575 F.3d 235 (3d Cir. 2009). But see C.B. v. Garden Grove Unified School District, 635 F.3d 1155 (9th Cir. 2011), where the court held that full reimbursement for private school placement may be granted even if the placement does not satisfy all of the child's educational needs.

[193] C.B. v. Special School District No. 1, 2011 U.S. App. LEXIS 8176 (April 21, 2011).

[194] See Frank G. v. Board of Education, 459 F.3d 356 (2d Cir. 2006), cert. den. 552 U.S. 985 (2007); Carmel Central School District v. V.P., 192 Fed. Appx. 62 (2d Cir. 2006); K.J. v Fairfax County School Board, 39 Fed. Appx. 921 (4th Cir. 2010).

[195] 20 U.S.C. §1412(a)(10)(C)(iii)(III). See C.G. and B.S. v. Five Town Community School District, 513 F.3d 279 (1st Cir. 2008), where the court held that the parents' "single-minded refusal to consider any placement other than a residential one" was unreasonable; C.H. v. Cape Henlopen School District, 606 F.3d 59 (3d Cir. 2010), where the court held that the parents' disregard of their obligation to cooperate and assist in the formation of an IEP was unreasonable.

[196] C.H. v. Cape Henlopen School District, 606 F.3d 59 (3d Cir. 2010); Anello v. Indian River School District, 355 Fed. Appx. 594 (3d Cir. 2009).

[197] Carmel Central School District v. V.P., 192 Fed. Appx. 62 (2d Cir. 2006); Frank G. v. Board of Education, 459 F.3d 356 (2d Cir. 2006) cert. den. 552 U.S. 985 (2007); M.M. v. School Board of Miami-Dade County, Florida, 437 F.3d 1085 (11th Cir. 2006).

[198] 471 U.S. 359 (1985).

[199] See e.g., Ferren C. v. School District of Philadelphia, 612 F.3d 712 (3d Cir. 2010); Reid v. District of Columbia, 401 F.3d 516 (U.S. App. D.C. 2005); Draper v. Atlanta Independent School System, 518 F.3d 1275 (11th Cir. 2008).

[200] M.C. v. Cent. Regional School District, 81 F.3d 389 (3d Cir. 1996).

[201] Reid v. District of Columbia, 401 F.3d 516 (U.S. App. D.C. 2005); Neena S. v. School District of Philadelphia, 2008 U.S.Dist. LEXIS 102841 (Dec. 19, 2008).

[202] Reid v. District of Columbia, 401 F.3d 516 (U.S. App. D.C. 2005).

[203] 42 U.S.C. §1983.

[204] Doe v. Todd County School District, 625 F.3d 459 (8th Cir. Nov. 12, 2010).

[205] See Padilla ex rel. Padilla v. School District No. 1, 233 F.3d 1268 (10th Cir. 2000); A.W. v. Jersey City Public Schools, 486 F.3d 791 (3d Cir. 2007); J.S. v. Isle of Wight County School Board, 402 F.3d 468 (4th Cir. 2005).

[206] D.D. ex rel. V.D. v. N.Y. City Board of Education, 465 F.3d 503 (2d Cir. 2006). For a more detailed discussion of IDEA and Section 1983 see Suzanne Solomon, "The Intersection of 42 U.S.C. §1983 and the Individuals with Disabilities Education Act," 76 Fordham L. Rev. 3065 (May 2008). See also Mark H. v. Lemahieu, 513 F.3d 922 (9th Cir. 2008), where the court found that parents could seek monetary damages under section 504 for a violation of FAPE.

[207] 29 U.S.C. §794a.

[208] 42 U.S.C. §1988.

[209] 468 U.S. 992 (1984).

[210] Id. at 1009.

[211] Id. at 1012.

[212] P.L. 99-372.

[213] 20 U.S.C. §1415(i)(3). For a discussion of P.L. 108-446 and attorneys' fees, see CRS Report RS22055, The Individuals with Disabilities Education Act (IDEA): Attorneys' Fees Provisions in P.L. 108-446, by Nancy Lee Jones.

[214] 532 U.S. 598 (2001).

[215] For more information about the Buckhannon decision, see CRS Report 98-921, The Americans with Disabilities Act (ADA): Statutory Language and Recent Issues, by Nancy Lee Jones.

[216] See P.N. and M.W. v. Clementon Board of Education, 442 F.3d 848 (3d Cir. 2006), cert. den., 549 U.S. 881 (2006); A.R. ex. rel. R.V. et. al. v. New York City Department of Education, 407 F.3d 65 (2d Cir. 2005); Department of Education, State of Hawaii v. Leialoha J. ex. rel. Presh'es J., 2008 U.S. Dist. LEXIS 87854 (D. Hawaii Oct. 29, 2008).

[217] See El Paso Independent School District v. Richard R., 591 F.3d 417 (5th Cir. 2009), cert. den., 130 S. Ct. 3467 (2010), where the Fifth Circuit overruled a district court's decision allowing attorneys' fees for a resolution session.

[218] District of Columbia v. Jeppsen and M.J., 514 F.3d 1287 (D.C. Cir. 2008).

[219] Weissburg v. Lancaster School District, 591 F.3d. 1255 (9th Cir. 2010).

[220] T.B. v. v. Bryan Independent School District, 628 F.3d 240 (5th Cir. 2010). See also, D.S. v. Neptune Township Board of Education, 264 Fed. Appx. (3d Cir. 2008).

[221] Bassman v. Chicago Public Schools, District #299, 2008 U.S. Dist. LEXIS 87469 (N.D. Ill. Oct. 29, 2008).

[222] Bingham et. al. v. New Berlin School District, 550 F.3d 601 (7th Cir. 2008).

[223] See Smith v. Fitchburg Public Schools, 401 F.3d 16 (1st Cir. 2005); P.N. ex. rel. T.N. v. Seattle School District, No. 1, 474 F.3d 1165 (9th Cir. 2007); Salley v. Trenton Board of Education, 156 Fed. Appx. 470 (3d Cir. 2005); Mr. L. ex. rel. M. v. Sloan and Norwalk

Board of Education, 449 F.3d 405 (2d Cir. 2006); Evans v. Grossmont Union High School District et. al., 197 Fed. Appx. 648 (9th Cir. 2006); Bassman v. Chicago Public Schools, District #299, 2008 U.S. Dist. LEXIS 87469 (N.D. Ill. Oct. 29, 2008).

[224] 458 F.3d 755 (8th Cir. 2006).

[225] A.H. v. South Orange Maplewood Board of Education, 153 Fed. Appx. 863 (3d Cir. 2005), cert. den. 549 U.S. 945 (2006).

[226] See, for example, S.N. ex. rel. v. Pittsford Central School District, 448 F.3d 601 (2d Cir. 2006); Whitney Ford ex. rel. v. Long Beach Unified School District, 461 F.3d 1087 (9th Cir. 2006); Van Duyn v. Baker School District 5J, 502 F.3d 811 (9th Cir. 2007).

[227] Weissburg v. Lancaster School District, 591 F.3d. 1255 (9th Cir. 2010).

[228] See Damian J. v. The School District of Philadelphia, 358 Fed. Appx. 333 (3d Cir. 2009), where the court of appeals declined to overrule the district court's award of attorneys' fees, finding that the determination of the fees was made following "a thoroughly reasoned and careful analysis."

[229] See, for example, Damian J. v. The School District of Philadelphia, 358 Fed. Appx 333 (3rd Cir. 2009); Crawford et. al. v. San Dieguito Union School District, 202 Fed. Appx. 185 (9th Cir. 2006); A.S. ex. rel. V.S. and G.S. v. Colts Neck Board of Education, 190 Fed. Appx. 140 (3d Cir. 2006); Aguirre v. Los Angeles Unified School District, 461 F.3d 1114 (9th Cir. 2006); Starkey ex rel. Starkey v. Somers Cent. Sch. Dist., 2008 U.S. Dist. LEXIS 104064 (S.D.N.Y. Dec. 23, 2008).

[230] See Gary G. v. El Paso Independent School District, 632 F.3d 201 (5th Cir. 2011) (attorneys' fees denied after rejection of a settlement agreement), El Paso Independent School District v. Richard R., 591 F.3d 417 (5th Cir. 2009), cert. den., 130 S. Ct. 3467 (2010)(attorneys' fees denied after rejection of a settlement agreement that included all the relief requested); V.G. by J.G. v. Auburn Enlarged Cent. Sch. Dist., 2008 U.S. Dist. LEXIS 99743 (N.D.N.Y. 2008), aff'd 349 Fed. Appx. 582 (2d Cir. 2009)(reduction of attorneys' fees after rejection of a settlement offer). However, a school district does not shield itself from attorneys' fees simply by making a settlement offer, and a party may still receive attorneys' fees if it is "substantially justified" in rejecting the settlement offer. See Hawkins v. Berkeley Unified Sch. Dist., 2008 U.S. Dist. LEXIS 94673 (N.D. Cal. Nov. 20, 2008). Additionally, evidence of a settlement agreement that was offered following confidential mediation but referencing the mediation session cannot be used to show that the party rejected a school district's settlement offer. See J.D. v. Kanawha County Board of Education, 571 F.3d 381 (4th Cir. 2009), cert den., 131 S.Ct. 107 (2010).

[231] Ector County Independent School District, 2011 U.S. App. LEXIS 6380 (5th Cir. March 28, 2011).

[232] See, for example, Kaseman v. District of Columbia, 444 F.3d 637 (D.C. Cir. 2006); Pullins v. Community Services for Autistic Adults and Children, 171 Fed. Appx. 867 (D.C. Cir. 2005); Whatley v. District of Columbia, 447 F.3d 814 (D.C. Cir. 2006); Jester v. Government of the District of Columbia, 474 F.3d 820 (D.C. Cir. 2007); Blackman et. al. v. District of Columbia et. al., 456 F.3d 167 (D.C. Cir. 2006). For examples of the appropriation provisions that cap IDEA fees in the District of Columbia, see 2006 District of Columbia Appropriations Act §122(a)(1), P.L. 109-115; Consolidated Appropriations Act, 2008, P.L. 110-161, § 819. This cap has been held not to be applicable to a class action as a whole but rather limits fees for individual students in the class. Blackman et al. v. District of Columbia, 633 F.3d 1088 (D.C. Cir. 2011).

[233] 20 U.S.C. §1415(i)(3)(B)(i)(II).

[234] 400 Fed. Appx. 947 (5th Cir. 2010).

[235] Children's Center for Developmental Enrichment v. Machle, 612 F.3d 518 (6th Cir. 2010).

[236] R.P. v. Prescott Unified School District, 631 F.3d 1117 (9th Cir. 2011).

[237] Id. at 135. The Ninth Circuit also observed that the district court had erred in holding the parents liable for bringing a suit for an improper purpose because they brought the suit in anger. Anger was not a motive listed in IDEA, and the court noted that anger may well be a legitimate reaction to a belief that rights have been violated.

[238] 591 F.3d 417 (5th Cir. 2009), cert. den., 130 S. Ct. 3467 (2010).

[239] 590 F.3d 898 (DC Cir. 2010).

[240] Id. at 902.

[241] 20 U.S.C. §1415(i)(3)(B).

[242] 548 U.S. 291 (2006).

[243] P.L. 99-372.

[244] H.Rept. 99-687, at 5.

[245] 548 U.S. 291, 295 (2006).

[246] 548 U.S. 291, 303 (2006). For a more detailed discussion, see CRS Report RS22465, The Individuals with Disabilities Education Act (IDEA): The Supreme Court Denies Expert Fees in Arlington Central School District v. Murphy, by Nancy Lee Jones.

[247] 20 U.S.C. §1415.

[248] 34 C.F.R. §§ 300.151-300.153.

[249] 34 C.F.R. §300.153(a). In Reinhardt v. Alburquerque Public Schools Board of Education, 595 F.3d 1126 (10th Cir. 2010), the court addressed a retaliation claim by a speech-language pathologist who had filed an IDEA complaint with the state, finding that the teachers advocacy on behalf of students with disabilities was protected under Section 504 of the Rehabilitation Act, 29 U.S.C. §794.

[250] 20 U.S.C. §1416.

[251] Keene v. Zelman, 337 Fed. Appx. 553 (6th Cir. 2009). Although the issue in Keene involved the award of attorneys' fees, the fees were awarded for deficiencies in the procedures for litigating due process notices. See also N.D. v. State of Hawaii, 600 F.3d 1104 (9th Cir. 2010), where the court found no violation of the stay put provision by Hawaii's decision to shut down the public school for 17 Fridays in the 2009-2010 school year. The court held that the stay put provision was not intended to cover system-wide changes in public schools that affect children with and without disabilities.

[252] 634 F.3d 1065 (9th Cir. 2011).

[253] Id.

[254] The Developmental Disabilities Assistance and Bill of Rights Act, 42 U.S.C. §15001 et seq.

[255] For a discussion of IDEA and the enforcement of systemic, not individual, complaints, see Monica Costello, "Systemic Compliance Complaints: Making IDEA's Enforcement Provisions a Reality," 41 U. Mich. J. L. Reform 507 (Winter 2008).

[256] Unified School District No. 259 v. Disability Rights Center of Kansas, 491 F.3d 1143 (10th Cir. 2007); Connecticut Office of Protection and Advocacy for Persons with Disabilities v. Hartford Board of Education, 464 F.3d 229 (2d Cir. 2006).

In: Education of Students with Disabilities   ISBN: 978-1-62257-996-9
Editors: H. Garlach and N. Darst   © 2013 Nova Science Publishers, Inc.

Chapter 4

ALTERNATE ASSESSMENTS FOR STUDENTS WITH DISABILITIES[*]

Erin D. Lomax

SUMMARY

The Elementary and Secondary Education Act (ESEA), as amended by the No Child Left Behind Act of 2001 (NCLB, P.L. 107-110), and the Individuals with Disabilities Education Act (IDEA, P.L. 108-446) both require all students with disabilities to participate in district and state assessments. Because student achievement on state assessments is used to determine Adequate Yearly Progress (AYP) in state accountability systems mandated by NCLB, schools are now held accountable for the achievement of all students, including students with disabilities. The authorization for NCLB expired at the end of FY2008, and the 111th Congress is expected to consider whether to amend and extend the ESEA. One focus of reauthorization may be reexamining how students with disabilities are included in accountability systems.

The current NCLB focus on accountability for the achievement of students with disabilities has led educators, administrators, and policymakers to reexamine the appropriateness of the general state assessment for measuring the achievement of certain students with disabilities. Although many students with disabilities are able to

---

[*] This is an edited, reformatted and augmented version of a Congressional Research Service publication, CRS Report for Congress R40701, from www.crs.gov, prepared for Members and Committees of Congress, dated January 7, 2011.

participate in the general state assessment, either with or without accommodations, other students with disabilities may not be able to participate fully in the general state assessment because of the nature and severity of their disability. These students may need an alternate assessment that is tailored to their needs and allows them to more accurately demonstrate what they know and can do.

There are currently five assessment options for measuring the achievement of students with disabilities: (1) general state assessment, (2) general state assessment with accommodations, (3) alternate assessment based on grade-level standards, (4) alternate assessment based on alternate achievement standards (AA-AAS), and (5) alternate assessment based on modified achievement standards (AA-MAS). The first three assessment options (general state assessment, general state assessment with accommodations, and alternate assessment based on grade-level standards) result in scores that may be counted in AYP calculations in the typical manner, as determined by a state's accountability system. Scores from the second two assessment options (AA-AAS and AAMAS) have restrictions on the way they may be counted in AYP calculations. These restrictions are outlined in regulations issued by the U.S. Department of Education (ED) and have numerous implications for state accountability systems.

The purpose of this report is to describe the ED regulations that allow states to use scores from alternate assessments for AYP calculations in accountability systems. This report also describes the current status of state implementation of alternate assessments and examines some of the challenges states have encountered in developing and implementing these assessments. The final section of this report discusses other policy proposals for measuring the achievement of students with disabilities and including them in accountability systems.

OVERVIEW

The Elementary and Secondary Education Act (ESEA), as amended by the No Child Left Behind Act of 2001 (NCLB, P.L. 107-110), and the Individuals with Disabilities Education Act (IDEA, P.L. 108-446) both require all students with disabilities to participate in district and state assessments.[1] Because student achievement on state assessments is used to determine Adequate Yearly Progress (AYP) in state accountability systems mandated by NCLB, schools are now held accountable for the achievement of all students, including students with disabilities. The authorization for NCLB expired at the end of FY2008, and the 111th Congress is expected to consider whether to amend and extend the ESEA. One focus of reauthorization may be reexamining how students with disabilities are included in accountability systems.[2] The current NCLB focus on accountability for the achievement of students with disabilities has led educators, administrators, and policymakers to reexamine the appropriateness of the general state assessment for measuring the achievement of certain students with disabilities. Although many students with disabilities are able to participate in the general state assessment, either with or without accommodations, other students with disabilities may not be able to participate fully in the general state assessment because of the nature and severity of their disability. These students may need an alternate assessment that is tailored to their needs and allows them to more accurately demonstrate what they know and can do. There are currently five assessment options for measuring the achievement of students with disabilities: (1) general state assessment, (2) general state assessment with accommodations, (3) alternate assessment based on *grade-level* standards, (4) alternate assessment based on *alternate* achievement standards (AA-AAS), and (5) alternate assessment based on *modified* achievement standards (AA-MAS). The first three assessment options (general state assessment, general state assessment with accommodations, and alternate assessment based on grade-level standards) result in scores that may be counted in AYP calculations in the typical manner, as determined by a state's accountability system.[3] Scores from the second two assessment options (AA-AAS and AA-MAS) have restrictions on the way they may be counted in AYP calculations. These restrictions are outlined in regulations issued by the U.S. Department of Education (ED) and have numerous implications for state accountability systems. The purpose of this report is to describe the ED regulations that allow states to use scores from alternate assessments for AYP calculations in accountability systems. This report also describes the current status of state implementation of alternate assessments and examines some of the challenges states have encountered in developing and implementing these assessments. The final section of this report discusses other policy proposals for measuring the achievement of students with disabilities and including them in accountability systems.

BRIEF LEGISLATIVE HISTORY
OF ALTERNATE ASSESSMENTS

Including students with disabilities in state assessments is a relatively new practice. As recently as the 1990s, students with disabilities were often excluded from general state assessments. The Improving America's Schools Act of 1994 (IASA, P.L. 103-382) and IDEA of 1997 (P.L. 105-17) were the first pieces of federal legislation that mandated the participation of students with disabilities in state assessments.[4] By mandating participation of students with disabilities in state assessments, the legislation sought to increase access to the general education curriculum for students with disabilities and, in turn, increase expectations and achievement of students with disabilities.

The use of alternate assessments within state assessment systems is also relatively new. In 1997, IDEA required states to develop alternate assessments for students with disabilities for whom the general state assessment was inappropriate. The alternate assessment was intended to be a more accurate measure of what some students with disabilities know and can do. The alternate assessment was intended to decrease the barriers of the general state assessments and allow students with disabilities to demonstrate their knowledge more accurately.

Several years after IASA and IDEA required students with disabilities to participate in state assessments, the No Child Left Behind Act of 2001 (NCLB) greatly increased the emphasis on student assessment, and the academic achievement of students with disabilities gained more attention. Under NCLB, student scores on state assessments are used to measure AYP. Scores on these assessments must be disaggregated by various subgroups, one of which is students with disabilities. Although NCLB requires states to develop at least one alternate assessment to use within their state assessment systems, the law did not explicitly outline how the alternate assessments should be used within an accountability system.

The combination of the requirement to include all students with disabilities in state assessment systems and NCLB's requirement that all subgroups of students meet AYP goals created a need for states to have more accurate assessments for all students with disabilities, including students with the most significant cognitive disabilities and other students with disabilities who were not expected to meet grade-level achievement standards within the academic year. For these students with disabilities, an alternate assessment may be more appropriate than the general state assessment. Because of the NCLB requirement to develop at least one alternate assessment, many alternate assessments were already used by states. Nonetheless, questions remained about who should be eligible to take alternate assessments and how scores from alternate assessments should be counted within state accountability systems.

To address these concerns, ED released regulations outlining the use of two types of alternate assessments for students with disabilities: alternate assessments based on *alternate* achievement standards (AA-AAS) and alternate assessments based on *modified* achievement standards (AAMAS). The regulations provide guidance to states on how to determine a student's eligibility for participation in alternate assessments and how to count scores from alternate assessments in state accountability systems.

ALTERNATE ASSESSMENTS: DESCRIPTION AND REGULATIONS

An alternate assessment is an assessment designed for students with disabilities for whom the general state assessment is inappropriate even when they are provided with appropriate accommodations. It is designed to be a more accurate measure of what students with disabilities know and can do. Alternate assessments differ from general state assessments in both form and complexity. The form of an alternate assessment varies depending on the needs of the student. The assessment may include teacher observation of the student, samples of student work that demonstrate mastery of specific content (e.g., portfolio assessment), performance on tasks produced in an "on-demand" setting (e.g., performance assessment), or other methods of collecting data on student achievement.

An alternate assessment is developed by adapting two parameters of the general state assessment: content standards and achievement standards. A *content standard* specifies what all students should know and be able to do. Content standards describe what teachers should be teaching and what students should be learning in academic areas, such as reading, mathematics, and science. An *achievement standard* is a predetermined level of performance that denotes proficiency within a given content area. Achievement standards describe how well a student must perform in order to be proficient within a content area. Determining achievement levels requires that achievement standards describe the competencies associated with varying levels of proficiency and set "cut scores" that categorize students into these levels. An example of a content standard for elementary mathematics may be: "Know the addition facts (sums to 20) and the corresponding subtraction facts and commit them to memory." The corresponding achievement standard may be a level of mastery that defines proficiency (e.g., number correct, 80% accuracy, 90% accuracy, and so on).

Understanding the difference between content standards and achievement standards is essential to understanding the way different types of alternate assessments are developed. ED regulations regarding the design of alternate assessments describe different methods for developing alternate assessments that vary according to (1) when it is appropriate to adapt and extend content standards *and* achievement standards, and (2) when it is appropriate to adapt *only* the achievement standards. In general, in AA-AAS, it is appropriate to adapt and extend content standards and achievement standards; in AA-MAS, it is appropriate to adapt only the achievement standards.

ED issued two sets of regulations concerning the development of alternate assessments and their use in state accountability systems. In December 2003, ED finalized NCLB regulations that authorized states to use results from AA-AAS in AYP calculations for students with the most significant cognitive disabilities.[5] Later, in April 2007, ED finalized NCLB regulations that authorized states to use results from AA-MAS in AYP calculations for other students with disabilities who were unlikely to reach grade-level proficiency within a year.[6] The following sections describe the regulations issued by ED concerning the development of AA-AAS and AA-MAS and their use in state accountability systems. In addition, Appendix A provides a table that summarizes the similarities and differences between AA-AAS and AA-MAS.

Alternate Assessments Based on Alternate Achievement Standards

AA-AAS are assessments designed to measure the academic achievement of students with the most significant cognitive disabilities. A state that uses AA-AAS must develop alternate achievement standards through a "documented and validated standards setting process," and ensure that the standards (1) are aligned with the state's academic content standards, (2) promote access to the general curriculum, and (3) reflect professional judgment of the highest achievement standards possible.[7] AA-AAS are subject to the same technical standards as the general state assessment, including the need for them to meet professional and technical standards for validity and reliability.[8]

AA-AAS may cover a narrower range of content and have a different set of expectations than the general state assessment based on grade-level expectations. The *content standards* of AA-AAS may be "extended" so that students with the most significant cognitive disabilities may be tested on content that is aligned with grade-level content standards but not fully representative of grade-level content standards. The content standards of the AA-AAS may be "substantially simplified" and may include prerequisite skills that would be necessary to master grade-level content. The *achievement standards* of AA-AAS may differ from a grade-level achievement standard in the level of expectation that is necessary to denote proficiency. Alternate achievement standards are subject to the same requirements as other academic achievement standards.

That is, alternate achievement standards must be aligned with the state's academic content standards, describe at least three levels of achievement, include descriptions of the competencies associated with each level, and include assessment scores (cut scores) that differentiate among the achievement levels.[9] A state may choose to develop alternate achievement standards for grade clusters (e.g., 3-5, 6-9, or 10-12) rather than for individual grades.

AA-AAS are used to assess students with disabilities[10] who have the "most significant cognitive disabilities." IDEA does not provide a federal definition of "significant cognitive disability," and students within any of the disability categories may be eligible to participate in AA-AAS.[11] ED describes students with the most significant cognitive disabilities as students who are "(1) within one or more of the existing categories of disability under the IDEA (e.g., autism, multiple disabilities, traumatic brain injury, etc.); and (2) whose cognitive impairments may prevent them from attaining grade-level achievement standards, even with the very best instruction."[12] ED estimates that approximately 9% of students with disabilities (approximately 1% of all students) have the most significant cognitive disabilities that may qualify them to participate in AA-AAS.

States are responsible for defining "most significant cognitive disability" and establishing criteria to identify the students with disabilities who are eligible to participate in AA-AAS. Based on guidance issued by the state, the final determination of eligibility for AA-AAS is made by a student's Individualized Education Program (IEP) team.[13] In addition to providing guidance on the students who may appropriately participate in AA-AAS, the state must (1) ensure that parents of those students are informed that their child's achievement will be based on alternate achievement standards, and (2) report to ED on the number and percentage of students taking alternate assessments.

ED regulations do not limit the number or percentage of students who may participate in AAAAS.

The regulations do, however, limit the number of proficient and advanced scores based on AA-AAS that may be used in AYP calculations within a state accountability system. The number of proficient and advanced scores based on AA-AAS may not exceed 1% of all students in the grades assessed in reading/language arts and in mathematics within the state accountability system.

This regulation is often referred to as the "1% rule" or the "1% cap," and it represents approximately 9% of all students with disabilities. The 1% cap applies to both LEAs and states but not to individual schools. Under certain circumstances, however, an LEA may request an exception from the state to exceed this cap.[14]

The 1% cap was developed through a process of proposed rules and public comment that occurred between August 2002 and December 2003. On August 6, 2002, ED first proposed that the number of proficient and advanced scores based on AA-AAS included in AYP calculations may not exceed 0.5% of all students in the grades assessed.[15] The "0.5% cap" became a final rule on December 2, 2002.[16] The 0.5% cap was based on scientific estimates of the prevalence of moderate, severe, and profound mental retardation. Moderate, severe, and profound mental retardation are often defined as intellectual functioning and adaptive behavior that are three or more standard deviations below the mean.

At that time, ED proposed an operational definition of "students with the most significant cognitive disabilities" to mirror that of moderate, severe, and profound mental retardation (i.e., students with intellectual functioning and adaptive behavior three or more standard deviations below the mean). Many commenters objected to the 0.5% cap, citing state and LEA variation in the prevalence of students with the "most significant cognitive disabilities." Based on these comments, ED proposed raising the cap to 1% of all assessed students.[17]

In addition, many commenters objected to the proposed operational definition of students with the "most significant cognitive disabilities" because of its implicit reliance on IQ tests (measuring "intellectual functioning" usually involves the use of traditional IQ tests). ED agreed that the definition would have placed unwarranted reliance on IQ tests and removed it. The final regulations maintained the 1% cap and removed the operational definition, allowing states to develop their own criteria for students with the "most significant cognitive disabilities."[18]

Alternate Assessments Based on Modified Achievement Standards

AA-MAS are assessments designed to measure the academic achievement of students with disabilities whose disabilities may prevent them from achieving grade-level proficiency within a year but who do not have the "most significant cognitive disabilities." A state that uses AA-MAS must develop modified achievement standards that (1) are aligned with the state's academic content standards for the grade in which the student is enrolled, (2) are challenging for eligible students, but may be less difficult than the grade-level academic achievement standards, (3) include at least three achievement levels, and (4) are developed through a documented and validated standards-setting process that includes broad stakeholder input.[19] AA-MAS are subject to the same technical standards as the general state assessment, including the need for them to meet professional and technical standards for validity and reliability.[20]

AA-MAS must be aligned with grade-level content standards. The *content standards* may not be "extended" or "substantially simplified," and they may not reflect prerequisite skills for grade-level content. AA-MAS must represent grade-level content standards. The assessment may, however, differ from the general state assessment in terms of the expectation of achievement (i.e., the achievement standard). The *achievement standards* of AA-MAS may differ from a grade-level achievement standard in the level of expectation that denotes proficiency. Modified achievement standards describe achievement expectations that are less difficult than grade-level expectations. An AA-MAS, therefore, covers the same grade-level content as the general state assessment, however, questions may be less difficult and the expectation of achievement can be modified. Modified achievement standards are subject to the same requirements as other academic achievement standards. They must be aligned with the state's academic content standards, describe at least three levels of achievement, include descriptions of the competencies associated with each level, and include assessment scores (cut scores) that differentiate among the achievement levels.[21] A state must develop modified achievement standards for each grade in which AA-MAS is implemented; it may not develop modified achievement standards for grade clusters (e.g., 3-5, 6-9, 10-12).

AA-MAS are used to assess students with disabilities as defined by IDEA[22] whose disabilities may prevent them from achieving grade-level proficiency within a year (the year covered by their IEP). Students in any of the disability categories described in IDEA may be eligible to participate in

AA-MAS.[23] Beyond the requirement that a student have a disability, a state must establish additional criteria for IEP teams[24] to use in determining whether a student should participate in AA-MAS. At minimum, the criteria must include three types of evidence. First, there must be objective evidence that demonstrates the student's disability has precluded him or her from achieving grade-level proficiency. This evidence may include performance on prior years' state assessments or other assessments. Second, the student's progress to date in response to appropriate instruction must indicate that that the student would not meet grade-level proficiency within the academic year, even if significant growth were to occur. This determination is made by a student's IEP team using multiple measures of the student's progress. Third, the student's IEP must include goals that are based on the academic content standards for the grade in which the student is enrolled (i.e., the student must have a "standards-based IEP").

As with AA-AAS, ED regulations do not limit the number or percentage of students who may participate in AA-MAS. The regulations do, however, limit the number of proficient and advanced scores that may be used in AYP calculations within a state accountability system. The number of proficient and advanced scores based on AA-MAS may not exceed 2% of all students in the grades assessed in reading/language arts and in mathematics within the state accountability system. This regulation is often referred to as the "2% rule" or the "2% cap," and it represents approximately 20% of all students with disabilities. The 2% cap applies to both LEAs and states but not to individual schools. Under certain circumstance, however, states and LEAs may exceed this cap.[25]

The 2% cap is based on several studies reporting that some students with disabilities, even when provided evidence-based instruction, may not achieve grade-level proficiency within an academic year. The studies estimated that the percentage of students with disabilities who may not reach grade-level proficiency is between 15% and 22%.[26] Again, the 2% cap translates into approximately 20% of all students with disabilities, which is reasonably similar to the results of the studies cited by ED.27 During the public comment period on the proposed rules, some commenters stated that the 2% cap was too low, however, many commenters stated that the 2% cap was too high, citing data reported by the National Center on Educational Outcomes.28 ED recognized that a greater number of studies to support the 2% cap was desirable, however, ED maintained that the 2% cap is appropriate and protects students with disabilities from being inappropriately assigned to participate in AA-MAS.[29]

Alternate Assessments in State Accountability Systems

The previous sections have discussed general features of alternate assessments, regulatory requirements for the development of AA-AAS and AA-MAS, eligibility for AA-AAS and AAMAS, and the basic concept of the 1% cap and 2% cap. The following sections discuss in greater detail how the use of alternate assessments can affect the calculation of AYP in state accountability systems. First, exceptions to the 1% cap and 2% cap are discussed. The next section discusses a process called redistributing scores that states must use if they exceed the 1% cap or 2% cap. A hypothetical example is offered to illustrate how a state may calculate the 1% cap and 2% cap and redistribute scores if it has exceeded the caps. The final section discusses state reporting requirements concerning student participation in alternate assessments.

Exceptions to the 1% Cap and 2% Cap

As discussed earlier, the 1% cap refers to the number of proficient and advanced scores from AAAAS that may count as proficient or advanced for AYP purposes. Similarly, the 2% cap refers to the number of proficient and advanced scores from AA-MAS that may count as proficient or advanced for AYP purposes. Under certain circumstances, an LEA or a state may exceed the 1% cap, the 2% cap, or both caps (i.e., the 3% total cap). Again, these caps do not apply to individual schools.

A state may grant an exception to the 1% cap for an LEA, provided that (1) the LEA documents that the incidence of students with the most significant cognitive disabilities exceeds 1% of all students in the grades assessed, (2) the LEA explains why the incidence exceeds 1% (e.g., special services within the LEA, or a small LEA in which even one student exceeds the 1% cap), and (3) the LEA ensures that all students with disabilities continue to participate in state assessments. The state must regularly review the appropriateness of this exception.[30] The state may not grant an LEA an exception to the 2% cap unless the LEA is below the 1% cap, and the exception to the 2% cap may only be made in the amount that the LEA is below the 1% cap. In general, an LEA is not permitted to exceed a total of 3% of proficient and advanced scores from alternate assessments (AA-AAS plus AA-MAS) that may count as proficient or advanced for AYP purposes; however, if the LEA was granted an exception to the 1% cap, the LEA may exceed the 3% total cap by the amount of the 1% cap exception.

A state may not request from the Secretary of Education (Secretary) an exception to the 1% cap or the 2% cap. A state may, however, exceed the 2% cap provided that it is below the 1% cap.[31] A state may not exceed the 3% total cap under any circumstances.

Table 1. summarizes the regulations surrounding when states and LEAs may exceed the 1% cap, the 2% cap, and the 3% total cap.

Table 1.When May a State or LEA Exceed the 1% and 2% Caps?

	AA-AAS (1% Cap)	AA-MAS (2% Cap)	AA-AAS and AA-MAS (3% Cap)
State	Not permitted.	Only if a state is below the 1% cap, but cannot exceed the 3% cap.	Not permitted.
LEA	Only if granted an exception by the SEA.[a]	Only if LEA is below 1% cap, but cannot exceed 3% cap	Only if granted an exception to the 1% cap by the SEA, and only by theamount of the exception.

Source: U.S. Department of Education, "Modified Achievement Standards," Non-Regulatory
   Guidance, July 20, 2007, (http://www.ed.gov/policy/speced/guid/ nclb/twopercent.doc).
[a.] SEA=State Educational Agency.

Redistributing Scores that Exceed the Cap

An LEA or state that exceeds either the 1% cap or 2% cap (without exception) must count all scores of students with disabilities in AYP calculations, including the scores that exceed the cap. However, a state must count the proficient and advanced scores that exceeded the cap as "non-proficient" for the purposes of AYP. In other words, if too many students have achieved proficient or advanced scores on AA-AAS and AA-MAS, the scores in excess of the allowable amount are treated as non-proficient scores. States must adopt a process for allocating these non-proficient scores in the AYP accountability calculations. The process of counting proficient and advanced scores as non-proficient scores for AYP purposes is called redistributing scores.

When the number of proficient and advanced scores exceeds the 1% cap or 2% cap, the state must redistribute these scores as non-proficient scores (hereafter referred to as "redistributed non-proficient scores"). The state must count the redistributed non-proficient scores in each applicable AYP subgroup at the school, LEA, and state level. ED does not mandate a procedure in regulations for redistributing scores. ED's non-regulatory guidance, however, provides a reference that describes four methods a state may use to redistribute scores: (1) random assignment, (2) proportional, (3) strategic, and (4) predetermined school cap.[32] These four methods of redistributing proficient and advanced scores are described below; however, they do not represent all possible methods.

The random-assignment method selects proficient and advanced scores at random to become redistributed non-proficient scores. All proficient and advanced scores from alternate assessments would have an equal chance of being redistributed. This method is relatively easy to understand and communicate to educators, and it can be done using a computerized random-number generator. Over time, random assignment should be impartial and fair because each score has an equal chance of being selected. On the other hand, random assignment can seem unfair in the short term when the selection of scores is uneven in a particular year (i.e., even when random assignment is used, a school may be randomly assigned a much higher number of scores to redistribute than another school simply due to chance). In addition, this method may be difficult to implement in small LEAs due to the small number of scores resulting from alternate assessments.

The proportional method requires a redistribution of proficient and advanced scores in proportion to the number of students in an LEA or school that participated in alternate assessments. LEAs or schools that tested a larger number of students using alternate assessments would be required to redistribute a larger number of proficient or advanced scores. This method may deter LEAs or schools from inappropriately testing a large number of students using alternate assessments. However, it may also unfairly penalize LEAs or schools that serve a disproportionate number of students with disabilities, and therefore, *appropriately* test a disproportionate number of students using alternate assessments.

The strategic method redistributes proficient and advanced scores in a manner that will result in the maximum benefit for each school. Using this method, scores may be redistributed in a way that allows a school to have a better chance of meeting AYP. For example, scores from students who belong to the fewest number of subgroups may be redistributed because a non-proficient score may have less of a negative impact on AYP. Similarly, scores from students who belong to subgroups in no danger of missing AYP may be redistributed. This method may aid schools in meeting AYP, however, it is difficult to implement and may be perceived as unethical.

The predetermined school-cap method redistributes proficient and advanced scores based on a school's historical percentage of students with disabilities. This method may work well for schools with a relatively stable population of students, however, minor fluctuations in student attendance may make the implementation of this method difficult. In addition, using a predetermined school cap could potentially perpetuate inappropriate historical identification of students with disabilities in some schools (i.e., if a school has historically identified students with disabilities inappropriately, and a predetermined school cap is based on historical numbers of students with disabilities, the school may be incentivized to continue to identify students inappropriately).

Appendix B provides a table that briefly summarizes the pros and cons of four methods for redistributing proficient scores that exceed the 1% and 2% caps. At times, it may be possible or beneficial for a state to use these methods in combination. For example, a state may choose to redistribute scores using a random-assignment method, which determines the number of scores per school that must be redistributed. At the school level, however, a strategic method could be employed to maximize the possibility that the school meets AYP goals.

Example: Calculating the Cap, Exceeding the Cap, and Redistributing Scores

The following example demonstrates how states and LEAs calculate the 1% cap and the process of redistributing proficient and advanced scores if the 1% cap is exceeded (without exception).[33] The 2% cap is calculated and enforced in a similar way.[34]

The 1% cap is calculated based on the number of students enrolled in the grades assessed for AYP. The grades assessed for AYP include grades 3 through 8 and one grade in high school (for this example, grade 10). If an LEA has a total enrollment of 10,000 students in grades 3 through 8 plus grade 10, no more than 100 proficient scores based on AA-AAS may count as proficient for AYP purposes. If the LEA had 150 students participate in AA-AAS, two scenarios could develop. In the first scenario, only 100 of the 150 students may obtain a proficient score. All of these scores would count as proficient in the calculation of AYP and the 1% cap would not be exceeded.[35] In the second scenario, all 150 students may obtain a proficient score. Only 100 of these scores may count as proficient scores in the calculation of AYP, and 50 of the proficient scores must be redistributed as non-proficient scores.[36] If the LEA does not receive an exception from the state, the LEA must redistribute 50 scores as non-proficient and count these redistributed non-proficient scores in AYP calculations for each applicable subgroup in the state accountability system.[37]

In the second scenario, participation in AA-AAS resulted in 150 proficient scores, and 50 scores must be redistributed as non-proficient scores for AYP purposes. In the hypothetical LEA above, suppose four schools were responsible for the scores from AA-AAS:

- School A: 50 proficient scores
- School B: 50 proficient scores
- School C: 25 proficient scores
- School D: 25 proficient scores

The state may direct the LEA to redistribute scores using the random-assignment method. Using a random-assignment method, the following outcome is possible: School A must redistribute 16 scores, School B must redistribute 20 scores, School C must redistribute 8 scores, and School D must redistribute 6 scores. Essentially, any random combination of 50 scores could be redistributed.

The state may, instead, direct the LEA to redistribute scores using the proportional method. Using the proportional method, the number of redistributed scores depends on a proportion that reflects the number of scores that must be redistributed compared to the total number of scores. In this example, 50 of 150 scores must be redistributed, which would result in a proportion of 1 to 3 (50 to 150). One third of the scores from each school must be redistributed: School A must redistribute 17 scores, School B must redistribute 17 scores, School C must redistribute 8 scores, and School D must redistribute 8 scores.

Redistribution methods (i.e., the random-assignment method and the proportional method) determine how many scores must be redistributed, but they do not always determine which scores must be redistributed. After using either the random-assignment method or the proportional method discussed above, LEAs may use a strategic method to determine which scores to redistribute in order to maximize their chances of meeting AYP goals.

At the state level, the interaction of the 1% and 2% caps can make the redistribution of scores more complicated. *Appendix C* provides a hypothetical example of how scores are redistributed in a state that uses both AA-AAS and AA-MAS.

Reporting Requirements

States are required to report to the Secretary separately on the participation of students with disabilities in state accountability systems. Specifically, each state must report the number of students with disabilities participating in (1) general state assessments, (2) general state assessments with accommodations, (3) alternate assessments based on grade-level academic achievement standards, (4) AA-AAS, and (5) AA-MAS.[38] States are required to prepare two different sections in a "report card" format that address (1) assessment data and (2) accountability data. In the assessment-data section, the state should report on the actual scores received by students who participate in alternate assessments, even if proficient scores have become redistributed non-proficient scores for the purposes of AYP. In the accountability-data section, states should apply the 1% cap and 2% cap in reporting proficient and non-proficient scores. That is, if a student obtained a proficient score that was deemed to be outside of the 1% cap or 2% cap, the score should be reported as non-proficient.

States and LEAs are also required to report to parents, teachers, and principals. The state's assessment system, including its alternate assessments, must produce individual student reports that allow parents, teachers, and principals to understand and address specific needs of students. For these reports, states and LEAs must report the actual scores received by students participating in alternate assessments, even if a student's score became a redistributed non-proficient score. That is, if a student with a disability scored "proficient," but this score was deemed to be outside of either the 1% cap or 2% cap, the state and LEA must still report to the parents, teachers, and principals that the student's score was "proficient."

STATE AND LOCAL IMPLEMENTATION OF ALTERNATE ASSESSMENTS IN STATE ACCOUNTABILITY SYSTEMS

In regulations dated December 9, 2003, ED stated that it intended "to issue a report on the implementation of this regulation after two years of implementation."[39] In response to this commitment, ED released a report from the Study of State Implementation of Accountability and Teacher Quality Under *No Child Left Behind* (SSI-NCLB).[40] The report presents findings concerning states' implementation of AA-AAS. The report's findings are based on surveys of state officials in school years 2004-2005 and 2006-2007, as well as extant data about states' implementation of NCLB assessment and accountability requirements. At the time of data collection, ED regulations regarding AA-MAS were not finalized. During the development of the AA-

MAS regulations, ED offered "2% interim policy options." When ED regulations regarding AA-MAS were finalized and released on April 9, 2007, they included a transition provision regarding modified achievement standards, which provided that states may (with approval from the Secretary) continue to use the 2% interim policy options through school year 2008-2009.[41] Since the 2% interim policy options are set to expire and states will be required to adopt the finalized ED regulations regarding AA-MAS, implementation results of this transitional provision will not be discussed.[42]

Development and Implementation of AA-AAS

In school year 2005-2006, all 50 states, the District of Columbia, and Puerto Rico had alternate assessments in reading and mathematics.[43] To comply with ED regulations regarding the development of new alternate achievement standards, states could keep their existing alternate assessment if they believed it to be consistent with regulations, develop a new alternate assessment, or modify an existing alternate assessment. In 2006-2007, 9 states reported keeping an existing alternate assessment, 18 states reported developing a new alternate assessment, and 15 states reported modifying an existing alternate assessment.[44] By August 2008, most states had received approval from ED on their AA-AAS within their state assessment and accountability plans. Fifteen states, however, did not receive approval. Of those not receiving approval, states typically had difficulty with the alignment (linkage) of content standards with alternate assessments, the technical quality of the alternate assessments (e.g., reliability, validity), and the documentation of a validated standards-setting process.

By April 2007, 50 states provided participation guidelines for IEP teams to use in determining which students were eligible to take AA-AAS. Forty-two of the 50 states used a "checklist" or "worksheet" method that allowed IEP teams to provide evidence that a particular student with a disability was eligible to participate in AA-AAS. All states required documented evidence that the student had a significant cognitive disability and received an extensively modified curriculum during instruction. States defined "most significant cognitive disability" using criteria that describe a student's intellectual and adaptive functioning. The most common criteria used to define "most significant cognitive disability" included (1) significantly subaverage intellectual functioning or cognitive ability (40 states), (2) deficits in adaptive behavior (35 states), (3) cognitive and adaptive deficits that adversely affect academic performance (19 states), and (4) cognitive and adaptive deficits that manifest before the age of 18 (23 states).

Thirty-one states also required IEP teams to use exclusionary criteria to determine eligibility for AA-AAS. Exclusionary criteria are criteria that may not be considered in determining eligibility for participation in alternate assessments. For example, in many states participation in AA-AAS may not be due to the student's specific disability category (e.g., autism, mental retardation); excessive absences; social, cultural, or economic differences; or expectations of poor performance on the general state assessment.

In school year 2005-2006, 49 states, the District of Columbia, and Puerto Rico used scores from AA-AAS to calculate AYP. Twenty-two states reported granting exceptions to the 1% cap to LEAs. Twenty-six states, the District of Columbia, and Puerto Rico did not grant exceptions to LEAs, in most cases because no LEAs requested exceptions.[45] The number of exceptions granted to LEAs by states varied from approximately 2 exceptions to approximately 100 exceptions. Of the 22 states that reported granting exceptions, the 1% cap was typically exceeded by a small amount. LEAs that exceeded the 1% cap by a larger amount tended to have low student enrollments in which just a few students participating in AA-AAS would exceed the cap.

The SSI-NCLB report did not collect data on the number of states that were required to redistribute scores that exceeded the cap or the methods of redistributing scores used by states. It appears, however, that some states have tested much higher proportions of their students with disabilities with AA-AAS than would be envisioned under ED policies. In general, ED estimated that the 1% cap translates into approximately 9% of students with disabilities, and several states reported assessing much more than 9% of students with disabilities using AA-AAS. In several isolated cases, the number of students with disabilities participating in AA-AAS exceeded 30% of all students with disabilities.[46] In addition, for school year 2005-2006, 10 states reported problematic data that did not clearly describe the percentage of students with disabilities who participated in AA-AAS.[47]

Development and Implementation of AA-MAS

There are fewer data available that describe the development and implementation of AA-MAS. Since ED released final regulations in April 2007, states have had approximately two years to adapt their assessment and accountability systems to be consistent with the regulations. As of January

2009, ED reported that eight states[48] administered AA-MAS in school year 2007-2008 and an additional 20 states were in the process of developing AA-MAS.[49]

The National Center on Educational Outcomes (NCEO) conducted a survey of states that have implemented AA-MAS.[50] The survey reports that nine states have publicly available participation guidelines for IEP teams to determine eligibility for AA-MAS. All nine states have written descriptive criteria for eligibility. In addition, some have flow charts or decision trees (four states) and checklists (three states). Eligibility criteria varied across states. The most common criteria included (1) student has an IEP (nine states), (2) student is learning grade-level content (seven states), and (3) decisions about the student are based on multiple measures of performance (seven states). Some states used exclusionary criteria as well. Again, exclusionary criteria are criteria that may not be considered to determine eligibility for participation in alternate assessments. For example, some states required that eligibility for AA-MAS not be dependent on (1) the student's disability category (e.g., learning disability, mental retardation) (six states), (2) excessive absences, social, cultural, language, economic, or environmental factors (four states), or (3) educational placement (three states).

To date, student participation rates within the states that implement AA-MAS are not readily available. Thus, at this time it is not possible to determine whether states are appropriately testing students with disabilities using AA-MAS, whether states are exceeding the 2% cap, and how states are redistributing scores, if necessary.

CHALLENGES IN DEVELOPMENT AND IMPLEMENTATION OF ALTERNATE ASSESSMENTS

The following sections describe several challenges states have encountered in the development and implementation of alternate assessments. Although all states now have approved assessment systems that incorporate AA-AAS and nearly all use results from these assessments in their accountability systems, most states are still in the development process of incorporating AAMAS. One difficulty that states faced in the development and implementation of alternate assessments was the limited statutory language provided in NCLB. The limited statutory language may have delayed states in the development of alternate assessments as they awaited regulations from ED.

Another challenge in developing alternate assessments was developing alternate assessments that met professional standards for technical adequacy, including validity and reliability. The lack of technical adequacy evidence delayed ED's approval of some state assessment systems, which further delayed the implementation of alternate assessments.

Limited Statutory Language and Timing of Regulations

NCLB does not include statutory language regarding alternate assessments. Section 1111 of NCLB outlines the requirements for state assessments, in general, which include the provision that state assessments must measure the achievement of all children. The statute allows for "reasonable adaptations and accommodations" for students with disabilities, however, the language maintained that students with disabilities must be tested relative to state academic content standards and achievement standards.[51] The use of adaptations and accommodations are not synonymous with the development and use of alternate assessments based on grade-level expectations, AA-AAS, or AA-MAS.[52]

NCLB was enacted in January 2002. Section 1908 of NCLB required the Secretary to issue regulations for Section 1111 "not later than 6 months after the date of enactment." ED regulations were subsequently released on July 5, 2002.[53] These regulations specify, for the first time, that states' assessment systems under NCLB must include at least one alternate assessment for students with disabilities. Alternate assessments were required to yield results in at least reading/language arts, and, beginning in the 2007-2008 school year, science. The regulations issued in July 2002 did not include language that allowed states to develop alternate or modified achievement standards, nor did they specify how results from alternate assessments could be used in state accountability systems.

Approximately a year and a half later, ED issued the December 9, 2003, regulations regarding the development and use of AA-AAS in state accountability systems (approximately two years after the enactment of NCLB). These regulations were the first to mention the development of alternate achievement standards, which allowed states, for the first time, to set different levels of expectations for students with the "most significant cognitive disabilities." The December 2003 regulations were also the first set of regulations to describe the 1% cap in counting proficient and advanced scores for AYP purposes.

Approximately three and a half years later, ED issued the April 19, 2007, regulations regarding the development and use of AA-MAS in state accountability systems (more than five years after the enactment of NCLB). These regulations were the first to mention the development of modified achievement standards for students with disabilities, and the first to describe the 2% cap in counting proficient and advanced scores for AYP purposes.

The timeline above describes a period of more than five years in which states were gradually given information on how to develop and use alternate assessments for students with disabilities in their accountability systems. During that period, states developed their own policies regarding the use of alternate assessments in accountability systems, which occasionally became inconsistent with subsequent ED regulations. When final ED regulations were released, states that had adopted policies inconsistent with regulations often had to redevelop alternate assessments, redevelop achievement standards, change their general testing practices, and resubmit their state assessment plans to ED for approval.

Technical Adequacy of Assessments

Alternate assessments are subject to the same technical adequacy requirements as all general state assessments under Section 1111 of NCLB. That is, alternate assessments must "be used for purposes for which such assessments are valid and reliable, and be consistent with relevant, nationally recognized professional and technical standards."[54] While there are, arguably, "recognized professional and technical standards" for standardized assessments of the general population,[55] there are no "recognized professional and technical standards" for individualized, alternate assessments of students with disabilities. There are types of validity and reliability evidence that are often relevant to alternate assessments, but the type of evidence needed to establish validity and reliability may need to be made on a case-by-case basis. Because alternate assessments take various forms, such as portfolios, checklists, teacher observations, and performance assessments, traditional evidence of validity and reliability may be inappropriate. The general state assessment is usually a standardized test that uses a combination of multiple-choice and constructed-response (e.g., short answer, essay) formats. Collecting validity and reliability evidence for a standardized test using multiple-choice and constructed-response formats is a well-established practice in the field of educational assessment. Collecting this evidence for individualized alternate assessments, however, is not well established.

In 2001, a research collaborative was convened to examine key issues in developing technically defensible alternate assessments for use in state accountability systems. The collaborative included experts in special education, curriculum, and measurement. This collaborative created a model framework that could be used to study the validity of alternate assessments.[56] By early 2008, 10 states had partnered with the collaborative to apply the model framework to their own alternate assessments. It is unclear at this time, however, whether the model framework is increasing approval rates of states' alternate assessments undergoing peer review.

During ED's peer review process for state assessment systems, the most common problems cited by reviewers were (1) insufficient evidence to show how alternate assessments were linked to grade-level content standards, and (2) inadequate evidence of the validity and reliability of the alternate assessments. In addition, some states had not adequately documented how the alternate assessment standards were adopted by the state, how the alternate achievement standards were set by the state, and how the results of the alternate assessments would be reported.[57]

ANALYSIS OF RECOMMENDATIONS FOR NCLB REAUTHORIZATION: STUDENTS WITH DISABILITIES

As this report has discussed, the inclusion of students with disabilities in state assessment and accountability systems is a relatively new practice. NCLB was the first federal law that held schools accountable for the academic achievement of students with disabilities, and the methods used to include these students have been evolving since its enactment. The reauthorization of NCLB may revisit issues related to the assessment of students with disabilities and the ways in which schools are held accountable for their academic achievement.

The Education Commission of the States (ECS) collected and synthesized recommendations for NCLB reauthorization from 15 national education organizations. ECS manages a database of these recommendations around 16 issue areas, one of which is "students with disabilities." Of the 15 surveyed organizations, 13 provided recommendations on the assessment of students with disabilities.[58] Some organizations advocated improving current practice, such as improving alternate assessments, maintaining the current 1% and 2% regulations, and increasing funding for the development of assessments for students with disabilities. Other organizations, however, proposed more substantial changes to current practice, such as reconsidering the 1% and 2% caps, increasing the role of IEPs in assessment and accountability systems, increasing the use of growth models for students with disabilities, and providing other policy flexibility in AYP determinations. An analysis of these proposed changes to current practice is provided in the following sections.

Reconsidering the 1% and 2% Caps

One possible issue for the reauthorization of NCLB may be the reconsideration of the 1% and 2% caps. As previously discussed, Congress did not originally include any statutory language on the use of alternate assessments in state accountability systems under NCLB. Congress may choose to revisit the issue and include statutory language that either increases or decreases the 1% and 2% caps. Increasing or decreasing the caps would have implications for the manner in which schools and LEAs are held accountable for the achievement of students with disabilities.

One commission recommended maintaining the 1% cap but decreasing the 2% cap to 1%.[59] Under this proposal, the number of proficient and advanced scores based on AA-AAS may not exceed 1% of all students assessed, and the number of proficient and advanced scores based on AA-MAS may not exceed 1% of all students assessed. Decreasing the 2% cap would reduce the amount of flexibility that states currently have in assessing students with disabilities and in determining how scores are included in the accountability system. In general, decreasing the 1% and 2% caps may further discourage states and IEP teams from inappropriately identifying students with disabilities and recommending their participation in alternate assessments. In addition, decreasing the caps may send a strong signal to educators that students with disabilities should have access to the general education curriculum and be measured against challenging academic standards.

Alternatively, Congress may choose to increase the caps, providing more flexibility to states in the assessment of students with disabilities. Increasing the 1% and 2% caps may protect schools and LEAs from failing to meet AYP due solely to the students with disabilities subgroup. It may also provide educators more flexibility in determining appropriate academic goals for students with disabilities, instead of being required to teach either extended or grade-level content standards of the state. Increasing the caps, however, may incentivize states and IEP teams to inappropriately identify students with disabilities and to recommend their participation in alternate assessments. It may also result in the exclusion of some students with disabilities from participation in the general education curriculum, which may deny them equal access to instruction and equal opportunity to achieve challenging academic standards.

ED has indicated that the current Administration is interested in maintaining the use of AA-AAS for students with the most significant cognitive disabilities; however, it does not support the continuation of AA-MAS for other students with disabilities.[60] ED has not made changes to the original regulations outlining the use of alternate assessments; however, this issue may receive attention from Congress during the reauthorization of the ESEA.

Role of IEPs

Several education organizations have proposed increasing the role of IEPs in state assessment and accountability systems. IDEA requires that each student with a disability be provided an IEP that outlines the provision of special education and related services. An IEP is a written document that provides descriptions of the student's current level of functioning, measurable annual goals, and methods for measuring the student's progress toward these goals.[61] Organizations that advocate increasing the role of IEPs propose using these annual goals and methods for measuring student progress in assessment and accountability systems. There is some disagreement, however, over the appropriate amount of independence and flexibility that should be granted to states and IEP teams for the development of annual goals, measurement of academic achievement, and determination of AYP.

At one end of the spectrum, states could be granted a considerable amount of flexibility to direct IEP teams to determine curricula, standards, and assessments for students with disabilities. Several organizations proposed allowing states to count students with disabilities as meeting AYP if they successfully completed their IEP goals.[62] Other organizations proposed allowing states to independently determine the percentage of students with disabilities that should participate in alternate assessments or "out-of-level" assessments based on the student's IEP.[63] In this scenario, states could use separate starting points for AYP projections based on each individual student's present level of achievement, as outlined in the IEP. These methods would provide states and IEP teams the flexibility necessary to develop truly individualized education plans for students with disabilities and allow the curriculum, standards, and assessments to be adapted to suit the needs of the student. On the other hand, the focus on meeting IEP goals for AYP may inadvertently lead to setting lower goals for students with disabilities, thereby lowering overall expectations of achievement for students with disabilities. Such an outcome would be inconsistent with the original intent of including students with disabilities in state assessment and accountability systems— increasing access to the general education curriculum, and, in turn, increasing expectations and achievement of students with disabilities.

At the other end of the spectrum, states may be granted some flexibility to direct IEP teams to choose specific curricula and assessments, however, the standards would be determined by the state. In this scenario, states could require the use of a "standards-based IEP" document, which would require IEP teams to write annual goals that are linked to the state's academic content standards. Traditionally, a student's IEP has been considered a highly individualized document that is not necessarily linked to the state's academic content standards. "Traditional" IEP goals tend to focus on developmental goals, such as "school readiness" and functional skills. As the emphasis on academic achievement of students with disabilities increased during the 1990s, the focus of many IEP goals shifted from "traditional" developmental goals to academic goals. Including academic goals on IEPs allows IEP teams to link the goals for students with disabilities to the state academic content standards in a way that was not possible with developmental goals. A "standards-based IEP," therefore, is a document in which students with disabilities have annual goals that are aligned with, or linked to, the state's grade-level academic content standards.[64] If students were assessed against standards-based IEP goals, they would, in essence, be assessed against state academic content standards. Requiring standards-based IEPs would provide an academic focus and structure for states and IEP teams to use when determining appropriate goals for students with disabilities. It would also allow some flexibility in the curricula chosen to teach these standards and the assessments used to measure the attainment of the standards. On the other hand, standards-based IEPs may not allow IEP teams enough flexibility to truly individualize goals and instruction, especially for students with significant cognitive disabilities. IEP teams may want to preserve some of the more traditional developmental goals for students with significant cognitive disabilities, and IEP teams may find it difficult to extend the state content standards in a meaningful way for these students.

In general, increasing the role of the IEP in assessment and accountability systems may reduce the redundancy in setting multiple sets of goals and objectives for students with disabilities. It may also simplify the reporting of the academic progress of students with disabilities by combining reporting requirements contained within IDEA and NCLB. Nevertheless, the variability in procedures used to set IEP goals and objectives may reduce their usefulness in accountability systems. IEP goals vary greatly in their rigor, level of challenge to the student, and relationship to the state content standards. Using IEP goals to determine AYP may also result in a diminished capacity to compare the achievement of students across schools, districts, and states, which may mask the overall achievement (or lack of achievement) of students with disabilities.

Growth Models[65]

A number of education organizations have proposed expanding the use of growth models in AYP determinations for students with disabilities.[66] Several organizations have proposed that AYP should reflect the academic "progress" of students with disabilities, independent of any ultimate goal (i.e., 100% proficiency by school year 2013-2014). Similarly, other organizations have proposed the use of individual student growth models that follow the progress of the same students over time at all performance levels. Such models would reward schools for improving the achievement of all students with disabilities, even those performing substantially below the proficient level.

In November 2005, the Secretary announced a growth model program in which states could use growth models to make AYP determinations. Fifteen states currently participate in the growth model pilot program. Requirements for the growth models in the pilot program, however, are relatively restrictive. In order to be considered for the pilot program, the growth models proposed by states must have met the following seven criteria:

1. Ensure that all students are proficient by 2013-2014 and set annual goals to ensure that the achievement gap is closing for all groups of students;

2. Establish high expectations for low-achieving students, while not setting expectations for annual achievement based upon student demographic characteristics or school characteristics;
3. Produce separate accountability decisions about student achievement in reading/language arts and in mathematics;
4. Ensure that all students in the tested grades are included in the assessment and accountability system, hold schools and districts accountable for the performance of each student subgroup, and include all schools and districts;
5. Be based on assessments in each of grades 3-8 and high school in both reading/language arts and mathematics that have been operational for more than one year, received approval through the NCLB peer review process for the 2005- 06 school year, and produce comparable results from grade to grade and year to year;
6. Track student progress as part of the state data system; and
7. Include student participation rates in the state's assessment system and student achievement on an additional academic indicator.

If these requirements are upheld in future growth model programs, it is unclear if the growth models would be flexible enough to credit states for improving the achievement of students with disabilities. Under the current requirements, it is not necessarily the case that schools and LEAs would meet AYP by improving the achievement of students with disabilities, even if the improvement was substantial. For example, if the ultimate goal of 100% proficiency by 2013- 2014 is maintained (criterion 1), in many cases students with disabilities would have to make unreasonably large gains in achievement each year to make AYP. Relatively significant gains in achievement may still result in failure to meet AYP goals for the school and LEA.

In addition, some of the criteria above may be inconsistent with the use of alternate assessments in growth models, especially for students with the "most significant cognitive disabilities" who participate in AA-AAS. For example, if the assessment system must "be based on assessments in each of grades 3-8"and "produce comparable results from grade-to-grade and year-to-year" (criterion 5), it is unclear how some AA-AAS fulfill this requirement. General state assessments would reflect a progression of skills and competencies from grades 3-8 that would represent what annual growth means for students without disabilities. Regulations outlining the development and use of AA-AAS, however, allow states to incorporate "out of level" testing for students with the "most significant cognitive disabilities" and use alternate achievement standards for grade clusters (e.g., 3-5, 6-9, 10-12). It is unclear how an "out of level" AA-AAS for a three to five grade cluster produces "comparable results from grade-to-grade and year-to-year." Using out of level tests and grade clusters make it more difficult to define what represents annual growth. The annual growth of students participating in AA-AAS, therefore, may not be adequately captured by this type of growth model.[67]

Other Policy Flexibility in AYP Determinations

Increasing the role of IEPs and the use of growth models are regularly mentioned as possible issues to consider when assessing students with disabilities for AYP purposes. Other policy flexibility in making AYP determinations, however, have been offered at a more general level. Rather than focus on methods for assessing students with disabilities, these other options tend to focus on how the scores of students with disabilities should count in AYP determinations.

For example, one option may be to allow extended time for students to be included in the "students with disabilities" AYP subgroup. That is, if a student is no longer eligible for special education because he or she has made academic improvements, the scores from state assessments for that student could still be counted in the "students with disabilities" AYP subgroup. Currently, regulations allow a student who was previously identified as having a disability but no longer receives special education services to be counted in the "students with disabilities" AYP subgroup for an additional two years.[68] Some proposals may favor including these students in the "students with disabilities" AYP subgroup for a longer period of time because it may increase the likelihood that the subgroup makes AYP. Allowing "declassified" students[69] to count in the "students with disabilities" AYP subgroup could be viewed as giving more credit to a school's effort to educate students with disabilities successfully so that they no longer require special education services. This provision may incentivize schools to move students in and out of special education based on academic performance, without concern over losing a "high-achieving special education student" from the "students with disabilities" AYP subgroup.

Another option may be to maintain the current "safe harbor" provision of NCLB. The safe harbor provision allows schools or LEAs that fail to meet the usual AYP requirements to be deemed to have made AYP if (1) among the subgroups not meeting AYP, the percentage of students who are *not* at the proficient or higher level in the school declines by at least 10%,[70] and (2) among the subgroups not meeting AYP, the students make progress on at least one other academic indicator included in the state's AYP standards.[71] If students with disabilities, as a subgroup, fail to meet AYP goals, the school or LEA may still be deemed to have made AYP if the above conditions are met.[72] This provision provides flexibility to schools and LEAs by providing a secondary route to meeting AYP. It does not, however, focus attention and resources on developing appropriate assessments for students with disabilities or attaining higher levels of achievement for students with disabilities.

APPENDIX A. CHARACTERISTICS OF ALTERNATE ASSESSMENTS

Table A-1. Characteristics of Alternate Assessments.
Similarities and Differences between AA-AAS and AA-MAS

	AA-AAS (1%)	AA-MAS (2%)
Achievement Standard	An alternate achievement standard is an expectation of performance that differs in complexity from a grade-level achievement standard, usually based on a very limited sample of content that is linked to, but does not fully represent, grade-level content. May be defined for grade clusters (e.g., 3-5, 6-8, 10-12).	A modified achievement standard is aligned to grade-level content standards for the grade in which a student is enrolled and challenging for eligible students, but may be less difficult than grade-level achievement standards. Achievement standards must include three levels of performance, cut scores that distinguish one level from another, and descriptors of the content-based competencies associated with each level. May not be defined for grade clusters. Must be defined grade-by-grade.
Setting Standards	Requires a "documented and validated standards setting process." A detailed description of the procedures used, the qualifications of panelists (which must include	Requires a "documented and validated standards setting process." A detailed description of the procedures used, the qualifications of panelists (which must include persons

Table A-1. (Continued)

	AA-AAS (1%)	AA-MAS (2%)
	persons knowledgeable about the state's content standards and experienced in standards setting, and special educators who are most knowledgeable about students with disabilities), the final cut scores, and performance level descriptors must be submitted for peer review.	knowledgeable about the state's content standards and experienced in standards setting, and special educators who are most knowledgeable about students with disabilities), the final cut scores, and performance level descriptors must be submitted for peer review.
Content Standards on which the Test is Based	"Extended" standards may include substantially simplified content, including pre-requisite skills.	Grade-level
Assessment	May include reduced coverage and/or simplification of grade-level content, based on "extended" standards. Format may permit variation in test content for individual students if results can be aggregated.	Built on grade-level content but with easier items.
Cap	State and LEA	State and LEA
Out-of-Level Assessments	Permitted only if consistent with the regulation (i.e., documented and validated standards-setting process employed).	Not permitted because out-of-level assessments do not assess grade-level content.
IEP	Must include annual measurable IEP goals and benchmarks or short-term objectives.	Must include annual measurable IEP goals that are based on grade-level content standards.
State Guidelines Define Who is Eligible	Students with the most significant cognitive disabilities. IEP team makes the decision regarding the appropriate assessment..	Student whose disability has precluded him or her from achieving proficiency, as demonstrated by objective evidence of the student's performance, and whose progress is such that, even if significant growth occurs, the student's IEP team is reasonably certain that he or she will not achieve grade-

	AA-AAS (1%)	AA-MAS (2%)
		level proficiency within the year covered by the IEP. IEP team makes the decision regarding the appropriate assessment.

Source: U.S. Department of Education, Modified Academic Achievement Standards, Non-Regulatory Guidance, July 2007, pp. 52-53, http://www.ed.gov/policy/speced/guid/nclb/twopercent.doc.

APPENDIX B. METHODS OF REDISTRIBUTING SCORES

Table B-1. Methods for Distributing Scores Exceeding Caps

Model	Pros	Cons
Random Assignment	Should be impartial and fair over time. Easy to computerize. Easy to understand/communicate.	Seldom regarded as fair when distribution is uneven in a particular year.
Proportional	Might deter inappropriate assignment of students to alternate achievement standards and modified achievement standards.	Might be hard to implement in small districts. Might penalize a school that has a large number of students with significant cognitive disabilities appropriately tested using alternate achievement standards. Might penalize a school that has a large number of students with disabilities appropriately tested using modified achievement standards.
Strategic	Might be perceived as providing the maximum benefit for schools.	Difficult to implement. Can be perceived as unethical or as using favoritism. Consistency might be hard to maintain over time. Assumes "correct" students assessed.

Table B-1. (Continued)

Model	Pros	Cons
Predetermined School Cap	Might be effective in LEAs with stable populations and special education services when alternate achievement standards and modified achievement standards have been applied conservatively.	an imbalance among schools. May perpetuate historical problems.

Source: Tiffany Martinez and Ken Olsen, Distribution of Proficient Scores that Exceed the 1% Cap: Four Possible Approaches, Mid-South Regional Resource Center, March 2004, ERIC# ED484423 at http://www.eric.ed.gov/.

Note: This table has been slightly modified from its original form to incorporate redistributing scores based on alternate achievement standards and modified achievement standards.

APPENDIX C. REDISTRIBUTING SCORES EXAMPLE

Table C-1. Examples Showing the Percentage of Proficient and Advanced Scores to be Redistributed in a State that Implements Both Modified and Alternate Academic Achievement Standards

	AA-AAS (1%)	AA-MAS (2%)	Proficient and Advanced Scores that Must be Redistributed as Non-Proficient Scores
LEA A			
	0.9%	2.6%	0.5%
Exceeds the 2% Cap			
LEA B			
	0.7%	2.3%	0%
Exceeds the 2% Cap			
LEA C			
	1.4%	1.5%	0.4%
Exceeds the 1% Cap			
LEA D			
			0.9%
Exceeds both the 1% and 2% Caps	1.3%	2.6%	(0.3% from AA-AAS)

Source: The example is reproduced from U.S. Department of Education , Modified Academic Achievement Standards, Non-Regulatory Guidance, July 2007, pp. 46-47, http://www.ed.gov/policy/speced/guid/nclb/ twopercent.doc.

Note: The example above assumes that LEAs have not been granted an exception from the state to exceed the 1% or 2% cap.

- *LEA A* does not exceed the 1% cap; it is 0.1% under the cap. However, LEA A exceeds the 2% cap by 0.6%. Because an LEA (or state) may exceed the 2% cap by the amount it is below the 1% cap, the LEA only needs to redistribute 0.5% of its proficient and advanced scores as non-proficient scores (0.9% + 2.6% = 3.5%; 3.5% - 3.0% = 0.5%).

- *LEA B* is under the 1% cap by 0.3% and over the 2% cap by 0.3 percent. An LEA or state may exceed the 2% cap provided that it does not have more than a total of 3% proficient and advanced scores from both types of alternate assessments (AA-AAS and AA-MAS). In this case, LEA B does not exceed that 3% limit, so it does not need to redistribute any scores.

- *LEA C* exceeds the 1% cap by 0.4%, but it is under the 2% cap by 0.5%. An LEA or state may not exceed the 1% cap (unless the LEA has an exception from the state), even if it has less than 2% of proficient or advanced scores on AA-MAS. Therefore, LEA C has 0.4% of its proficient and advanced scores from AA-AAS that must be redistributed as non-proficient scores.

- *LEA D* exceeds both the 1% and 2% caps (by 0.3% and 0.6%, respectively). Therefore, LEA D has 0.9% of its proficient and advanced scores from its alternate assessments that must be redistributed as non-proficient scores. (1.3% + 2.6% = 3.9%; 3.9% - 3.0% =0.9%). Note that 0.3% must be from AA-AAS scores since LEA D was 0.3% over the 1% cap (unless the LEA has an exception from the state).

End Notes

[1] For more information on assessments in elementary and secondary education, see CRS Report R40514, Assessment in Elementary and Secondary Education: A Primer, by Erin D. Lomax.

[2] For an overview of NCLB reauthorization issues, see CRS Report RL33749, The No Child Left Behind Act: An Overview of Reauthorization Issues for the 111th Congress, by Rebecca R. Skinner.

[3] For more information on AYP, see CRS Report RL32495, Adequate Yearly Progress (AYP): Implementation of the No Child Left Behind Act, by Rebecca R. Skinner.

[4] Legislation mandated the participation of students with disabilities in district-wide assessments as well. Because the focus of this report is on state assessments used in AYP calculations, the practice of including students with disabilities in state assessments is highlighted.

[5] U.S. Department of Education, "Title I – Improving the Academic Achievement of the Disadvantaged; Final Rule," 68 Federal Register 236, December 9, 2003.

[6] U.S. Department of Education, "Title I – Improving the Academic Achievement of the Disadvantaged; Individuals with Disabilities Education Act (IDEA); Final Rule," 72 Federal Register 67, April 19, 2007.

[7] 34 C.F.R. §200.1(d).

[8] 34 C.F.R. §§200.2(b) and 200.3(a)(1).

[9] 34 C.F.R. §200.1(c).

[10] As defined by IDEA, §620(3).

[11] Under IDEA, the term "child with a disability" includes a child with mental retardation, hearing impairments (including deafness), speech or language impairments, visual impairments (including blindness), deaf-blindness, serious emotional disturbance, orthopedic impairments, autism, traumatic brain injury, specific learning disability, multiple disabilities, other health impairments, or developmental delay. Note that "developmental delay" is restricted within the law to include only children between the ages of six and nine years old. Students in any of the IDEA disability categories would be eligible to participate in AA-AAS if they met state criteria for "most significant cognitive disability."

[12] U.S. Department of Education, Alternate Achievement Standards for Students with the Most Significant Cognitive Disabilities, Non-Regulatory Guidance, August 2005, p. 23, http://www.ed.gov/policy/elsec/guid/altguidance.pdf.

[13] An IEP is a written statement for each student with a disability that includes a description of the special education and related services required by a student with a disability. For a complete description of the elements of an IEP, see IDEA §614(d)(1)(A). An IEP team is a group of individuals who develop, review, and revise the IEP for a student with a disability. The IEP team includes, at minimum, a parent of the child, one general educator, one special educator, a public representative who is qualified to provide or supervise the delivery of individualized instruction, and an individual who can interpret the instructional implications of evaluation results. Other individuals may be included as part of an IEP team, including the student with a disability if appropriate, at the discretion of the parent or public agency. For a complete description of the IEP team, see IDEA §614(d)(1)(B).

[14] Exceptions to the 1% cap are discussed in a future section: "Exceptions to the 1% Cap and 2% Cap;" 34 CFR Part 200 regulations dated December 9, 2003, originally allowed states to request a waiver to the 1% cap. In 34 CFR Part 200 regulations dated April 19, 2007, however, the rule was changed and states are no longer permitted to request an exception to exceed the 1% cap.

[15] U.S. Department of Education, "Title I – Improving the Academic Achievement of the Disadvantaged; Proposed Rule," 67 Federal Register, August 6, 2002.

[16] U.S. Department of Education, "Title I – Improving the Academic Achievement of the Disadvantaged; Final Rule," 67 Federal Register, December 2, 2002.

[17] For a summary of the scientific evidence used to support the "0.5% cap," see U.S. Department of Education, "Title I – Improving the Academic Achievement of the Disadvantaged; Proposed Rule," 68 Federal Register 13798-13799, March 20, 2003.

[18] U.S. Department of Education, "Title I – Improving the Academic Achievement of the Disadvantaged; Final Rule," 68 Federal Register 236, December 9, 2003.

[19] 34 C.F.R. §200.1(e).

[20] 34 C.F.R. §§200.2(b) and 200.3(a)(1).

[21] 34 C.F.R. §200.1(c).

[22] IDEA, §602(3).

[23] See footnote 11.

[24] See footnote 13.

[25] Exceptions to the 2% cap are discussed in the section "Exceptions to the 1% Cap and 2% Cap."

[26] Kristen L. McMaster, Doug Fuchs, and Lynn S. Fuchs, et al., "Responding to Non-responders: An Experimental Field Trial of Identification and Intervention Methods," Exceptional Children, vol. 71 (2005), pp. 445-463; Joseph K. Torgenson, A.W. Alexander, and Richard K. Wagner, et al., "Intensive Remedial Instruction for Children with Severe Reading Disabilities: Immediate and Long-term Outcomes from Two Instructional Approaches," Journal of Learning Disabilities, vol. 34 (2001), pp. 33-58; G. Reid Lyon, Jack M. Fletcher, and Lynn S. Fuchs, et al., "Learning Disabilities," in Treatment of Childhood Disorders, ed. E. Mash & R. Barkley, 3rd ed. (New York: Guilford Press, 2006), pp. 512-594.

[27] The studies in footnote 26 excluded students with the "most significant cognitive disabilities," therefore, the estimates of students with disabilities who may not reach grade-level proficiency are in addition to students with the "most significant cognitive disabilities."

[28] A.T. Clapper, A.B. Morse, and S.S. Lazarus, et al., 2003 State Policies on Assessment Participation and Accommodations for Students with Disabilities, National Center on Educational Outcomes, Synthesis Report 56, Minneapolis, MN, 2005.

[29] U.S. Department of Education, "Title I – Improving the Academic Achievement of the Disadvantaged; Final Rule," 72 Federal Register 17765, April 19, 2007.

[30] 34 C.F.R § 200.13(c)(5).

[31] A state may exceed the 2% cap if it is below the 1% cap without being granted an official exception from the Secretary.

[32] U.S. Department of Education, Modified Academic Achievement Standards, Non-Regulatory Guidance, July 20, 2007, p. 44, http://www.ed.gov/policy/speced/guid/nclb/twopercent.doc; Tiffany Martinez and Ken Olsen, Distribution of Proficient Scores that Exceed the 1% Cap: Four Possible Approaches, Mid-South Regional Resource Center, March 2004, ERIC# ED484423 at http://www.eric.ed.gov.

[33] Throughout the example, "proficient and advanced" scores will be referred to as "proficient" scores.

[34] This example is adapted from U.S. Department of Education, Alternate Achievement Standards for Students with the Most Significant Cognitive Disabilities, Non-Regulatory Guidance, August 2005, pp. 32-35, http://www.ed.gov/policy/ elsec/guid/altguidance.pdf. For a specific example on the 2% cap, see U.S. Department of Education , Modified Academic Achievement Standards, Non-Regulatory Guidance, July 2007, pp. 42-45, http://www.ed.gov/policy/speced/ guid/nclb/twopercent.doc.

[35] If any number less than 100 students attained a proficient score, this scenario would be applicable.

[36] If any number between 101 and 150 students attained a proficient score, the number of scores exceeding 100 would be redistributed.

[37] Although the state is ultimately responsible for redistributing scores, the state has flexibility to permit LEAs to redistribute scores provided that the practice is consistent with state policy. The 1% cap also applies at the state level. The state may not exceed the 1% cap under any circumstances; therefore, all scores exceeding the 1% cap at the state level must be redistributed.

[38] 34 C.F.R. §200.6(a)(4).

[39] U.S. Department of Education, "Title I – Improving the Academic Achievement of the Disadvantaged; Final Rule," 68700, December 9, 2003; Note that these regulations address the development and use of AA-AAS in state accountability systems; however, regulations regarding the development and use of AA-MAS were not released until April 19, 2007.

[40] Amy Elledge, Kerstin Carlson Le Floch, and James Taylor, et al., State and Local Implementation of the No Child Left Behind Act, Office of Planning, Evaluation, and Policy Development; U.S. Department of Education, Volume V – Implementation of the 1 Percent Rule and 2 Percent Interim Policy Options, Washington, DC, January 2009, http://www.ed.gov/rschstat/eval/disadv/nclb-disab/nclb-disab.pdf.

[41] 34 C.F.R. §200.20(g).

[42] For more information on implementation of the "2% interim policy options," see Amy Elledge, Kerstin Carlson Le Floch, and James Taylor, et al., State and Local Implementation of the No Child Left Behind Act, Office of Planning, Evaluation, and Policy Development; U.S. Department of Education, Volume V – Implementation of the 1 Percent Rule and 2 Percent Interim Policy Options, Washington, DC, January 2009, pp. 29-34, http://www.ed. gov/rschstat/eval/ disadv/nclb-disab/nclb-disab.pdf.

[43] Three states had not yet developed alternate assessments for all grades assessed for AYP purposes (i.e., grades 3-8 and once in high school).

[44] 42 states reported data.

[45] One state survey respondent was unsure if any exceptions to the 1% cap were granted to LEAs.

[46] See Exhibit C.4 of Amy Elledge, Kerstin Carlson Le Floch, and James Taylor, et al., State and Local Implementation of the No Child Left Behind Act, Office of Planning, Evaluation, and Policy Development; U.S. Department of Education, Volume V – Implementation of the 1 Percent Rule and 2 Percent Interim Policy Options, Washington, DC, January 2009, p. 85, http://www.ed.gov/rschstat/eval/disadv/nclb-disab/nclb-disab.pdf.

[47] States varied in the way they calculated participation rates of students with disabilities who were tested using AAAAS. For more information, see S.J. Thompson, C.J. Johnstone, and M.L. Thurlow, et al., 2005 State Special Education Outcomes: Steps Forward in a Decade of Change, National Center on Educational Outcomes, Minneapolis, MN, 2005, http://cehd.umn.edu/nceo/OnlinePubs/2005StateReport.pdf.

[48] Another source reports that, as of December 2008, nine states had developed AA-MAS (see Sheryl S. Lazarus, Christopher Rogers, and Damien Cormier, et al., States' Participation Guidelines for Alternate Assessments Based on Modified Academic Achievement Standards (AA-MAS) in 2008, National Center on Educational Outcomes (NCEO), Synthesis Report 71, Minneapolis, MN, December 2008, http://cehd.umn.edu/nceo/OnlinePubs/Synthesis71/ Synthesis71.pdf.

[49] See State Status Chart at http://www.ed.gov/policy/elsec/guid/stateletters/ssc.xls.

[50] See footnote 47.

[51] ESEA, Section 1111(a)(3)(C)(ix)(II).

[52] Adaptations and accommodations are generally thought of as changes in testing materials and procedures, however, the test content and questions remain the same. Examples of adaptations and accommodations include changes in the presentation of a test (e.g., repeating directions, providing directions in Braille), changes in the response to test items (e.g., using a scribe), changes in setting (e.g., study carrel, separate room), use of additional equipment (e.g., calculator, amplification device, manipulatives), and use of flexible timing and scheduling (e.g., extended time, frequent breaks).

[53] U.S. Department of Education, "Title I – Improving the Academic Achievement of the Disadvantaged; Final Rule," 67 Federal Register 129, July 5, 2002.

54 ESEA, Section 1111(a)(3)(C)(iii).

55 For example, see AERA, APA, NCME, "Standards for Educational and Psychological Testing," (Washington, DC: American Psychological Association, 1999).

[56] Rachel Quenemoen, A Brief History of Alternate Assessments Based on Alternate Achievement Standards, National Center on Educational Outcomes, Synthesis Report 68, Minneapolis, MN, September 2008, p. 17, http://cehd.umn.edu/ nceo/OnlinePubs/ Synthesis68/Synthesis68.pdf.

[57] Amy Elledge, Kerstin Carlson Le Floch, and James Taylor, et al., State and Local Implementation of the No Child Left Behind Act, Office of Planning, Evaluation, and Policy Development; U.S. Department of Education, Volume V – Implementation of the 1 Percent Rule and 2 Percent Interim Policy Options, Washington, DC, January 2009.

[58] For the full text of ECS's "Students with Disabilities (SWD) Summary of Recommendations NLCB Reauthorization" see http://nclbmb.ecs.org/reports/Report.aspx?id=1572.

[59] Commission on No Child Left Behind, Ensuring Students with Disabilities Achieve Academic Success, http://www.aspeninstitute.org/sites/default/files/content/docs/ commission% 20on%20no%20child%20left%20behind/ DisabilitiesBackgrounderFINAL5.8.07.pdf.

[60] Statements made about AA-AAS and AA-MAS are based on information provided by the U.S. Department of Education at a meeting with staff from the House of Representatives on March 25, 2010.

[61] An IEP must include additional elements that are not discussed in this report. For a full description of the requirements of an IEP, see IDEA §614(d).

[62] NGA, CCSSO, and NASBE, Joint Statement on the Reauthorization of the No Child Left Behind Act (NCLB), http://www.nga.org/Files/pdf/0704NCLBSTATEMENT.PDF.

[63] NCSL and AASA, Joint Statement of the National Conference of State Legislatures and the American Association of School Administrators on ESEA Reauthorization, http://ecom. ncsl.org/statefed/nclb/NCSLAASAJointStatement.htm.

[64] For more information on standards-based IEPs, see Eileen Ahearn, Standards-Based IEPs: Implementation in Selected States, National Association of State Directors of Special Education, May 2006, http://www.projectforum.org/ docs/Standards-BasedIEPs-ImplementationinSelectedStates.pdf.

[65] A complete discussion of growth models is beyond the scope of this report. For a more thorough discussion of growth models, see CRS Report RL33032, Adequate Yearly Progress (AYP): Growth Models Under the No Child Left Behind Act.

[66] See, for example, NGA, CCSSO, and NASBE, Joint Statement on the Reauthorization of the No Child Left Behind Act (NCLB), http://www.nga.org/Files/pdf/0704NCL BSTATE MENT.PDF; NASSP, NASSP No Child Left Behind Legislative Recommendations, http://www.principals.org/s_nassp/bin.asp?CID=969&DID=52898&DOC=FILE.PDF; and Commission on No Child Left Behind, Ensuring Students with Disabilities Achieve Academic Success, http://www.aspeninstitute.org/sites/default/files/content/ docs/commis sion%20on%20no%20child%20left%20behind/ DisabilitiesBackgrounderFINAL5.8.07.pdf.

[67] It is possible in some cases, however, to include scores from AA-AAS in a growth model that meets the criteria above. At least one state has a growth model that incorporates scores from students with the most significant cognitive disabilities who participate in alternate assessments.

[68] 34 C.F.R. § 200.20(f)(2)(i)(B).

[69] A "declassified" student is a student who was once identified with a disability and received special education services but no longer requires such services. The Office of Special Education Program's Annual Report to Congress provides information on the percentage of students ages 6-12 who received special education services in 2000 but were declassified by 2002. The percentage of declassification ranged from 2% (traumatic brain injury, autism) to 34% (speech or language impairments). On average, 17% of students with disabilities were

declassified from 2000 to 2002. For more information on declassification, see U.S. Department of Education, 28th Annual Report to Congress on the Implementation of the Individuals with Disabilities Education Act, 2006, Volume 1, January 2009, pp. 71-74, http://www.ed.gov/about/reports/annual/osep/2006/parts-b-c/28th-vol-1.pdf.

[70] In practice, the 10% threshold is difficult to meet and some have recommended reducing this to 3%-4%. See, for example, Robert L. Linn, Issues in the Design of Accountability Systems, National Center for Research on Evaluation, Standards, and Student Testing, CSE Technical Report 650, Los Angeles, CA, April 2005, http://www.eric.ed.gov/ ERICDocs/data/ ericdocs2sql/content_storage_01/0000019b/80/1b/b4/91.pdf.

[71] Under NCLB, state AYP systems must include at least one indicator, other than achievement test scores. For senior high schools, the additional indicator must be the graduation rate. A typical additional indicator for elementary and middle schools is the attendance rate; For more information on "safe harbor," see CRS Report RL33032, Adequate Yearly Progress (AYP): Growth Models Under the No Child Left Behind Act.

[72] In 28 states with available data in 2004-2005, 35% of schools missed AYP for the "students with disabilities" subgroup and 8% of schools missed AYP solely for the "students with disabilities" subgroup. See Amy Elledge, Kerstin Carlson Le Floch, and James Taylor, et al., State and Local Implementation of the No Child Left Behind Act, Office of Planning, Evaluation, and Policy Development; U.S. Department of Education, Volume V – Implementation of the 1 Percent Rule and 2 Percent Interim Policy Options, Washington, DC, January 2009, http://www.ed.gov/ rschstat/eval/disadv/nclb-disab/nclb-disab.pdf.

INDEX

A

academic performance, 58, 152, 162
academic progress, 3, 160
access, 6, 7, 26, 46, 61, 96, 97, 99, 108, 121, 138, 140, 157, 158, 159
accessibility, 98
accommodations, x, 13, 14, 15, 17, 18, 19, 34, 42, 43, 136, 137, 139, 150, 154, 170
accountability systems, x, 13, 21, 23, 25, 26, 28, 42, 45, 135, 136, 138, 139, 140, 145, 149, 152, 153, 154, 155, 156, 157, 158, 159, 160, 169
achievement test, 98, 172
adaptations, 154, 170
adaptive functioning, 151
Adequate Yearly Progress (AYP), x, 39, 42, 135, 136, 167, 171, 172
ADHD, 54, 94
adjustment, 94
administrators, x, 135, 137
adult education, 83
advancement, 96
advocacy, 33, 34, 108, 121, 133
age, 27, 38, 45, 50, 51, 54, 57, 58, 65, 71, 78, 80, 87, 89, 152
agencies, viii, 2, 6, 24, 52, 69, 76, 79, 86, 97
alphabet, 124
American Psychological Association (APA), 170
American Recovery and Reinvestment Act, 19, 36, 88
American Recovery and Reinvestment Act of 2009, 88
American Samoa, 87
Americans with Disabilities Act (ADA), 54, 81, 93, 108, 112, 113, 118, 129, 131
anger, 133
aphasia, 54
appropriations, 80, 87, 93, 119
Appropriations Act, 119, 132
arbitration, 75
assessment tools, 13, 56
asthma, 54
attachment, 94
audit, 77
authorities, 70, 80, 123
authority, 22, 24, 47, 62, 69, 74, 75, 89, 104, 105, 108, 109, 112, 114
autism, 40, 55, 94, 123, 141, 152, 168, 171
awareness, 51

B

background information, 5, 6, 12, 21, 29, 39
banks, 127
barriers, 83, 138
base, 71, 72
behavioral assessment, 100
behavioral problems, 62, 63

behaviors, 37, 70
benchmarks, 164
benefits, 51, 92, 97, 100, 101, 104, 108, 125, 126
bipolar disorder, 94
blindness, 53, 55, 93, 168
Braille, 42, 170
brain, 53, 54
Bureau of Indian Education (BIE), ix, 50, 87

C

case law, 124
catalyst, 118
CEC, 34, 47
certification, 26, 29, 30, 31, 32, 45, 63
CFR, 40, 41, 42, 44, 168
challenges, xi, 136, 137, 153
Chicago, 43, 131, 132
Chief Justice, 129
childhood, 37
city, 101, 111, 112, 115, 123, 125, 128, 131
civil action, 68, 128
civil law, 68
civil rights, viii, ix, 49, 113
civil rights statute, viii, 49, 113
classes, 64, 84, 94, 95, 103, 123
classroom, viii, ix, 2, 3, 8, 9, 17, 19, 28, 31, 33, 34, 39, 43, 50, 61, 65, 72, 99, 103, 105
clusters, 141, 143, 162, 163
cognitive ability, 151
cognitive impairment, 40, 141
collaboration, 34
color, 117
Commonwealth of the Northern Mariana Islands, 87
communication, 37, 81, 82
community, 83
compensation, 31, 46
competitive grant program, 19, 43, 44
complexity, 20, 35, 40, 139, 163
compliance, viii, 2, 20, 22, 24, 71, 77, 92, 100

composition, 60
comprehension, 82
computer, 64
conduct disorder, 94
confidentiality, 109
conflict, 16, 17, 25, 35, 43, 99
conflict of interest, 35
conformity, 41, 54, 96
congress, viii, x, 1, 2, 5, 6, 10, 11, 12, 16, 17, 18, 19, 21, 26, 27, 28, 29, 33, 35, 43, 45, 47, 49, 51, 84, 86, 91, 93, 97, 104, 105, 113, 117, 119, 120, 121, 135, 136, 157, 158, 167, 171
consensus, 126
consent, 38, 56, 82, 85, 112, 115
Consolidated Appropriations Act, 87, 132
constitution, 111, 117
constitutional issues, 127
construction, 74
Consumer Price Index, 87
controversial, 117
controversies, 98
cost, ix, 49, 61, 66, 67, 69, 71, 72, 74, 85, 103, 112, 114, 115
counsel, 61, 62, 102, 109
Court of Appeals, 94, 119
covering, 30
curricula, 158, 159
curriculum, 6, 7, 8, 26, 29, 33, 59, 60, 61, 98, 99, 138, 140, 151, 156, 157, 158, 159

D

daily living, 83
damages, 112, 117, 129, 131
danger, 107, 147
data collection, 62, 71, 150
database, 156
DEA, v, vii, viii, x, 1, 3, 40, 41, 44, 47, 49, 50, 80, 81, 83, 84, 85, 86, 91, 92, 121, 124, 126, 127, 129, 130, 131, 133, 135, 136, 168
decision trees, 153
deficiencies, 86, 133
deficit, 54, 94

delinquent students, vii, 1
demographic characteristics, 161
denial, 98, 101, 102, 108, 116, 118, 125
Department of Education, xi, 11, 36, 39, 42,
    43, 44, 45, 51, 52, 80, 84, 86, 88, 89,
    101, 105, 106, 108, 110, 116, 121, 122,
    123, 124, 125, 131, 136, 137, 146, 165,
    166, 167, 168, 169, 170, 171, 172
Department of Justice, 23, 25, 95
Department of the Interior, 87
depression, 94
deprivation, 117
detention, 107
developmental factors, 56
diabetes, 54
disadvantaged students, vii, 1, 3, 22, 24
disclosure, 114
discrimination, 113, 129
disorder, 54, 81, 94
dissenting opinion, 97, 123
distribution, 54, 165
District of Columbia, ix, 50, 71, 89, 119,
    121, 122, 123, 124, 128, 131, 132, 151,
    152
diversity, 47
drugs, 69, 70, 105
due process, ix, 22, 38, 49, 65, 67, 68, 69,
    70, 82, 85, 86, 93, 95, 101, 104, 107,
    108, 109, 110, 113, 120, 127, 128, 133
dyslexia, 54
dysthymic disorder, 95

EIS, 63, 83, 84
Elementary and Secondary Education Act
    (ESEA), vii, x, 1, 3, 135, 136
elementary school, 29, 41, 54, 85, 89, 96,
    114
elementary teachers, 30
eligibility criteria, ix, 50
emergency, 29, 30, 32, 64
employment, 30, 38, 52, 60, 83
enforcement, 20, 24, 44, 71, 72, 74, 76, 77,
    107, 109, 133
enrollment, 74, 85, 115, 148
environment, ix, 34, 47, 50, 60, 62, 63, 64,
    75, 84, 94, 97, 103, 116
environmental factors, 153
environments, 65, 79
equal opportunity, 158
equipment, 27, 42, 73, 74, 170
equity, 5, 6, 42
ethnic groups, 22, 24, 37, 75, 89
ethnicity, 36, 62, 74, 88
evidence, 38, 73, 75, 82, 95, 100, 123, 132,
    144, 151, 154, 155, 156, 164, 168
examinations, 58
exclusion, 103, 158
exercise, 28, 75
expenditures, 73, 74, 75, 88
expertise, 61
expulsion, 36, 70, 104
external validation, 45

E

earnings, 112
economic disadvantage, 58, 81
economics, 32, 45, 84
educational assessment, 42, 156
educational career, 98
educational experience, 3, 26, 27, 51
educational opportunities, 98, 109
educational services, ix, 22, 25, 49, 51, 70,
    92, 97, 107, 116
educators, vii, viii, x, 2, 4, 33, 46, 104, 107,
    135, 137, 147, 157, 164

F

Fairbanks, 97
fairness, 42, 114
families, 78
federal funding, vii, viii, x, 1, 3, 19, 39, 49,
    50, 71, 73, 74, 78, 91, 92, 95, 104, 113,
    121
federal government, 21, 40, 42, 71
federal law, 43, 110, 156
Federal Register, 44, 167, 168, 169, 170
federal regulations, 61
financial, 73, 111, 113, 116
financial resources, 73

financial support, 73
firearms, 105
flaws, 100
flexibility, 5, 26, 40, 157, 158, 159, 162,
    163, 169
fluctuations, 147
food, 127
force, 104
Ford, 132
foreign language, 32, 45, 84
formation, 130
formula, ix, 50, 71, 72, 82
free appropriate public education (FAPE),
    ix, x, 3, 49, 50, 78, 91, 92, 108
funds, ix, x, 1, 3, 14, 19, 21, 23, 25, 39, 49,
    50, 51, 52, 62, 63, 66, 71, 72, 73, 74, 76,
    78, 83, 85, 87, 88, 91, 92, 95, 103, 111,
    120, 121, 123, 124, 127, 157

G

GAO, 127
general education, viii, 2, 3, 4, 6, 8, 9, 10,
    12, 27, 28, 31, 33, 34, 39, 41, 59, 60, 62,
    63, 84, 138, 157, 158, 159
genetic disease, 122
geography, 32, 45, 84
grades, 13, 14, 41, 94, 98, 123, 141, 142,
    144, 145, 148, 161, 170
grading, 96
grant programs, 19
grants, viii, ix, 39, 49, 50, 51, 52, 71, 72, 73,
    78, 79, 104, 111, 113
Greece, 128
growth, 35, 47, 144, 157, 160, 161, 162,
    164, 171
growth models, 157, 160, 161, 162, 171
guardian, 120
guidance, 10, 14, 19, 35, 40, 84, 89, 92, 139,
    141, 146
guidelines, 14, 15, 19, 151, 153

H

harassment, 108, 128
Hawaii, 106, 131, 133
health, 53, 61, 65, 94, 168
health services, 61
hearing impairment, 55, 93, 168
high school, 3, 4, 13, 14, 21, 22, 23, 24, 26,
    27, 28, 36, 38, 45, 57, 81, 148, 161, 170,
    172
high school diploma, 26, 27, 45, 81
higher education, 38, 79
history, 32, 45, 84, 120, 121
house, 42, 106, 127, 171
House of Representatives, 42, 171
Hunter, 123
hyperactivity, 54, 94

I

IASA, 138
ideal, 123
identification, viii, 2, 16, 22, 24, 37, 38, 40,
    58, 62, 64, 66, 68, 75, 77, 82, 88, 89,
    102, 148
impairments, 55, 65, 93, 94, 168
improvements, 162
incarceration, 45
incidence, 62, 145
independence, 158
independent living, 52, 60, 83
individual students, 4, 132, 164
individualized instruction, 27, 63, 168
individuals, 54, 61, 113, 121, 122, 168
Individuals with Disabilities Education Act,
    v, vii, viii, x, 1, 3, 9, 15, 25, 32, 36, 40,
    41, 44, 47, 49, 50, 80, 81, 83, 84, 85, 86,
    88, 91, 92, 121, 122, 124, 126, 127, 128,
    129, 130, 131, 133, 135, 136, 168, 172
induction, 34
infants, 51, 52, 78, 84, 105, 129
inflation, 71, 87
informed consent, 56
injury, 53, 54, 69, 70, 105

institutions, 61, 64, 79
instructional methods, 83
instructional time, 28
intelligence, 98
intervention, 23, 25, 57, 58, 70, 74, 76, 78,
    79, 83, 84, 89, 105, 107
issues, vii, viii, ix, x, 2, 4, 5, 18, 27, 50, 68,
    69, 91, 93, 105, 107, 109, 110, 111, 112,
    113, 119, 121, 122, 130, 156, 162, 167

J

judicial decisions, x, 51, 91, 93, 100, 109
jurisdiction, 110

K

kindergarten, 62, 89

L

language impairment, 53, 65, 93, 168, 171
laws, vii, 2, 4, 5, 12, 20, 21, 117
lawyers, 120
lead, 11, 18, 26, 34, 35, 79, 159
learning, 4, 8, 33, 35, 53, 54, 57, 58, 63, 65,
    77, 81, 83, 94, 106, 139, 153, 168
learning disabilities, 54, 81, 94
learning environment, 58
learning outcomes, 63
legal issues, 83, 84, 85, 86
legislation, 12, 42, 138
level of education, 96
limited English proficiency, vii, 1, 22, 57,
    58
literacy, 10, 37
litigation, 112, 119
local educational agency (LEA), ix, 21, 22,
    34, 36, 41, 43, 45, 50, 56, 57, 58, 59, 60,
    62, 64, 66, 67, 68, 69, 70, 72, 73, 74, 75,
    77, 80, 81, 82, 83, 85, 86, 87, 88, 89, 98,
    109, 110, 114, 116, 117, 118, 119, 121,
    142, 145, 146, 147, 148, 149, 150, 161,
    163, 164, 166, 167

logistics, 33
Louisiana, 124

M

maintenance of effort (MOE), ix, 50, 83
majority, viii, 2, 7, 31, 33, 34, 37, 38, 46,
    115, 120
Mars, 127
Marshall Islands, 87
MAS, x, 13, 16, 18, 35, 41, 42, 136, 137,
    140, 143, 144, 145, 146, 149, 150, 152,
    153, 154, 155, 157, 158, 163, 164, 166,
    167, 169, 170, 171
materials, 42, 56, 170
mathematics, viii, 2, 3, 4, 6, 8, 9, 13, 14, 19,
    20, 21, 23, 24, 27, 29, 30, 32, 43, 45, 82,
    84, 139, 142, 144, 151, 161
matter, 30, 46, 67
measurement, 32, 33, 34, 46, 156, 158
media, 76, 122
mediation, ix, 22, 24, 38, 39, 49, 65, 67, 68,
    69, 72, 75, 86, 92, 105, 108, 109, 132
mediation process, ix, 49, 67, 72
medical, 62, 72, 83, 97, 101, 102, 103, 126,
    130
memory, 139
mental health, 97
mental retardation, 58, 65, 81, 93, 142, 152,
    153, 168
mentoring, 34
methodology, 61
Miami, 130
migrant students, vii, 1
Minneapolis, 127, 169, 170, 171
Missouri, 129
models, 63, 82, 83, 160, 161, 171
modifications, 34, 59, 124
motor skills, 8

N

National Center for Education Statistics, 80
National Survey, 81

natural disaster, 73
negative effects, 104
No Child Left Behind, vii, x, 1, 3, 36, 39,
    40, 41, 42, 43, 44, 45, 84, 98, 99, 124,
    135, 136, 138, 150, 167, 170, 171, 172
nonprofit organizations, 79
nursery school, 126

O

occupational therapy, 102
officials, 66, 95, 105, 117, 150
omission, 16
opportunities, 22, 25
overlap, 23, 25, 113
oversight, 75

P

P.L. 110-325, 122
pain, 117
parental consent, 38, 56, 57, 58, 81, 82, 89,
    101, 107
parental involvement, 112
pathologist, 58, 133
pathology, 61, 102
peer relationship, 8
peer review, 156, 161, 164
percentile, 97
performance indicator, viii, 2, 3, 22, 24, 77
permit, 7, 57, 89, 105, 121, 164, 169
persuasion, 114
Philadelphia, 110, 122, 129, 130, 131, 132
physical education, 61
pilot study, 35
policy, viii, xi, 2, 5, 20, 31, 32, 39, 40, 42,
    45, 84, 136, 137, 146, 151, 157, 162,
    165, 166, 168, 169, 170
policy issues, viii, 2, 5
policy options, 151, 170
policymakers, x, 31, 135, 137
pools, 103
poor performance, 152
population, vii, 1, 71, 87, 147, 155

portfolio, 139
portfolio assessment, 139
post traumatic stress disorder, 94
potential benefits, 62
poverty, 72, 82
precedent, 115
prejudice, 110, 120
preparation, 31, 79, 120
preschool, 3, 37, 41, 51, 52, 54, 78, 96
preschool children, 37, 51, 52
president, 39
principles, x, 16, 42, 47, 91, 92
private schools, 56, 66, 85, 114, 115, 119,
    130
probability, 78
problem behavior, 8
problem solving, 82
procedural right, 111, 114
professional development, 62, 79
professionals, 57, 79, 83
profit, 121
protection, 54, 121
psychological processes, 81
psychologist, 58
public education, ix, x, 3, 41, 49, 50, 52, 54,
    75, 77, 78, 81, 91, 92, 95, 96, 97, 102,
    103, 107, 108, 111, 115, 117, 121
public schools, 6, 9, 21, 40, 106, 127, 133
Puerto Rico, ix, 50, 71, 89, 151, 152

Q

qualifications, 31, 86, 163

R

race, 36, 62, 74, 88
random assignment, 146, 147
reading, viii, 2, 3, 4, 6, 8, 9, 10, 13, 14, 20,
    21, 23, 24, 27, 29, 32, 45, 57, 58, 82, 84,
    97, 121, 139, 142, 144, 151, 154, 161
reading comprehension, 82
reality, 31
reasoning, 103

recognition, 70
recommendations, 114, 125, 156
recreation, 61, 102
redistribution, 147, 149
redundancy, 160
reform, 40, 46, 133
regulatory requirements, 145
rehabilitation, 61, 102
Rehabilitation Act, 42, 54, 81, 93, 108, 113, 117, 129, 133
reimburse, 85, 115
rejection, 132
relatives, 118
reliability, 140, 143, 151, 154, 155, 156
relief, 105, 113, 118, 119, 127, 132
reserves, 71, 87
resolution, 38, 39, 67, 68, 75, 86, 92, 98, 108, 109, 110, 118, 120, 126, 131
resources, 60, 163
response, 42, 57, 58, 63, 93, 117, 144, 150, 155, 170
response format, 155
restrictions, xi, 13, 17, 42, 62, 136, 137
restructuring, 22, 25
retaliation, 108, 133
retardation, 53, 65, 142
retirement, 74
rewards, 21, 44
rights, ix, 49, 50, 51, 52, 54, 66, 67, 69, 78, 82, 85, 92, 98, 101, 108, 111, 112, 113, 117, 121, 133
risk, 63, 72, 74, 87, 103
rules, 43, 142, 144

S

safety, 69, 104
sanctions, 21
schizophrenia, 94
school activities, 83
school enrollment, 72, 85
school performance, 94
schooling, 64, 103
science, 6, 9, 14, 30, 32, 41, 45, 84, 139, 154

scope, 42, 113, 121, 171
SEA, 63, 68, 72, 73, 74, 76, 79, 80, 110, 114, 117, 121, 146
secondary education, vii, viii, 1, 2, 3, 6, 29, 32, 39, 83, 167
secondary school education, 41, 54, 96
secondary schools, vii, 1, 3, 12, 89
secondary students, 3
senate, 82, 106, 110
September 11, 43
service provider, 4, 10, 26
skin, 127
social relationships, 37
social skills, 8, 27
speech, 4, 58, 61, 65, 93, 102, 133, 168, 171
spelling, 93
spending, ix, 50, 73
spina bifida, 102
standard deviation, 142
statute of limitations, 128
statutes, 113, 117, 124, 128
statutory authority, 110
statutory provisions, 20, 89, 115
storage, 172
structure, 51, 112, 159
student achievement, x, 7, 14, 17, 20, 21, 25, 32, 33, 34, 41, 47, 60, 63, 135, 136, 139, 161
student enrollment, 152
subgroups, 3, 4, 22, 24, 27, 43, 138, 147, 162
subtraction, 139
supervision, 38, 41, 54, 75, 89, 96
supplement, not supplant (SNS) requirements, ix, 50, 73, 74, 80
support services, 96, 121
Supreme Court, 81, 86, 92, 93, 95, 96, 98, 99, 102, 104, 105, 107, 111, 112, 113, 115, 116, 117, 118, 120, 121, 130, 133
suspensions, 36, 63

T

tactics, 119
teacher effectiveness, 5, 31, 32, 34, 46

teacher performance, 31
teacher preparation, 33
teachers, viii, 2, 3, 4, 5, 8, 9, 26, 28, 29, 30,
    31, 32, 33, 34, 45, 46, 47, 60, 62, 63, 84,
    106, 133, 139, 150
teams, 15, 28, 35, 47, 106, 151, 152, 153,
    157, 158, 159
technical assistance, 23, 25, 71, 76, 79
techniques, 67, 106
technology, 72, 79
tension, 4
tenure, 46
test items, 170
testing, 14, 15, 147, 153, 155, 161, 170
therapy, 61, 122
threshold level, 22
time frame, 56
Title I, 3, 6, 13, 21, 23, 41, 84, 87, 167, 168,
    169, 170
Title II, 84, 87
toddlers, 51, 52, 78, 84, 105, 129
training, 31, 38, 60, 62, 79
transparency, 77
transport, 109
transportation, 61, 102
traumatic brain injury, 40, 55, 94, 141, 168,
    171
tuition, 115, 116
tutoring, 109

U

uniform, 3, 29, 77
united, 87, 117, 130
United States, 87, 117, 130

V

vocalizations, 104
vocational education, 83

W

waiver, 40, 73, 74, 88, 168
walking, 54
war, 56
Washington, 45, 110, 121, 170, 171, 172
weapons, 69, 70, 105
withdrawal, 107
witnesses, 120

Y

yield, 56, 154